To

Ruby Lee Session, her sons and daughter,

the family that never gave up,

and the innocents who remain behind bars.

A PLEA FOR JUSTICE:

The Timothy Cole Story

FRED B. MCKINLEY

EAKIN PRESS Waco, Texas

FIRST EDITION
Copyright © 2010
By Fred B. McKinley
Published in the United States of America
By Eakin Press
A Division of Sunbelt Media, Inc.
P.O. Box 21235 🕮 Waco, Texas 76702
e-mail: sales@eakinpress.com
💻 website: www.eakinpress.com 💻
ALL RIGHTS RESERVED.
1   2   3   4   5   6   7   8   9
ISBN 978-1-935632-04-7
ISBN 1-935632-04-3
Library of Congress Control Number 2010927054

CONTENTS

Appendices

FOREWORD

In 1985, Tim Cole, a college student at Texas Tech University in Lubbock, was arrested on a brutal rape charge. A decent young man with his whole life ahead of him, he was convicted, sentenced, and sent to prison, where he died during an asthma attack. He was entirely innocent of the crime of which he was accused.

Those of us who work to free the innocent in Texas confront a great many problems: the legal system is a stacked deck, there is no real funding for the work, there are too many people who have been framed in this state, and too few volunteers to work at getting them released. The worst problem of all, however, is the lack of public support.

As the founder of, and chief counsel for, the Innocence Project of Texas, I travel all over the state trying to garner support for our movement. From Rotary clubs and rallies, church groups and caucuses, I've learned that freeing the innocent is not a popular cause. I've come to realize that most people believe very few of their fellow citizens are falsely convicted. They think the problem, such as it is, is being handled by the system. Finally, they're convinced that nothing like this could ever happen to them.

A PLEA FOR JUSTICE: The Timothy Cole Story demonstrates how misguided such thinking is. Objective and detailed, the book reveals the facts of this tragic case. McKinley's authorial voice is not overheated, rhetorical, or angry, and he grinds no political axes. Instead, he sets out a balanced account of just what happened. By telling the story as an honest reporter, McKinley has done more to reveal the flaws of the Texas system than any reform advocate or "movement person" ever could.

More than once, those of us who worked on Tim's case said someone should tell the true story of what happened to him. We knew that if the story, which was far deeper than the one described by headlines and thirty-second TV spots, could *just get out there*, more people would come to understand that what happened to Tim Cole was by no means a rare aberration. We knew that if all the facts of this case were revealed, the public might have a lesson in injustice and what it takes to fix it.

As it turns out, Fred B. McKinley is the writer who has told the story. Anyone who wants to know the truth about how our criminal justice system really works should read this book. Anyone who wants to know what the system does to its victims should also read it. When told well, as in these pages, truth has the power to change people's minds.

Until that day, some of us will keep fighting for the Tim Coles of the world, but now, armed with this book, we'll do so with more faith than we had before.

—JEFF BLACKBURN
Chief Counsel
Innocence Project of Texas

Acknowledgments

My longtime mentor and friend, Dr. Ralph A. Wooster, Distinguished Professor Emeritus of History at Lamar University in Beaumont, Texas, directed all of his students, including me, to use extreme caution when relying on secondary resources, and through my years of writing, I have come to more appreciate the wisdom of his advice. "When possible," he said, "always utilize primary sources." He explained his reasoning—these provided the most factual accounts, because they were written at, or near the time, of one's particular research topic.

While reviewing existing material about the Timothy Brian Cole case, including limited interviews, newspaper articles, and internet sources, whether printed or recalled twenty-some years after the fact, I have attempted to follow Dr. Wooster's counsel. In this situation, however, we have one of the best primary resources available, in the form of the 99th District Court Reporter's Notes produced by the late Bobby G. Rogers, described as the "godfather of all local court reporters: the last one to use shorthand, pen and ink." Rogers's entries reflect the actual words of the trial judge, opposing counsel, and witnesses at a time when memories were fresh and untainted by revisionist editing and selective process.[1]

Realizing the extreme difficulty created by revisiting painful memories, I take this opportunity to issue a special note of gratitude to Ruby Lee Session and her sons, Cory Session and Kevin Kennard, who agreed to meet with me and share personal details about Tim's life. My admiration for these individuals runs deep.

During the development stages of the book, I had the pleasure of making the acquaintances of Natalie Roetzel, Executive Director, and Jeff Blackburn, Chief Counsel of the Innocence Project of Texas, who lead and direct the activities of a remarkable organization of conscience, comprised of "dedicated student-volunteers" and "experienced legal advocates" that continue to champion the rights of those wrongly convicted and incarcerated. From the beginning, Natalie and Jeff lent their support to this project and permitted me full access to their files. Without their cooperation, this work would have fallen well short of its intended mark.[2]

My heartfelt appreciation goes out to those in the Lubbock Police Department who aided in my research, especially to Chief Dale A. Holton for allowing complete transparency. I also appreciate Captain Greg Stevens, Public Information Officer, for his contributions. From the outset, Greg spent hours running down leads, contacting his peers at the Lubbock County Sheriff's Office, and then furnishing copies of investigative reports and photographs, some never published until now.

I would also like to thank Barbara Sucsy, Lubbock County District Clerk, and her staff for scanning Tim Cole's entire case file, thereby granting me online access by way of an excellent system provided and maintained under the supervision of David Slayton and Dean Stanzione, Lubbock County Director and Assistant Director of Court Administration, respectively. Moreover, David was instrumental in helping me locate the exhibit file which not only shed light on previously recorded material, but also exposed one of the great myths associated with the original police photo spread that arguably led to an unjust conviction.

I extend a personal acknowledgment to Elliott Blackburn, reporter for *The Lubbock Avalanche-Journal*. His coverage, ranging from investigating the Tim Cole case in its initial stages to the writing of a prize-winning, three-part series titled "Hope Deferred," speaks not only of his professionalism, but also that of his editor, Terry Greenberg, and the paper for which they work.

Some readers may question whether I tried to interview other major participants in this case. I did locate and talk with a few of the jurors, but unfortunately, they claimed to remember nothing about the trial. Even John Tabor, co-counsel for the defense, said that he could not recall whether he served as second chair. Finally, both Mike Brown, who still practices law in Lubbock, and Judge Jim Bob Darnell of the 140th District Court of Lubbock, refused to grant interviews. Likewise, a former detective with high-profile status during the investigation said that he could see neither the value nor the purpose of answering additional questions.

Many others also deserve credit, specifically the following, who provided suggestions, support, information, photographs, and leads. To any whom I may inadvertently have left out, please accept my sincere apology.

In alphabetical order by first names:
Aaron Chamberlain, Texas State Law Library, Austin, TX
Adam Leiber, Assistant Attorney General, Open Records Division, Austin, TX
Adrienne Richey, Reference & Tech Services Librarian, Texas State Law Library, Austin, TX
Alexandra Gongora, Deputy Clerk, Lubbock County District Clerk's Office, Lubbock, TX
Ashton Morgan, Press Center, Office of the Governor, Austin, TX
Beverly Daughtry, Publisher, *The Elgin Courier*, Elgin, TX
Carolyn F. Moore, President, Lubbock County Bar Association, Lubbock, TX
Celina Franco, Appellant Clerk, Lubbock County District Clerk's Office, Lubbock, TX
Charlie Baird, Judge, 299th Judicial District Court, Travis County, Austin, TX
Charlotte Null, Records System Manager, Lubbock Police Department, Lubbock, TX

Chuck Lanehart, Attorney-at-Law, Lubbock, TX

Darren Lindly, Corporal, ID Section, Lubbock Police Department, Lubbock, TX

David Henderson, Officer, Property Crimes Section, Lubbock Police Department, Lubbock, TX

Debbie Ray, Deputy Program Monitor, Department of Criminal Justice, Huntsville, TX

Debi Pettiet, Court Reporter, 99th District Court, Lubbock, TX

Dennis R. Reeves, Capital Public Defenders Office, Lubbock, TX

Donna L. Clarke, Assistant Criminal District Attorney, Lubbock, TX

Ellen Alfano, V.P. & Deputy Executive Editor, the *Fort Worth Star-Telegram*, Fort Worth, TX

Eric Ferrero, Director of Communications, the Innocence Project, New York, NY

Erik Brown, Assistant General Counsel, Department of Criminal Justice, Huntsville, TX

Erin Heine, *The Elgin Courier*, Elgin, TX

Gilbert "Gib" Weaver, Superintendent, TTUISD, Lubbock, TX

Glenn H. Utter, Chair, Department of Political Science, Lamar University, Beaumont, TX

Heidi Templeton, Director of Public Relations, Truman State University, Kirksville, MO

Jackie Chavez, Lubbock Chamber of Commerce, Lubbock, TX

Jana Birchum, Photographer, Austin, TX

Jason Clark, Public Information Officer, Department of Criminal Justice, Huntsville, TX

Jeanne Fairman, Executive Secretary, Lubbock County Bar Association, Lubbock, TX

Jennifer C. Cohen, Assistant General Counsel, Texas Department of Public Safety, Austin, TX

Jerry Wayne Johnson, Snyder, Texas

John C. Akard, Judge, President-Elect, Lubbock County Bar Association, Lubbock, TX

John Lipe, Service Hydrologist, National Weather Service, Lubbock, TX

Judy Mills, Deputy Clerk, Lubbock County Clerk, Lubbock, TX

Julia Childs, Director of Marketing, *The Lubbock Avalanche-Journal*, Lubbock, TX

Justin Weaver, Meteorologist-in-Charge, National Weather Service, Lubbock, TX

Kelly Pinion, Lubbock County Clerk, Lubbock, TX

Kelly Rowe, Sheriff, Lubbock County, TX

Kevin Cullen, Editor, *The Daily Toreador*, Texas Tech University, Lubbock, TX

Kimberly Vardeman, Assistant Librarian, Texas Tech University Library, Lubbock, TX

Leslie Prather-Forbis, Texas State Law Library, Austin, TX

Lisa Wood, Archives Clerk, Lubbock County District Clerk's Office, Lubbock, TX

Lourdes Justiniani, Open Records Section, Department of Criminal Justice, Austin, TX

Lupe Ponciano, Intake Coordinator, the Innocence Project of Texas, Lubbock, TX

Maria Ramirez, Legal Support Director, Texas Board of Pardons and Paroles, Austin, TX

Marilyn Lutter, Administrative Assistant, Lubbock District Attorney's Office, Lubbock, TX

Marti Ruby, Official Court Reporter, 299th Judicial District Court, Travis County, Austin, TX

Mary Ann Archer, William Mitchell College of Law, St. Paul, MN

Michelle Lyons, Director of Public Information, Department of Criminal Justice, Huntsville, TX

Neal R. Axton, William Mitchell College of Law, St. Paul, MN

Nick Vilbas, Texas Tech Law Student, the Innocence Project of Texas, Lubbock, TX

Nneka Kanu, Assistant Attorney General, Open Records Division, Austin, TX

Patricia Clark, Archivist, Special Collections Library, Texas Tech University, Lubbock, TX

Patrick Aten, Assistant to the City Council, City of Lubbock, Lubbock, TX

Rachel Williams, Records Division, Department of Criminal Justice, Huntsville, TX

Rebecca Garza, City Secretary, City of Lubbock, Lubbock, TX

Rhonda Devitt, Court Coordinator, 140th District Court, Lubbock, TX

Ronald Seacrist, Chief of Police, Texas Tech University, Lubbock, TX

Ronny L. Clinton, Lubbock, TX

Sally Ann Post, Director, Communications and Marketing, Texas Tech University, Lubbock, TX

Sammy W. Smith, Deputy District Clerk, Lubbock County District Clerk's Office, Lubbock, TX

Sandra K. Murphy, Administrator, Department of Criminal Justice, Huntsville, TX

Sheri W. Lewis, Associate Director, *The Daily Toreador*, Texas Tech University, Lubbock, TX

Stephen Stephanian, Digital Media Specialist, Office of the Governor, Austin, TX

Sue Faison, Court Coordinator, 99th District Court, Lubbock, TX

Sue Moreno, Lubbock Police Department, Lubbock, TX

Thomas J. Nichols, Director of Police and Safety Services, Lubbock ISD, Lubbock, TX

Timothy L. Hendricks, Office of the Registrar, Texas Tech University, Lubbock, TX

Ute Schechter, Earl Gregg Swem Library, The College of William & Mary, Williamsburg, VA

Whitney Stark, Communications Director, the Innocence Project of Texas, Lubbock, TX

And finally, I commend Kris Gholson, publisher at Eakin Press, for his unbiased support of the text, Janis Williams, editor, Pat Molenaar, book designer and typesetter, and Kim Williams, cover designer, because without their combined efforts, none of this would have been possible.

— FRED B. McKINLEY
Burleson, TX
April 15, 2010

INTRODUCTION

"Beware how you take away hope from another human being."
– OLIVER WENDELL HOLMES

Exactly what does the commonly-used term *justice* represent in today's society? *The Random House College Dictionary* describes it as "the quality of conforming to principles of reason, to generally accepted standards of right and wrong, and to the stated terms of laws, rules, agreements . . . in matters affecting persons who could be wronged or unduly favored." The interpretation of such verbiage, however, can be perplexing, and it is no small wonder that even a great legal mind such as late Chief Justice of the Supreme Court Warren E. Burger wrestled with the concept when he said that in the pursuit of justice, "Guilt or innocence becomes irrelevant in the criminal trial as we flounder in a morass of artificial rules poorly conceived and often impossible of application."[1]

With confusion deeply entrenched in our legal system, imagine a twenty-four-year-old black man, an army veteran recently enrolled in Texas Tech University in Lubbock, being placed in a police line-up, and then identified, beyond the shadow of a doubt, as the person who raped a fellow student. And later, as he heard the slamming of steel doors behind him, one can only envision what went through his mind – and the utter fear that he experienced. Timothy Brian Cole felt abandoned by an institution in its bid for a quick verdict, and he was not alone in his assessment. Many argue still that the legal establishment of

1

Lubbock County, Texas, charged with protecting *all* citizens, refused to consider *all* of the evidence in this particular case.

Many of us are blamed, at some point, for something that we did not do. I can recall two such events in my own life, one of which led to the only traumatic instance of corporeal punishment received during my school career. Of course an experience like that, though it seemed severe at the moment, doesn't compare to incarceration.

As a criminal investigator with the Attorney General's Office, Louisiana Department of Justice, I transported those whom I arrested to various parish prisons throughout the state, and afterward, I often remarked to my wife that the sounds and sights of these experiences sent cold chills through my body. I knew, though, that upon entering the walls of confinement, I would leave as soon as I completed the formal booking process. But Tim Cole's plight was far more extensive.

During his myriad pleas of innocence at the time of his arrest on the charge of aggravated sexual assault, as well as throughout his trial, subsequent conviction, and sentencing to twenty-five years, Tim Cole held firm to the notion that eventually justice would prevail and that he would taste freedom once more. His devoted mother and several siblings had faith in the system, too, but that trust would soon waver, and then shatter with the passage of time. This narrative attempts to put in perspective Tim Cole's tragedy and that of a family, honor bound, engaged in an epic mission to restore his good name.

The *New York Times*, in its Sunday, July 19, 2009, Health Guide Section, discussed the crime of rape:

- According to most estimates, 80-90% of rapes are not reported to authorities. Current trends project that 1 in 3 American women will be sexually assaulted at some point during her life.
- The typical rape victim is a 16-24 year-old woman. Anyone, however — man or woman, adult or child — can be the victim of rape. Most commonly, the assailant is a 25-44 year-old man who plans his attack. He usually chooses a

woman of the same race. Nearly half the time, the victim knows the rapist at least casually, by working or living near him. Alcohol is involved in more than 1 out of 3 rapes.
- Over 50% of rapes occur in the victim's home. The rapist breaks into the victim's home or gains access under false pretenses, such as asking to use the phone or posing as a repairman or salesman.
- Rape is a violent act, and most commonly committed by a male upon a female. However, some cases of rape have been reported in which a woman has raped a man. Rape also may occur between members of the same sex. This is more prevalent in situations where access to the opposite sex is restricted (such as prisons, military settings, and single-sex schools).
- Rape is an act of violence expressed through sex, but is not primarily about sex.[2]

The primary rape of March 24–25, 1985, detailed in this book represents but one of the 8,364 recorded cases in Texas for that year, and while it does not fit many of the stereotypes spelled out above, it nonetheless proves that a rapist will resort to any deception to gain access to unsuspecting prey. And it is only through due diligence, being constantly aware of one's surroundings, and continued education that potential victims can limit their exposure to such risks. By taking these precautions, citizens can substantially reduce one of our nation's top crime statistics.[3]

Within portions of the text, some readers may find the limited graphic language extremely offensive, but these particular words and expressions in unedited form are used exactly as found in the original trial transcripts, court testimony, and police reports. To replace them with less objectionable ones, in my opinion, would diminish the full impact. Rape is neither gentle nor pretty.

In order to further protect all rape victims discussed, I have used fictitious names, excluding that of Michele Jean Murray who has so courageously chosen to participate in public forums.

Regardless, all true identities were obtained without deceptive means from open public records; therefore, legal precedent stands. Please refer to the landmark Supreme Court ruling in *Cox Broadcasting Corp. v. Cohn*, 420 U.S. 469 (1975) for further information.[4]

During the closing months of 1984 and extending through March 25, 1985, a number of violent rapes occurred around Texas Tech in Lubbock, Texas. Females, both students and employees of the university, along with those who worked in the general area, were caught up in a wave of terror in the persona of the *Tech rapist*. *The Lubbock Avalanche-Journal* sensationalized the crimes, and the campus newspaper, *The University Daily*, not only ran complete accounts of the attacks and printed composite sketches drawn with the aid of rape victims, but also included suggestions about how to enhance individual security. In great numbers, authorities received tips, including reports from those who witnessed conversations between black men and white women. As a result, the few African-American males attending the university found it difficult to escape strict, personal scrutiny, and according to Reggie Kennard's firsthand observation: "If you [an African-American] walked the campus at night, you were going to get stopped. One of the black students would say, 'Hey, you look like the Tech rapist.'"[5]

While Lubbock unquestionably experienced such felonies before, during, and after those discussed in this text, the five within this particular time frame were given unparalleled attention by both Tech and Lubbock Police Departments, and for good reason. Of course, investigations would have occurred anyway, but one has to consider the monetary aspect. Texas Tech and Lubbock are joined at the hip, and therefore the university represents an integral part of the neighboring economy, given that it generates thousands of jobs and multi-millions in revenue. Kent Hance, the current system chancellor, put it best when he said, "Texas Tech University and the city of Lubbock are interconnected. What happens on campus impacts our community." Bottom line: city fathers and Tech officials needed to convince those who sent their daughters and granddaughters to the South Plains for a higher education that safety was job one.[6]

Relative to the arrests and indictments of various individuals mentioned in these pages, it is not my intent to prove or disprove the associated allegations, or sway the reader's opinion, except as regards Timothy Brian Cole. The purpose: clarity. Each of you has probably seen investigative television dramas that painstakingly lay out a scenario, in which the reporter and producers thicken the plot by including a reenactment of the crime and subsequent arrest. Well-staged interviews solicit responses from prisoners, witnesses, family members, friends, investigators, police officers, sheriffs, deputies, FBI agents, and representatives of other law enforcement outfits. Then, for good measure, remarks by famous trial lawyers, profilers, consultants, and those who administer lie detector tests are added to create more suspense, and with the conclusion of the trial, jurors gather and explain in great detail why they voted a certain way. When all is said and done, regrettably, not one of the viewers who spent an hour or more watching the program really knows whether the person who received the punishment is guilty, because no one has come forward to not only admit guilt, but have that guilt indisputably confirmed. As a reasonable alternative, I offer this. After completing this book, each reader will know exactly who committed the primary rape discussed — and why.

And lastly, what about the charges of mishandling by the Lubbock Police Department — and the district attorney who personally prosecuted the defendant? Many of these assertions are found in today's media even though it has been more than twenty years since Tim Cole's arrest. At this stage, I will simply make an observation from a historian's point of view. Our country's past is filled with horrific wrongdoings that we would like to have the opportunity to change for the better. Unfortunately, do-overs are not possible here. Besides, nothing can ever erase the deep wounds inflicted, the living nightmares created, and the misfortunes laid at the doorstep of the innocent victims discussed in the chapters that follow. Yet there is hope, for even now, there are lessons to be learned from Tim Cole, if only we would first consider and then put them into practice. After all, this is what Tim wanted, nothing more, nothing less.

CHAPTER ONE

THE BEGINNING

"How a person masters his fate
is more important than what his fate is."
– KARL WILHELM VON HUMBOLDT

Life is never fair, nor is it easy. Throughout millennia and for countless reasons, too many of our children die at birth, some before reaching maturity, while others not only grow into adulthood but live out their remaining years as successful members of society. In stark contrast, numerous individuals continuously struggle for various reasons, including but not limited to: illness, alcohol, drugs, certain economic and/or ethnic backgrounds, making bad choices — or just being in the wrong place at the wrong time. And as hard-luck cases, scores are caught up in a rip current from which they cannot escape. In my estimation, Timothy Brian Cole falls within the confines of this ill-fated category.

Tim, as his family and friends called him, was born to Ruby Lee Cole and Ernest James Kennard on July 1, 1960, in the Washington County seat of Brenham, Texas, located midway between Austin and Houston, during the final stage of President Dwight David Eisenhower's term of office and less than three months before the first Kennedy–Nixon debate that would set the tone for future American presidential campaigns. In 1960, Brenham boasted a population of 7,740, but these numbers would soon see a rapid rise "triggered by the influx of Houston-area and rural Washington County residents, expansion of processing and light industry, and the advent of new manufacturers, encouraged by the Brenham Industrial Foundation, established in 1953."[1]

Tim's mother and Kennard had four more children: daughter, Karen Michelle, born November 22, 1961, and sons Kevin Scott, Reginald Eugene (Reggie), and Rodney Joseph, born May 5, 1963, September 13, 1964, and November 10, 1965, respectively. But when the union dissolved, Ruby and three of her children moved in 1966 to Fort Worth, Texas. The two others, however, stayed behind with Ruby's mother and grandmother in Brenham, because at this point, Ruby did not want to uproot Karen who'd just started kindergarten, or Tim who'd just begun first grade.[2]

Ruby then married a Bell Helicopter employee, Dewitt Ray Session, and the couple gave birth to Sean Curtis on December 15, 1967, followed by Cory Dewitt on December 27, 1968. In 1969, when Tim and Karen rejoined the family in Fort Worth, Ruby and Dewitt had a total of seven children living with them, the oldest being Tim.[3]

Somewhere early on, whether by genetics or his parents' strong Christian training—probably more of the latter—Tim Cole developed a deep sense of family responsibility, a trait uncommon for most children his age, and he always sought to make the lives of his mother, stepfather, brothers, and sister a little easier. Still nothing more than a child himself, he took on the job of caring for those closest to him. His brother Reggie chuckled and said, "Tim was 10 going on 25. He was the man of the house, and what he said went."[4]

Everyone depended on him, including his stepfather, Dewitt, and his mother, Ruby, who by day taught classes within the Fort Worth Independent School District, and by night and weekends worked to complete a college degree. Tim, with a trademark infectious smile, "woke his siblings, cooked breakfast, packed lunches and made sure they went to school on time," Reggie said. "In the evening, he made sure the house was clean, homework was done, and with a wet belt, discipline was

Timothy Brian Cole in fifth grade
—Courtesy Ruby Lee Session

kept on the rare occasion someone stepped out of line."[5]

In Fort Worth, Tim attended Riverside Elementary and Riverside Middle School. He completed one year at Carter-Riverside High, before transferring to O. D. Wyatt, where he played basketball and graduated. But Tim was much more than a sports jock. He excelled in the classroom and as a member of a debating team sponsored by the local Optimist Club.[6]

However, he suffered with asthma, and his mother recalled that often she awoke "to the sound of her child struggling for air in the middle of the night and rushing him to the emergency room." Even so, the malady rarely slowed down the youngster, nicknamed "Ears," as evidenced by his fifth-grade picture, who became the "neighborhood sports hero and role model," as well as "a front-yard quarterback and a trash-talking competitor on the basketball court." His younger siblings followed along and tried to emulate his every move, even down to his method of dress. Never a selfish individual, Tim made sure that everyone, regardless of age or size, got to participate in the game of the day.[7]

By the time Tim graduated from high school in May 1978 and readied for college, his mother said that the asthma had improved to the point that "a quick spray of his atomizer quelled any breathing problems." He enrolled in September at Texas Tech University in Lubbock, and even though he had not been awarded a basketball scholarship, he still dreamed of playing for the Red Raiders, then coached by longtime great Gerald Myers. While he failed to make the team, he stayed on at Tech until May 1980. In January of the following year, he transferred to the University of Texas at San Antonio, hoping that he might have better results there, but when he still did not make the cut, he left school in May 1981.[8]

Timothy Brian Cole in senior prom attire
—Courtesy Ruby Lee Session

Without his parents' knowledge, Tim enlisted on September 3, 1981, for a four-year hitch in the U.S. Army. He completed basics at Fort Sam Houston in San Antonio, and at Fort Bliss in El Paso, he received specialized air defense artillery training. Before arriving at his next assignment in Fort Dix, New Jersey, he had accumulated and wore proudly on his uniform a sharpshooter badge with an automatic rifle bar, an expert badge with a hand grenade bar, an army service ribbon, and assorted others, including a crossed-muskets medallion indicating that he served in the infantry. At Fort Dix, Tim earned several commendations and certificates, among them one from the National Safety Council and another for attending a customer relations seminar.[9]

But Private First Class Tim Cole, with medical supply specialist (medic) training, never fit into the military regimen. He was too much of a loner, and he sorely missed his family back in Fort Worth. Soon, depression set in, and he turned to alcohol for relief. Unfortunately, this led to his leaving the army on January 14, 1983, after serving only slightly more than sixteen months. However, the honorable discharge certificate reflects the separation date as September 2, 1985, which would have been at the end of the original enlistment term.[10]

Upon returning to his hometown, Tim tried desperately to find a steady job and earn enough money not only to pay his way, but also to help with his family's finances. This, however, proved a difficult task. Later on during his trial, he explained:

> Well, my first job I got was in March of 1983. I was working for Nesbitt Building Maintenance cleaning up at [the] Miller Brewery Company on the South Freeway in Fort Worth . . . . The car that I had at the time broke down, so . . . the only way that I could get around was to catch the bus. . . . I got a job working at the Caravan of Dreams in downtown Fort Worth, a jazz club, and I worked there from September of 1983 until my father helped me get a job working at Bell Helicopter installing telephones for a company called Cen-Tel.

Timothy Brian Cole in uniform
— Courtesy Ruby Lee Session

Two months later, though, Tim found himself unemployed once more when Cen-Tel Business Systems' contract with Bell ended. He never held another job for the remainder of 1984.[11]

Sometime during that year, he picked up a copy of *Money Magazine*. An article

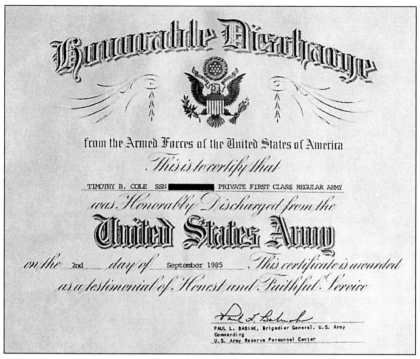

Timothy Brian Cole's Honorable Discharge
—Courtesy Ruby Lee Session

pointed out that he might be eligible to receive a guaranteed student loan and use the proceeds to go to college. Hope returned to the young man, and when he received notice that his loan application had been approved, for the first time in a long while, he felt that his life had turned a corner. Initially, he leaned toward attending Texas Southern University in Houston, but after thinking it over, he soon decided to complete his education at Texas Tech, where he retained a sophomore classification before enlisting in the army. Besides, he would join another brother, already enrolled there, and they could live together—which would both save money and allow him to maintain his strong family ties. "He came because I was in Lubbock," Reggie said. "Because I was the middle child . . . Tim was always real protective of me . . . I was the smallest one. So he always felt like he needed to keep an eye on me."[12]

When Tim arrived in Lubbock, in the northwest part of the state on January 1, 1985, he was not yet twenty-five years old, and although still young by any measure, the army veteran now focused more on his future than when he had lived here previously. He earnestly wanted to make up for lost time, complete a college degree, and get on with a professional career. As planned, he moved into a two-bedroom garage apartment at 1306 Avenue W, sharing with Reggie and another roommate named Quincy Johnson, and as soon as he could, he registered at Tech with a major in political science.[13]

In 1985, whites outnumbered blacks by more than eight to one in Lubbock, and out of a total of 21,676 students enrolled at

Map of Texas
—Courtesy Holiday Inn, Park Plaza, Lubbock

Texas Tech during the spring semester, only 498 were African-Americans. Of those, most were male. These glaring statistics would become more relevant as Tim Cole of Fort Worth, the young man with a thin build, standing six-feet tall, and weighing close to 155 pounds, arrived to attend his first lecture. This meant, as events unfolded, that he was part of an even smaller pool of individuals from which police drew suspects while investigating a crime perpetrated by a black man, particularly when one of them—Tim Cole—had an arrest record.[14]

After moving in with Reggie and Quincy Johnson, Tim found his surroundings to be somewhat less than favorable for keeping up class assignments. Both of his new roommates liked to have a lot of friends over, and as with many college kids living away from home and off campus, partying sometimes becomes the key focus, rather than concentrating on studies. But Tim was different in this respect. At first, he argued constantly with Quincy about the loud music played on the stereo and his late night hours that interfered with school, and frequently, he escaped to read in more peaceful settings. He finally talked with Reggie about the issue, but it did nothing to alleviate the prob-

Garage apartment at 1306 Avenue W as it appears today
—Photograph by Fred B. McKinley

lem with Quincy. When Tim gave up on his demands for quieting the raucous activities, others mistakenly assumed that he had learned to block out the annoying sounds. This is what Reggie concluded when he said, "He would sit at the table as if it didn't even bother him." The noise did matter, but what was Tim to do? Without the income or means necessary to move to another place, he adapted the best he could. To Reggie, Tim seemed too uptight and serious, and he often urged his older brother to get out more and relax. "Tim rarely left the house," Reggie said, "except to work or go to school or eat with his roommates."[15]

CHAPTER TWO

QUAGMIRE

"Everyone is a prisoner of his own experiences.
No one can eliminate prejudices — just recognize them."
— EDWARD R. MURROW

December 27, 1984 symbolized a critical component of Tim Cole's hellish nightmare, even though he had yet to arrive in Lubbock. Because on that Thursday, about five minutes past midnight, Velma Chavez, a twenty-six-year-old Hispanic nurse, finished a long shift at Lubbock General Hospital's Burn Unit. She was tired and eager to get home. Velma entered her vehicle, a 1979 brown Chevrolet Malibu station wagon that she had left earlier at the facility's south parking lot. She slid behind the wheel and started to close the door, but before she could pull it to, a black male came out of nowhere and overpowered her, pushing her over to the passenger side and commanding her to lie on the floor and keep her head down. He held a three- or four-inch knife, which he threatened to use if she failed to do exactly as instructed.[1]

Rain had been falling for four hours, and it was still misty and damp as the intruder drove to an out-of-the-way area in the northwest part of town. He stopped in a field far from the main road and ordered Velma to get out on the driver's side. After doing so, she found herself "standing in mud." Next, she was directed to get into the back seat, and while she removed her pants, her attacker said, "If you make the wrong move I'll bash your head in with this knife and run the blade into your skull."

He then raped her. When it was over, he demanded money and took what little cash Velma had in her purse—$11.00. While stuffing the bills into his pocket, the rapist "asked Ms. [Chavez] to kiss him and hold him tight." And then he had the audacity to follow-up with "if she had had enough?" By this time, understandably, Velma would have agreed to anything to get home safely, so she responded the only way she could have. She answered yes to the question.[2]

Afterward, the assailant left her, crying, scared, and dirty, to walk through the mist to the intersection of North Quaker and Loop 289, where at 12:46 a.m., she waved over D. Clements, a Texas Tech University policeman. When the officer inquired whether he could lend assistance, she screamed, "He's going to kill me."[3]

When she finally calmed down, Velma told the officer what had happened. As she finished detailing her horror, she expressed concern for her future safety, because her rapist had said, "Remember I know you and I know where you live so you don't tell no one or I will kill you."[4]

Clements took her back to the hospital where she worked, to the emergency room for treatment. For some strange reason, the rapist returned her automobile to Lubbock General, where police later recovered her bag, less the $11.00, still in her car. Detectives took the terrified nurse's statement in which she described her assailant as having perhaps a day's growth of beard, a large nose, and brown eyes, standing between five-feet ten and six feet, weighing about 160 pounds, aged between eighteen to twenty-five, and sporting a black Afro about an inch long. When asked what he was wearing, Velma explained that her attacker had on blue jeans, a blue jacket, and a terry-cloth type shirt, but she could not remember the color of the latter.[5]

A few days later, on Sunday, January 13, 1985, an eighteen-year-old white Tech coed walked to her car in the D-8 West parking lot, across from the Texas Tech Law School Building, around 10:15 p.m. Her name was Tana Murphy, the daughter of a vice president employed by the First City Bank of Lewisville. At her car, a 1976 Ford LTD, an African-American man asked for a boost from her battery, and before she could respond, he

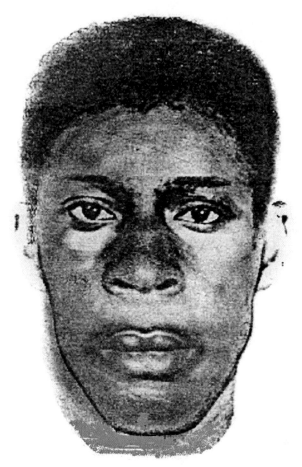

Above: *State's Exhibit No. 53*
Composite by Velma Chavez with assistance of
Sgt. Torres and Detective Supervisor Jay Parchman,
Texas Tech Police Department
—Sources: *Texas v. Cole*, vol. IX, 61;
Exhibit File No. 85-403, 151,
99th District Court, Lubbock.

Right:
A – Velma Chavez' Abduction Site
B – Tana Murphy's Abduction Site

took control of her and the car, abducting her. He drove to north Lubbock and stopped on a dirt road south of FM 1294, near the location of the Farmer's Depot. Tana tried to fight him off and escape, but he threatened to kill her if she kept pulling this type of stunt, so she yielded to his demands. He raped her four times. As during the attack of December 27, the assailant held a small pocket knife, described as having brown handles.[6]

All during the assault, the rapist kept telling Tana that he just needed someone to talk to. And afterward, curiously enough, he provided an extraordinary amount of information about himself, intended probably to throw a future investigation off track. He gave his name as Wayne, said he was from Houston, and that he was a Tech student living on campus at Weymouth Hall. He mentioned that he had been kicked off the university basketball team. Then he left Tana Murphy at the corner of Main Street and Flint Avenue and returned her car, minus the keys, to the

State's Exhibit No. 51
Composite by Tana Murphy with assistance
of Detective Supervisor Jay Parchman,
Texas Tech Police Department
—Sources: *Texas v. Cole*, vol. IX, 58;
Exhibit File No. 85-403, 151,
99th District Court, Lubbock.

same lot where it had originally been parked. Tana described her assailant as a cigarette smoker, about six feet tall, of medium build, with a short black Afro. He was clean cut with a thin mustache, and he wore a dark jacket, white short-sleeved shirt, blue jeans, and bronze-brown cowboy boots.[7]

Three weeks after Velma Chavez' rape, police received some well-timed tips from individuals who had recently seen a composite sketch of the assailant on local television. Authorities acted on the information, and by January 18, police had located and arrested twenty-two-year-old, Terry Lee Clark, a native of Washington County, Mississippi, who had previous altercations with the law in both his home state and later in Galveston. After serving several months of a seven-year sentence, Clark obtained a parole on condition that he would seek rehabilitation at the Eagle's Wing Halfway House, located at 500 E. Broadway in Lubbock. Tana Murphy and Velma Chavez viewed separate line-ups held at the Lubbock County Sheriff's Office, and both branded Clark as their common attacker. In spite of the apparent strong eyewitness identification, though, it appeared that Clark might be freed, because prosecutors worried that the testimony of the two women would not hold up in court. But even though the victims' charges were eventually dropped, Clark remained in jail because of a stronger case that had originated one day prior to his arrest, involving a third victim, Virgie Odom. Brad Underwood, Chief of the Felony Division of the District Attorney's Office, announced that a magistrate ruled "there was sufficient evidence to hold [him] . . . ."[8]

Nevertheless, a troubling loose end still dangled, at least according to Detective Supervisor Jay Allen Parchman of the Texas Tech Police Department, who held out doubts that Clark's

State's Exhibit No. 9
Mug shot of Terry Lee Clark, January 18, 1985
—Courtesy Lubbock County District Attorney

capture would stop the string of rapes, and he suspected there were at least two men involved, maybe copying each other. Parchman became even more wary when, on February 22, one of his officers, Gary Fisher, ran across an individual whom he thought he recognized "walking in the D-2 east parking lot of Horn Hall." Acting on impulse, Fisher stopped and interviewed this person who "stated that his name was Wayne Johnson and that he lived in Weymouth Hall." Furthermore, Johnson bragged that "he strongly resembled Rob Evan, a Texas Tech basketball coach, and that this explained why he looked familiar to Officer Fisher." When he read Fisher's report, Parchman connected the dots: in the Murphy rape, the attacker had also identified himself as a student living at Weymouth Hall named Wayne, who claimed an association with Tech basketball. "Since all this so closely paralleled the other information contained in this case as related by Tana [Murphy]," Detective Parchman said, "I felt it essential to show Mr. Johnson's picture to [her]. . . ."[9]

So he made a trip to Denton to talk with Tana about the possibility and to obtain a blood sample, but when she viewed a spread that included Jerry Wayne Johnson's photograph, plus six individual shots of him "as he appeared on February 22nd," she assured Parchman "that she had never seen this man before in her life." But the detective did not give up so easily. Before terminating the interview and returning to Lubbock, he showed her a picture of Johnson's western boots. Upon close inspection, though, Tana said that these "didn't remind her of the [ones] that her assailant had worn."[10]

Regardless, for the time being, most members of the Lubbock Police Department heaved a collective sigh of relief. They had caught their man, they thought, and Terry Lee Clark's arrest would put an end to the crime spree attributed to the infamous so-called *Tech rapist*. While the detective division concentrated on making a case against Clark, Tim Cole continued to have troubles of his own making.[11]

On Saturday, January 19, at about 6:00 a.m., Tim frantically flagged down Corporal Troy W. Sosebee of the Lubbock Police Department, who was driving his regular patrol route in front of the notorious Alamo Pool Hall and Motel, located at 608

Idalou Road on the east side of town. The place had long been considered a haven for drug dealers. Two armed men had robbed him, Tim said, and he wanted to file a complaint. Sosebee noted that Tim had been drinking, and that concerned him enough to ask for immediate backup. Officer Rosanna Bagby arrived on the scene, and she saw Tim place his hands inside his overcoat. She asked him not only to remove them, but also to keep them in plain sight. When Tim unexpectedly refused, she searched him, and in his right pocket, she found a five-shot .38 caliber revolver holding four live cartridges. From the smell of the barrel, both officers agreed the gun had been recently fired, but the spent shell casing was never recovered. Also on Tim's person were two baggies of marijuana and one package of cigarette papers.[12]

During questioning, Tim admitted that he had met two guys, whom he'd never seen before, at the Thriller Bar at 2114 East Broadway Street. Over drinks, one suggested that Tim join them at another "happening" party, and he foolishly agreed. The three got into a black and silver Cadillac and drove to the Alamo Pool Hall, where after a while, Tim followed one of the men outside to negotiate a drug sale. They stopped behind the building, and Tim bought $15.00 worth of marijuana. In doing so, he placed himself in peril. This time it almost turned deadly when the drug dealer suddenly drew a small revolver and hit him on the back of the head with it. He fired a shot into the air to make a stronger statement, and next he took Tim's wallet, which contained his driver's license, Tech identification card, some personal papers, and photographs.[13]

Although still dazed from the blow, Tim saw his mugger get back into the Cadillac with the second man, and they sped off toward some unknown destination. Patrons inside the pool hall claimed they'd heard a shot from outside, but no one could offer extra details. One witness, however, provided a possible lead on the car and said that it might be parked at the rear of another motel, this one at 2600 Parkway. There officers found a white and blue 1973 four-door Cadillac owned by a man and wife who were registered guests, but it did not prove to be the one driven by the robbery suspects.[14]

Without incident, Bagby and Sosebee transported Tim to the county lockup, where they booked him for unlawfully carrying a weapon and possession of marijuana, both misdemeanors under Texas law, punishable by a fine not to exceed $4,000 and/or county jail time for up to one year. Tim had a smile on his face, even as a deputy took his mug shot. Yet the young man had no inkling of how this inopportune episode of bad judgment would drastically impact his future, considering that his name, date of birth, social security number, address, and other particulars now became part of the system—the database of the Lubbock Police Department, where investigations begin and end.[15]

After Tim's release that same day, another name surfaced—

State's Exhibit No. 8
Mug shot of Timothy Brian Cole, January 19, 1985
—Sources: *Texas v. Cole*, vol. IX, 9;
Exhibit File No. 85-403, 151,
99th District Court, Lubbock.

George M. White
—Courtesy Lubbock
Police Department

one that would soon play an important part in the young man's prospects. George White, a wily Lubbock Police Department veteran with almost eighteen years on the force, called Tim at home and asked him to stop by the station to clear up some details in his robbery report. As he sat down with the corporal, Tim's accounts showed inconsistency. Now he said that he asked a group of people at the Thriller to take him home. There were at least five occupants, including himself and one female, in the car that he currently recalled as silver and maroon. On top of that, he could not say whether a man or woman sold him the marijuana. He looked through several mug books, but no one stood out. White promised to notify Tim if anyone was brought in for questioning. The investigation lay dormant until April 9, when police used the incident against him, and finally on September 10 of the following year, Tim pleaded guilty to both misdemeanor counts, after which charges were dismissed. By then, unfortunately, this issue had become the least of his worries.[16]

As it turned out, Detective Parchman's previous hunch proved correct. With Terry Clark still behind bars, either the *Tech rapist* or someone operating with the same distinctive pattern (*modus operandi*) struck again. At 6:30 p.m. on Friday, February 1, a black male came up from behind—surprised and then overpowered eighteen-year-old Trina Barclay, another white Tech student as she entered her car at the St. John's United Methodist Church parking lot at 1501 University

Avenue, across from Weeks Hall. He commandeered her 1980 Pontiac Sunbird, forced her to the passenger's side, drove to a secluded spot located about one-half mile south of FM 2641, and stopped on a dirt road.[17]

The attacker warned Miss Barclay not to look him in the face or make any cries for help. At first he "kept telling her he was not going to hurt her. He just wanted someone to talk to," and that he was headed to his trailer. But all of a sudden, he turned violent. While waving a small-bladed pocket knife with brown and white wooden handles, he warned, "Don't make any moves or I'll cut your fucking face."[18]

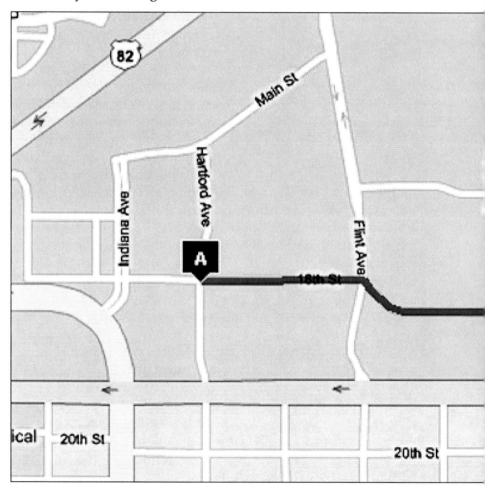

After the man broke the interior light with his knife, he told her to get into the back seat and remove her clothing. He did likewise and began the attack, penetrating her vagina and ejaculating prematurely. Next, both parties got dressed. The rapist drove a short distance and stopped on another dirt road, where he assaulted the young woman once more. Subsequently, he made her take the wheel, and when she reached a point near

Below: *A – Tana Murphy's Abduction Site*
B – Trina Barclay's Abduction Site

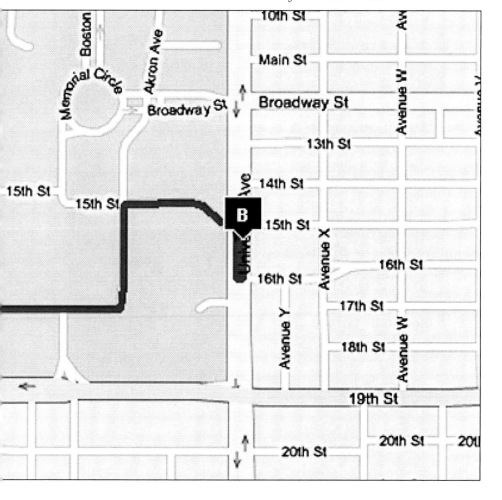

16th Street and Avenue X, the man got out of the car and started running.[19]

Trina told policeman Roberto Garcia, who took her report, that he used the word "fuck" in every sentence. She described her assailant as having a short Afro, and no facial hair or mustache. Furthermore, she said he wore a black leather jacket, blue jeans, light shirt, perhaps a tee shirt, and a dark baseball cap with a white bill. He was between eighteen and twenty-five years old, six feet tall, with a medium build. Trina added that his body contained no apparent scars.[20]

Even before police detectives could finish their paperwork, much less begin the slow investigative process to solve the latest case, a fourth aggravated sexual assault occurred just two days later. At 5:15 a.m. on Sunday, February 3, Margaret Russo, a thirty-two-year-old white night manager left her job at the Denny's Restaurant on Avenue Q. As she walked toward her parked car, a black male in his twenties, standing six feet tall and weighing around 165 pounds, caught her completely off guard. He made her lie on the floor-

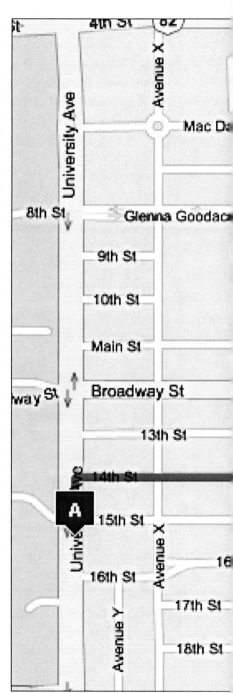

A – Trina Barclay's Abduction Site
B – Margaret Russo's Abduction Site

board, hijacked her 1985 two-door Dodge Mirada, and then drove to 500 N. Quirt Avenue. He said, "All I want to do is fuck you."[21]

He brandished a small-bladed pocket knife with brown and white handles, and he threatened to cut Margaret's throat if she failed to cooperate. After that, he twice raped her vaginally and forced her to perform oral sex on him, none of which resulted in an ejaculation.[22]

Margaret's attacker told her that he wanted money, and he thought that she was on her way to the bank to make the restaurant's night deposit of between $4,000 and $5,000. When he found out otherwise, he settled for a package of Marlboro cigarettes. During the tragic encounter, he continually used foul, vulgar language, including the word "fuck." When the man finished with her, he asked, appallingly, "You've never been raped before have you?"[23]

Margaret said no, and then her assailant drove toward the 100 block of Avenue O, where he left her on foot. He explained that she could retrieve her car at the American State Bank parking lot later, and before he drove off, he provided "directions to find her way back to Denny's." Actually, the automobile was recovered in a lot behind the very restaurant from which she had been abducted.[24]

Miss Russo supplied police with additional information about the physical traits of her attacker. Besides having brown eyes, short curly hair, a large mouth, and soft speech, he wore a black jacket, white-striped shirt, and a black medallion on a necklace that kept hitting her on the chin while he was on top of her. Lubbock police showed her two photo displays and some loose pictures of possible suspects. Margaret demonstrated just how uncertain she was by hesitantly pointing to three: Paul Ward, Vernon Ray Love, and Maurice Vester, but she made no positive identification. If fact, she admitted that she probably never could for the simple reason that her attacker never let her get a good look at him.[25]

Faced with an ever-growing threat on their hands, Tech police announced a marked increase in campus security, including random officer patrols and the addition of a second shuttle bus to be dispatched on demand. Brenda Arkell, a spokesperson for the department released a statement. "We really want to encourage . . . female students to call the Police Department if they need a ride to or from class, the parking lot, the dorm or anywhere on campus," she said. "We're going to do everything we can to make these measures effective."[26]

Larry Ludewig, Associate Vice President for Student Affairs and Dean of Students, added, "We want the campus community to know the administration is aware of the current doubts about campus security, and we are taking concrete steps to alleviate that problem."[27]

All the same, attention to the near state of hysteria produced unexpected consequences. On February 12, campus police received a report from another Tech student, who described her previous night's abduction and rape as almost identical to the ones recently covered by local media. During questioning, however, she broke down and confessed that she had fabricated the account. Her admission came too late, though, because the story had already hit the papers and airways. University Police Detective Jay Parchman commented on the severity of such false reports. "Things like this have a much broader impact than Texas Tech," he said in a statement. "It affects the city of Lubbock and the whole county. City police will step up their patrols in this area, and it will scare a lot of people needlessly."[28]

Barely three months into the new semester at Tech, on March 6, Tim's fragile life began first to unravel, and then spiral completely out of control. Late in the evening, he had gone to the school library to study, and afterward, he walked over to the Biology Building. At 11:25 p.m., Ken Myers of the Custodial Department telephoned campus police and reported that some of his crew had found a young student asleep in classroom 101. They woke him up, and then informed him he could not remain in the building. According to the offense report, the student, identified as Tim Cole, began acting strangely and scared them away. Two campus police officers, Fisher and Walker, responded to the call. When Tim began to cry and shake, "as if he were cold," he explained that "he was under a lot of pressure and that he had a lot of problems."[29]

Walker wrote, "The subject advised that he would go to the office with us and try to get some help, because he thought that he needed to see a psychiatrist."[30]

While being escorted from the premises, and after reaching the sidewalk, Tim said, "No, no, no!" and he ran. Both policemen followed. They tackled and restrained him, and then took him to the campus police station.[31]

When asked why he ran, Tim chose to remain silent, but his crying and shaking continued. He didn't explain this at the time, but he was having a tough time at school, and he believed that bad grades might jeopardize his guaranteed student loan, the one financial lifeline keeping him afloat. And another underlying reason for his bizarre behavior emerged later when he said, "I come from a large family . . . I have two brothers that don't really work, or anything of that nature, and they are not really taking any pressure off of my parents . . . I hadn't found a job, [so] I was beginning to wonder why did I come back down here to Texas Tech to go to college." The mood swings, however, can be fully explained. Tim Cole suffered from schizophrenia, "a chronic, severe, and disabling brain disorder that affects about 1.1 percent of the U.S. population age 18 and older in a given year."[32]

Walker left Tim at the station while he went out to talk to Reggie about the episode. Both Reggie and Quincy accompanied the officer on the return trip to campus, and Reggie spoke with his brother for a long while. After he assured police that Tim was okay, the three left for home. No official action was ever taken, except to refer the behavioral issue, the "need for psychological counseling," to the dean of the university.[33]

Saturday, March 23, was a big day for Tim Cole. After interviewing several times with the same prospective employer since the previous Wednesday, he had landed a job, if only that of a dishwasher at the Elephant Restaurant and Bar on 19th Street, just six blocks from where he lived. But he was happy, because he would bring in extra income and maybe relieve some of the demands he had put on himself to help with his family's finances. Tim was so excited that he marked the day on the calendar he and his roommates had hung on their kitchen wall. The notation read, "Work Saturday 9:00 a.m."[34]

The first day on a new job is usually hectic for anyone, and Tim's experience was no different. "The [electric] dishwasher kept backing up, and it was putting water all over the floor in the area where I had to wash the dishes," he said. "The assistant manager kept telling me to mop up the floor, and also keep up with the dishes at the same time . . . ."[35]

But the day's troubles would not end here. While trying to do everything as fast as possible—washing dirty dishes, mopping floors, and stacking silverware—Tim punctured his right thumb with a fork. Plus, he put in more hours than the schedule called for, because no staff member showed up to take his place. Accordingly, Tim did not get off work until 6:30 in the evening.[36]

At the end of his shift, he thought that everything had gone pretty well, considering that he brought in some overtime—which he certainly welcomed. He drove next door to Arby's Restaurant, where his brother Reggie worked the counter, and passed by the drive-in window. He received a free Coke, and then he went home. At about 3:00 the next afternoon, Sunday, March 24, Tim turned on the television and watched a spring season U.S.F.L. (United States Football League) game that lasted until about 5:30. Next, he walked downstairs to his bedroom to get some sleep, but not before asking Reggie to wake him up at 10:00. Reggie left the apartment about 9:30 p.m. to walk his female guest back to the Tech campus, and then he stopped by Arby's to get something to eat. He told his friends that he wanted his order to go—he had to be home shortly to awaken his brother. At about 10:05, he stirred Tim from a deep sleep, and he vividly recalled the instance. "They [the television newscasters] were talking about how President Reagan was going to the Senate to lobby for MX missiles," Reggie said. "I was in [the] Air Force R.O.T.C. at the time, and we had just been studying the same thing."[37]

Between 10:30 and 11:00 p.m., a friend of Tim's named Marlo Jones, who worked at Mr. Gatti's Pizza on University Avenue, came by for a visit. Tim remembered well the particular hour, just as Reggie had, because a newscast reported a segment about the MX Missile Program, considered controversial at the time by many, but supported overwhelmingly by President Ronald Reagan's administration.[38]

As soon as he got there, Marlo sat down on a bean bag chair and asked whether there was any beer in the house. "This isn't a convenience store," Tim answered, "because everybody seems [to] like coming to our apartment to get a beer . . . after work." Tim referred to the matter as a good-natured argument, because soon, he handed Marlo a beer, and the two friends "laughed it off."[39]

Beginning about 12:00 midnight, Tim's roommate Quincy brought to the apartment his fellow Arby's employees, among them Jackie Boswell, Leslie Thompson, and the store manager, Mike Cates, who soon challenged Reggie to a drinking match. Reggie broke out a bottle of bourbon, and the contest began. Jackie did not like alcohol, so she did not participate. Quincy drank quite a bit, Marlo and Leslie had a couple of Michelob beers, but as for Mike, he took no time at all to become completely inebriated with the stronger liquor.[40]

For his part, even with all the group activity in the living room, including "drinking and having a good time," Tim sat at the kitchen table, studying hard for an upcoming biology lab exam. He "stayed up until time to go to class" the following Monday morning, March 25, something he termed as routine.[41]

CHAPTER THREE

INTO THE ABYSS

*"I screamed for maybe twenty seconds, because then
he started saying that he was going to kill me, and
so I thought that maybe if I quit screaming
that he, at least, wouldn't . . . ."*[1]
– MICHELE JEAN MURRAY

With the public clamoring at a fever pitch for stronger, more aggressive police action to identify the *Tech rapist* and get him off the streets, another Tech student, twenty-year-old sophomore Michele Jean Murray, a graduate of Robert E. Lee High School in Baytown, Texas, became his fifth victim and the third to be attacked on a Sunday.[2]

Between semesters, Michele lived with her parents in Bellview, near Baytown, "a highly industrialized city of oil refining, rubber, chemical, and carbon black plants, on Interstate Highway 10 and State Highway 146, thirty miles east of downtown Houston in southeastern Harris and western Chambers counties." On Sunday, March 24, 1985, at a little before 8:00 p.m., Michele returned to campus after spending a weekend visiting a cousin who lived in Abernathy, about fifteen minutes north of downtown Lubbock. She unpacked her car, left it in the dorm parking lot, and took her belongings to her room in Doak Hall. She spent the next two hours cleaning, straightening up, and putting everything away.[3]

35

Since the previous August, Michele had driven a blue four-door Oldsmobile Cutlass Brougham, a classy mid-sized automobile. She wasn't comfortable leaving it parked in the dorm lot during weekdays, she stressed, because "they only issue a certain amount, and I didn't get [here] in time to get a parking permit before I . . . enrolled in school." Therefore, in order to avoid a fine, Michele did what she did every Sunday night. She moved her car to the St. John's United Methodist Church parking lot, across University Drive and a short walk from the dorm, a practice shared by many of her classmates.[4]

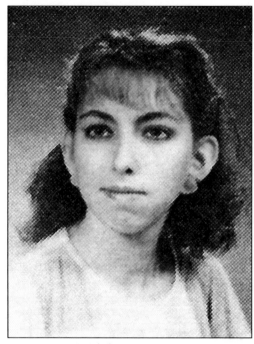

Michele Jean Murray
—Courtesy Texas Tech
University Library

As Tim Cole and his brother Reggie watched the news broadcast in their apartment, a few blocks way, Michele entered the church lot at about 10:00 p.m. The closer spots that she normally chose were taken, so she "parked approximately a third of the way from the entrance on the north . . . and the [one] on the south end . . . behind the Shell station." Even before she had come to a complete stop and turned off the ignition, she caught a glimpse of a man's shadow through her rearview mirror. He came closer, finally reaching the driver's side. At first, Michele refused to roll down her window, but in order to hear what he said, she cautiously lowered it half way. The stranger, an African-American man, explained that "he wanted someone . . . to help him boost his car off with some jumper cables."[5]

"I didn't even know if I had any," Michele replied, "as it was my parents' car, and even if I did, I wouldn't know how to use them."[6]

Given all the publicity concerning the rash of recent rapes, why did Michele throw caution to the wind? "I remember thinking," Michele said, "that before I even saw him . . . , I figured I would be really safe because . . . it seemed like there was even more light than there usually was. Besides, he looked like a Tech student, and I just didn't think that it—I guess I am . . . so naïve that I didn't think anything would happen." In fact, lighting conditions around the parking area had improved tremendously since the previous February 18, when a man named Lloyd Price, acting on behalf of St. John's, contacted Leon Henry, an electrical contractor, to install additional quartz lighting.[7]

Jim Bob Darnell, the district attorney for Lubbock County, agreed with Michele's opinion of herself. "That's the one thing I remember about that girl," he said. "She was probably more naïve about her surroundings than any other person I can remember."[8]

Upon hearing Miss Murray's response about having no jumper cables, the man said nothing and seemed to stare off into space. Unexpectedly, a small brown car, perhaps a Toyota Corolla driven by a male, passed behind them. "Why don't you ask him?" she inquired. "He is a guy, because I . . . don't know anything about cars."[9]

Before Michele could react though, the black man reached inside the car, unlocked the door, pulled a knife, held it to her neck, grabbed her hand, and demanded that she scoot over to the passenger's side. No matter how hard she tried to escape his grasp, the attacker held tight as she struggled, and he didn't let go until Michele gave a hard bite to his right thumb. Immediately, he gained complete control of her upper body and pushed it downward toward the floor. The young victim, only five feet, three inches tall, tearfully explained the terror that she underwent in these few, tense seconds. "I couldn't get away, because he had a knife, and plus, he was ten times stronger than me. Then, he started calling me a fucking bitch about ten or fifteen times." Michele had never been so scared, and for the first time in her life, she thought she was going to die. All of the hazy visions of brutal rape scenes depicted in movies and on television flashed before her eyes. She shook violently, her heart raced, then pounded, a strange metallic taste filled her mouth, which by now seemed as dry as the parched earth around Lubbock during summer months. "I was screaming, because I thought maybe that guy in the car would hear me, or somebody would hear me. He told me if I kept screaming that I wasn't going to come back alive. So I just got real quiet."[10]

Within thirty seconds, maybe less, the man reached for the keys still in the ignition, started the motor, backed up, and began to drive. With her head still in a downward position, and her assailant holding a knife to the side of her face, Michele had no idea which direction they were traveling. For the next few minutes, the fellow tried to carry on a conversation by asking things about her college major, her name, and where she lived. Michele tried to humor him by saying she was an education major. She gave her actual age, but a fake name, and a non-existent address. When the man said that he was also enrolled at Tech, she asked what he was studying, to which he issued a strange response, something about "hurdles." He started to rant about how the university mistreated black students, and Michele suspected that he was high on drugs. But when he bragged about being "on probation and

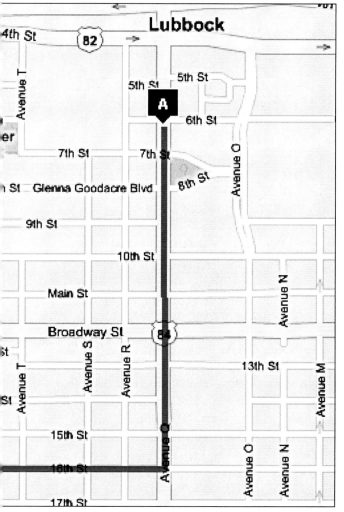

A – *Margaret Russo's Abduction Site*
B – *Michele Murray's Abduction Site*

had a sentence for 40 years for killing other women," she became utterly terrified.[11]

When the car did stop, finally, she raised her head high enough to tell that they were parked in an open field far from the Texas Tech campus, but close enough that she could see the glow of city lights. During that particular day, Lubbock had experienced beautiful — and somewhat unusual — weather for this time of year. Temperatures reached a high of seventy-eight degrees, and it was clear. By now, however, a little past 10:00 p.m., winds were blowing out of the southeast at only fifteen miles per hour, and with the sun having set three hours earlier, it had cooled to a comfortable fifty-six degrees. Visibility up close, nonetheless, remained extremely poor, because the phase of the moon on March 24 revealed a "waxing crescent [increasing in size] with 9% of the . . . visible disk illuminated."[12]

Michele timidly asked the man what he wanted, and without hesitation, he gave a cold, blunt reply. "Let's get it on." When she said that she had no idea what he meant, his answer sent shivers up her spine. "I want to screw you." Though inexperienced, Michele knew her only chance now was to talk her way out of this.[13]

"I am a virgin," she said. "I'm saving myself for marriage." But she could see her assailant didn't care about this. He just laughed and ridiculed her, saying flatly that he did not believe it. All twenty-year-old women, he argued, have had sex. Though Michele's nerves were shattered, she tried to appear calm. After all, he still held the knife in his right hand.[14]

Once again, Michele heard his sickening demand. "I want to screw you just once," he said, "then I'll take you back alive." Torn between fear of losing her life or losing her virginity, she chose to save her life.[15]

It took all the strength that Michele could muster to maintain her sanity and then bear what followed. "I was in the passenger seat," she said, "and he was in the driver's." The man took off his pants and ordered that she do likewise. Michele continued with the sordid details. "Then he tried to penetrate, but he couldn't, and then, he got mad and told me if it didn't go in, that he was not going to take me back alive. He told me to get it hard," she tearfully explained, "and he told me to suck him off." The young woman felt the cold steel of the knife blade touch her back as she bent over and complied.[16]

A few minutes later, the rapist performed oral sex on Michele. Still unsatisfied, he ordered her to change positions and take off her top, bra, and panties. He removed his shirt as well. While recalling these events, Michele could barely whisper, "We got in the back seat of the car . . . and he made me perform oral sex on him again." To her, it seemed that it took at least an hour or more for the man to obtain an erection. "Eventually it got hard," she said, "and he did penetrate after that. Once he penetrated and it stayed in, I kept crying because it hurt . . . ." Later, she revealed that her attacker admitted — referring to her virginity — that he did finally believe her, but relative to whether he had an orgasm or not, she had no clue.[17]

Following what seemed an eternity, he told Michele to start putting on her clothes, and he would as well. When he said "that he was going to drive the car back to a friend of his," Michele's thoughts turned once more to the possibility of worse things to come. She feared that a second man would now take his turn with her. But after hearing "that he would let her take the car from there," she hoped that he would at the very least, let her live.[18]

The two finished dressing, and the assailant, with the knife still clutched in his right hand, started the car. They began to move — but to what destination? As they continued driving, Michele sat upright in the passenger's seat. Even though she could somewhat see the nearby surroundings, including some shanty houses, as she described them, she had no idea where they were or where they were going. He did presumably stop at the friend's house, but Michele was so frightened that she could not later recall any details, except that he took $2.00, all the money she had in her purse, along with a gold Timex watch and a small diamond ring, for a total estimated value of $132. Michele expressed regret at losing her jewelry, but this was a simple thing, she thought, since at least she was alive. When the man got out of the car, he said that she could get back to campus on her own. She asked, "Well, how do I get back?" When she rephrased the question to, "I don't know how to get back," he responded with a gesture. "He pointed me toward the loop . . . ." A sobbing Michele explained what happened next. "I was driving away as fast as I could . . . ." At first she looked in her mirror long enough, she said, "Just to make sure he kept going in the opposite direction from me."[19]

By the time Michele reached the safety of her dorm, it was a little past 1:00 a.m. on Monday, March 25, and during the span of three hours since her abduction at 10:00 the previous evening, she had gone through an unimaginable experience. She ran to the locked doors, and banged like mad until she got the night watchman's attention. When he opened up, she said, "I told him I had been raped, and he called the Tech police." While waiting for authorities to arrive, Michele called an ex-roommate, Joan Wigness, who lived in nearby Weeks Hall. She gave a verbal statement to campus police before making her way up to her room. There, she made the most difficult call ever, the one to her mother to explain what had just happened. Shortly, Julie Smith, the resident assistant who "was also with the Rape Crisis Center," joined Michele in her room to help begin the long odyssey toward healing.[20]

Smith suggested that Michele gather some extra clothes, and then she, along with Joan and her roommate, accompanied her to Lubbock General Hospital, where they were met by Jennifer Ann Rosson, another volunteer with the Rape Crisis Center. Jennifer noted that Michele was extremely tense and nervous, as rape victims commonly are. Rosson described her appearance: "She had her hands very close in her lap. She had her elbows in close to her body. She was holding a Kleenex that she would use. She had the sniffles. She had been crying and her eyes were very red, and very swollen." Over the next five or six hours, Rosson comforted, counseled, and listened to Michele, and during this period, she completed an intake form that provided details about the crime. "She was shaking all over," Rosson said. "I don't re-call that she ever stopped shaking when we were together."[21]

Jamie Herrera, a Lubbock patrolman for about five years, worked the midnight shift, and at 1:54 a.m. on March 25, he was dispatched to the hospital. He found Michele "emotionally dis-

Jamie Herrera
—Courtesy Lubbock
Police Department

turbed, crying, confused." During the interview that lasted between one and two hours, Herrera said that Michele "didn't actually understand what was going on. She was upset. It was very easy for her to break down and cry during that period of time," and in fact she did, several times.[22]

A cursory glance revealed cuts on Michele's chest and hands, scratches on her leg, multiple bruising on her thighs and calves, and some vaginal blood on her clothing. None of the injuries, however, appeared to have come by way of the assailant's knife. Between intermittent periods of breaking down, crying, the distraught coed provided, as best she could, a complete description of her attacker, the man who mocked her and stole her virginity. He was black, about twenty-three or twenty-four years old, less than six feet tall, probably more like five feet, six inches, with a round, regular face, medium build, and a short Afro—cropped so close in fact that when she tried to pull it during the struggle to get out of the car, she could not grab hold. The man, she said, "had buggy eyes, and that is the thing that I remembered most about him." Additionally, he wore a watch of some kind, blue jeans, a yellow terry cloth pull-over shirt with a collar, and thick beach thongs that partly covered his feet. Asked whether her attacker wore a beard or mustache, Michele said no. It was more like a couple of days' growth. She also mentioned that he had smoky breath, only natural since he lit up a cigarette before, during, and after the attack.[23]

Dr. Phillip Swanson, an emergency room physician, performed a gynecological exam, taking swabs from the vagina and combings from pubic hair, as well as anything else that might aid police in identifying Michele's attacker. The Rape Crisis Center workers delivered her underwear and warm-up top and bottoms to the Department of Public Safety's Lab for analysis, and later in the day, Rosson took Michele to the city's health department for a blood test. Officer Herrera searched her car, where he found one whole Winston cigarette and part of another that had been smoked. And because the young victim mentioned that the assailant used her car's lighter, the officer dusted it for fingerprints. In a puzzling development that may have permanently altered this investigation, Jimmie Riemer, who worked in the police department's Identification Section, wrote in his report of March 25, "This date the latent prints were checked and found to have no ID value, so the latent card was destroyed. No latent fingerprints in this case at this time." One has to ask why Herrera did not place the actual cigarette lighter into evidence, and why would any identification technician, much less one with nineteen years on the job, destroy *anything* taken from a crime scene?[24]

Jimmie D. Riemer
—Courtesy Lubbock Police Department

With this latest assault now making local news, considerable speculation arose amongst the general public that cast doubt on whether authorities had actually arrested the *Tech rapist*, when they took Terry Lee Clark into custody back on January 18.

After all, even though Clark remained behind bars, the rapes nevertheless continued. Rumors ran rampant, and "stories about the legitimacy of Clark's arrest were fueled by the refusal of police officers to say they were 100 percent sure Clark was the assailant [on the cases prior to Michele Murray's]." Jay Parchman, Detective Supervisor of the Texas Tech Police Department, sought to offset such conjecture by pointing out to the press that three rape victims had positively identified Clark in separate line-ups. Too, he said, Clark had received, on February 5, grand jury indictments for the aggravated sexual assaults of Tana Murphy and Velma Chavez.[25]

True, another rape with characteristics similar to many of the others had occurred, and for the second time in less than two months, someone had abducted a Tech student from the same church parking lot, right across from campus. Lubbock Police Chief Tom Nichols knew something had to be done, and fast, to restore the public trust, so on Wednesday, March 27, his staff assigned Detective Joe Nevarez, who had been with the force since

March 1969, to begin the investigation of the most recent sexual assault. According to Nevarez, he asked Michele to meet him at the police station, and at 1:00 p.m. on the 27th, she arrived in the company of Jennifer Rosson. The discussion lasted an hour and a half, after which the detective took her full statement that explained the events of March 24–25. Michele also looked through several mug books but disappointingly, she failed to identify anyone. Then she and Nevarez worked

Thomas J. Nichols, Chief of Police from Feb. 19, 1983 to Feb. 9, 1990
—Courtesy Lubbock Police Department

for about thirty minutes on a composite that they hoped would describe the assailant, enough anyway to at least generate some worthwhile tips.[26]

With that part of the official procedure completed, the detective took Michele back to the scene of her abduction in the

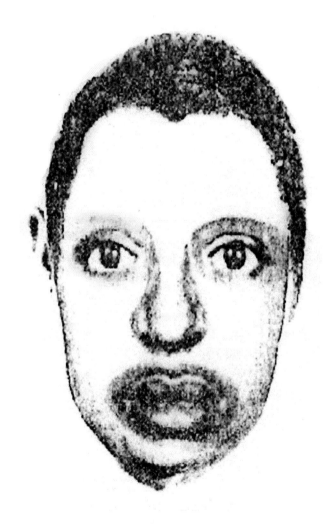

State's Exhibit No. 3

—Sources: *Texas v. Cole*, vol. IX, 4;
Exhibit File No. 85-403, 151,
99th District Court, Lubbock

José (Joe) Nevarez
— Courtesy Lubbock
Police Department

church parking lot. As with any good investigation, one should start from scratch, and this is exactly what Nevarez did. He asked Michele to tell him everything she could remember, to show him exactly where she had parked, and the route she thought they might possibly have taken that terrible night. Since she had previously described the area where the assault occurred to be near a "neighborhood of some small, run-down houses," they drove out to the east side of town, searching for anything that might lead them to the spot of the rape. Michele tried to help, but she simply didn't know. So she returned to her dorm and anxiously awaited word about an arrest that might allow her to carry on with a small degree of normalcy.[27]

CHAPTER FOUR

THE MOTH EFFECT

"The purpose for your participation in this
surveillance was to cause some black male
to seek you out, was it not?"[1]
– MIKE BROWN, ATTORNEY-AT-LAW, TO ROSANNA BAGBY

There has long been the human fascination with the moth, and for as many as four thousand years, the Chinese have used one of its species in silk production. Early on, children are introduced to the time-tested adage "like a moth to a flame," which originated as a teaching tool to keep us out of harm's way. After observing, at dusk or nighttime, this beautiful creature fluttering around bright lights in backyard gardens and on patios, everything begins to make sense. By one simple act of flirtation, Tim Cole became a victim of his own rendition of the Moth Effect, and afterward, he became forever interconnected to each of the five women in Lubbock, who had been raped between December 27, 1984 and March 25, 1985.[2]

The turning point of the investigation came on Sunday, March 31, 1985, the date that Detective Ronnie L. Goolsby took charge of the Murray case. Goolsby, a ten-year detective, felt the need for an innovative spark, so he immediately devised and submitted to his boss, Lieutenant Dean P. Summerlin, a bold plan whereby a massive surveillance effort would be initiated to draw out a credible suspect. Actually, this maneuver was nothing more than an undercover sting operation. The new strategy, which Summerlin readily endorsed, called for nine officers to be stationed at various points. One of them, a female, would be bait. But first, Goolsby created a chart that centered on the five aggravated sexual assaults attributed to the *Tech rapist*, involving Velma Chavez, Tana Murphy, Trina Barclay, Margaret Russo, and now Michele Murray. While reviewing the traits of each crime, the detective noted a great number of similarities between one assault and the next. He summarized these in a report:

> On each of the five separate offenses above, the victim was confronted as she was either getting into her car on a parking lot or was already in her car. On each occasion the suspect would produce a small pocket knife and move the victim over in the passenger seat so that the suspect could commandeer the vehicle and take the victim to a secluded area either North or East of the City and sexually assault the victim.
>
> The suspect would then drive the victim's vehicle back into town and in three of the five cases, would put the victim out a short distance from where the suspect would return the vehi-

Ronnie Goolsby
—Courtesy Lubbock
Police Department

Dean Summerlin
—Courtesy Lubbock
Police Department

cle. The other two cases, the suspect let the victim drive to an area and he would jump out of the vehicle and run. With the chart completed, it was shown that the suspect favored the weekend on Friday and Sunday nights. Two of the assaults took place on the St. John's United Methodist Church parking lot in the 1500 block of University (2-11 and 2-30).[3]

Earlier that same Sunday, Lt. Summerlin contacted an assistant pastor at St. John's and received approval to obtain a key that would allow police access to an upstairs office, where they would have an easy view of the parking lot. At about 6:00 p.m., the operation commenced with Summerlin, Goolsby, Nevarez, Corporals Billy Hudgens, George White, and Pat Nesbitt, Officer Rosanna Bagby, along with Texas Tech personnel, Jay Parchman and Gene Minnick, assuming their respective positions. Summerlin and Nevarez took the church office. White further explained, "That night, myself and several other officers maintained a surveillance in the area of 16th and University, for the purpose of observing foot traffic and persons in that area, to see if a suspect could be identified."[4]

Billy Hudgens
—Courtesy Lubbock
Police Department

Pat Nesbitt
—Courtesy Lubbock
Police Department

Teddy Daniels
— Courtesy Lubbock
Police Department

Stated simply, they were casting a net to seek out any black male who might make contact with a white female undercover operative, specifically Patrol Officer Bagby, who said, "I would park my vehicle [on the church parking lot], get out and walk across to one of the dorms, I think it was Weeks, then I would wait awhile and walk back." She repeated this routine at least five times that night, extending until 12:30 the following morning, with no success.[5]

In the meantime, information originated from other sources, and the university's beefed-up security measures began to yield dividends. On Wednesday afternoon, April 3, Corporal Teddy Daniels of the Lubbock Police Department handled a telephone call from Lisa Osteriech, an instructor at Texas Tech. She reported that at about 11:35 that morning, as she and student teacher Laura Shelton were walking to their car parked in an alley in the 1400 block of University, a smooth-talking, well-dressed black male, who fit the widely distributed composite description, walked up and began telling them how pretty they were. He wanted to shake their hands. His curious behavior set off alarms, and the two ladies stepped back. When Osteriech knocked on the door of a nearby apartment for assistance, the man quickly left, and neither of the women suffered injury, other than being frightened.[6]

Although disappointed with its previous outing, the surveillance team tried again, this time on Friday, April 5, with Goolsby, Bagby, Hudgens, Sergeant Randy Ward, Corporals George Parramore, Teddy Daniels, and Aubrey Stark, and Detectives Lloyd Brown and Randy Franklin participating.

Bagby began walking the streets at 7:00 p.m., but as before, no one attempted contact with her. At 1:00 a.m., Goolsby called his officers together and ordered them to go home, saying they'd try again later.[7]

Ever since Tim had arrived back in the South Plains, he'd dealt with one setback after another, but as April 6 ended, nothing provided the slightest hint that, within the span of the next five days, he would incur the wrath of the police department's unique version of the *Four Horsemen of the Apocalypse*: Goolsby, White, Nevarez, and Bagby.

On Sunday, April 7, Tim awoke as usual, Lubbock remained on edge, and Ronnie Goolsby strained under enormous pressure to identify and arrest the *Tech rapist*. However, now the detective had even more cause for concern. After getting off work at 4:30 that morning, Brenda Jones, a twenty-year-old white employee of Pinocchio's Pizza, rode her bike northbound on University en route to her apartment. A large red automobile, with red interior, pulled in front of her and slowed down. When she tried to pass, a black male jumped out of the vehicle, grabbed her, and pushed her to the pavement, causing minor abrasions on her hand. While screaming, "You bitch, you fucking whore, you better stop or I'll hurt you," he pulled her toward the driver's side door and tried to force her inside. But the young woman put up quite a fight and simply refused to be abducted. According to her, the attack lasted no more than sixty to ninety seconds.[8]

Whether the assailant saw another car coming or experienced some other distraction, Brenda was not sure, but at any rate, something scared him off. He quickly got back into his car and sped off down 47th Street. Brenda ran to her apartment building for help. She didn't even take the time to pick up her bike, glasses, or keys still lying in the middle of University. At her apartment, neither her roommate nor the security guard who lived upstairs was home, so she frantically searched for a telephone. After finding one, she put in a call for help. About that time, a paper boy came by, and he stayed with her until police arrived. They took her back to the scene of the crime, and luckily all of her personal belongings were recovered, unharmed, right where she left them. Miss Jones described her attacker as a black male in his early twenties, weighing between 145 and 150 pounds, and standing less than six feet. He wore a short Afro, and he had no facial hair. She had memorized his license plate, which she said was DGB411.[9]

Officers were unable to trace that particular combination, or any form thereof, so they asked Brenda to come by the station. At 4:00 that same afternoon, she tried to help with a composite drawing, but the attempt didn't pan out. Detective Goolsby then showed her books that contained from fifty to seventy-five mug shots of known black male sex offenders and rapists. Unfortunately, she could not make a positive identification so, for the time being, the investigation stalled.[10]

Naturally, the fact that the *Tech rapist* continued to operate right under their noses infuriated Ronnie Goolsby. Then he had a brainstorm. He decided to reassemble the surveillance team and make another run, but this time, he would extend the net. What soon followed kicked off a chain of events that could well have been plucked from a crime novel. Instead of having Bagby concentrate on the circuit from the church parking lot to Weeks Hall and back, her supervisor now ordered her to walk the area farther down University Avenue, which included Mr. Gatti's Pizza, a local haunt for college kids. Beginning at roughly 7:30 p.m., Goolsby deployed his squad in three separate vehicles. He teamed up with Corporal Nesbitt in one, he assigned Corporal Parramore to ride with Detective Nevarez in a second, and Corporals Hudgens and White rode in the third. Goolsby described the operation in its earliest stages:

> Parramore and Nevarez were in a white Thunderbird parked on Mr. Gatti's Pizza parking lot and as they had first pulled up to begin the surveillance, they observed a beige/brown 4dr Buick Electra 225, Tex registration of AXG99, which shows it to be registered to a 1974 Buick 4drHT to Timothy B. Cole of 1306 Ave. W., Lubbock. Det. Nevarez told this officer [Goolsby], that they had observed the B/M driving the Buick on the Church parking lot of 1500 University and that the veh. had stopped beside a white female who was walking across the parking lot. The black male appeared to be attempting

conversation with the female for a brief period of time and then the vehicle pulled off the lot.[11]

Police radios were abuzz with activity, pulses quickened, and the intensity thickened like fog. Conversations between Goolsby and the others contained remarks that indicated their hard work might finally be paying off. This could be the one, they said, and with a little luck, it would just be a matter of time before they'd find out for sure. At this moment, in the eyes of the police, it seemed as if for-

George Parramore
— Courtesy Lubbock Police Department

tune became their new partner, their new best friend. Maybe it was true that the third time's the charm. And then, they got another break, one that appeared like manna from heaven.

Parramore and Nevarez looked at each other in near disbelief as they saw the 1974 Buick slowly pulling into the Mr. Gatti's parking lot at 16th and University, close to where they sat in the Thunderbird. As the lone black occupant stepped out of the car, they got a good look at him.

He wore "a tweed sport coat and tan 'golfing cap', blue jeans and unknown shoes." They watched him walk into the pizza parlor and then take a seat on the north end of the building, next to the window, where he had an unobstructed view of University Avenue, and specifically the St. John's parking lot. At this time, no one on the stakeout team had any way of knowing that Tim actually came in to visit his friend Marlo Jones, who had yet to arrive, so Tim sat at his customary spot and waited. Watching, Goolsby concluded he couldn't pass up the opportunity to close this controversial case. He decided to go for the *coup de grâce*, the decisive stroke, and send in the decoy.[12]

At 9:00 p.m., Rosanna Lue Bagby entered Mr. Gatti's dressed as if she were a Tech student. She wore skorts, described as a skirt/shorts combo, a shirt, a jacket, and tennis shoes. Bagby saw Tim sitting alone at a bare table, staring out at the traffic. She explained what she did next:

> They [Goolsby and White] had said that there was this person in there sitting at the window, so I walked in and ordered a Dr. Pepper, sat down slightly in front of him, with my back to that person. [I] just sat there for awhile waiting, kind of watched the videos for awhile and drank my Dr. Pepper, just enough time to get noticed, and I got up and left.[13]

According to Rosanna, she remained in the restaurant for about ten minutes, with her back to Tim, and only one table between them. She made no attempt to talk to him, and neither did he try to strike up a conversation. After leaving, she strolled north on University, first past a Shell station, and then a Texaco. "He [Marlo Jones] did not come within a reasonable amount of time," Tim said, "so I got into my car and headed down 14th Street to [the] 14th Street Bar and Grille." On the way, in an ironic twist, he spotted the girl that he had just seen at the pizza place, but obviously, he didn't recognize her as the same police officer who had arrested him at the Alamo Pool Hall, early on January 19.[14]

As she crossed 14th Street, Tim pulled up behind her, and this is when Rosanna heard someone say, "Hey, come here."[15]

Cautiously and with full knowledge that her fellow squad members were nearby and ready to assist her at a split second's notice, the young patrol officer took a deep breath, turned, walked over to the vehicle, and looked long at the driver, whom she described as "a black male, [with] medium colored skin, [he] had a short black Afro, [and] his eyes were slightly protruded. He was of thin build; he was wearing a beige sports jacket, and a tweed button down hat. He was neat in person and dress."[16]

During a ten-minute conversation between the two, Tim acted as most single young men might have in a similar situation. He had seen a pretty girl with red hair and blue eyes, obviously alone, maybe unattached, and he wanted to make her acquaintance. First, he asked her name, and Rosanna gave her real one. He gave his name as Timothy, and he reached forward, politely, and shook her hand. He wanted to know why she left Mr. Gatti's so quickly. She replied that the person who was supposed to meet her there never made it. Tim commented, "You shouldn't have left. We could have had some beers, or something." The chitchat continued. It was established that they both attended Tech. He was a junior and she a senior. They discussed where they were each from. Tim asked Rosanna if she wanted a ride, but she said no. He pointed to the nearby bar and grill and asked, "Would you want to go have some beers or party some?" Rosanna declined, and then she asked his name again. After replying, "Timothy, Timothy Brian Cole," he shook her hand for the second time. He wanted her telephone number, but she did not give it. Once more, he offered the undercover officer a ride, but with another rejection, Tim simply said, "Bye." At this point, he drove eastbound on 14th Street.[17]

Even at her present pay grade, Rosanna Bagby was not just some ordinary rookie patrol officer with a high school education. She held a Bachelor of Science degree from Northeast Missouri State University [now Truman State University] in Kirksville, having majored in criminal justice and sociology. For her, the Lubbock Police Department represented the first step of a remarkable journey that would eventually take her to the rank of lieutenant within the high profile Texas Department of Public Safety's

Rosanna Bagby
—Courtesy Lubbock Police Department

Special Crimes Unit, then to the office of Bastrop County Sheriff, and finally to her own law practice. But on this day in April 1985, the assignment to the surveillance squad represented the single most important event in her young career.[18]

Soon Hudgens and White drove to where Bagby stood waiting, and she entered their unmarked vehicle. As they parked in the 1300 block of University Drive, the three discussed what Tim Cole said, his actions, and the next step in the investigation. Something stuck in the back of Rosanna's mind that reminded her of something one of the rape victims had said about her attacker, that he had buggy eyes. Bagby explained later, after viewing the composite shown previously as State's Exhibit No. 3, that she felt sure that she had met the same man. Without batting an eyelash, the patrol officer told Hudgens and White, "I thought he was the person we were looking for." Sadly, for all intents and purposes, the search for Michele Murray's rapist ended with Rosanna's statement that consisted of ten words. But it should be noted that at this time, Rosanna Lue Bagby occupied the lowest level on the department's ranking charts. She made no command decisions, and therefore she did not, nor could she, call off any future surveillance activity. Nevertheless, her declaration, when combined with the fact that she had previously arrested Tim Cole, contributed to the overall belief that further stakeouts would be unnecessary.[19]

While Bagby, Hudgens, and White continued to discuss the encounter with Cole, they spotted his vehicle slowly moving toward them. "He had made the block and come back to see where I had gone," Rosanna surmised. "I had to duck down in the car so he wouldn't see that I had gotten in . . . ."[20]

Within minutes, Detective Goolsby called a meeting behind the International House of Pancakes, located at 6th Street and Avenue Q. Present in addition to himself were White, Hudgens, Bagby, Nevarez, Nesbitt, and Parramore. Their goal was to determine how to proceed with the most promising suspect developed thus far. Hudgens immediately went back to the police station. There, he located Tim's previous arrest record that involved the marijuana and weapon charges at the Alamo Pool Hall the past January 19. He was surprised to note that

Bagby was one of the arresting officers. Now he needed a mug shot. Hudgens searched the files, but he found nothing. Perhaps another source would yield one, but that would have to wait until the next day. Meanwhile, the current surveillance ended at midnight, and it would never be reconvened, because building a case against Tim Cole became the primary task.[21]

Goolsby's team must have been caught up in the heat of the moment, as the mounting expectations of the public at large, as well as university and city officials and the police hierarchy stoked the flames and demanded quick action. Thus Tim Cole became a person of interest, then graduated to a suspect, and ultimately became the prime target, all within a matter of two hours. The young man from Fort Worth entered the eye of the perfect storm.

State's Exhibit No. 22: Lubbock Police Department Photo Spread
—Sources: *Texas v. Cole*, vol. IX, 23;
Exhibit File No. 85-403, 151, 99th District Court, Lubbock

Early on Monday, Goolsby "went to the Lubbock Sheriff's Office and obtained a color photo of Timothy Brian Cole (displayed previously as State's Exhibit No. 8)." He placed it into the number two slot of an array, but the detective claimed that he could not use this one, because Tim had exposed his teeth in a wide grin (see State's Exhibit No. 22). Oddly, Detective Goolsby had presented this particular photo spread to Brenda Jones that afternoon, and on Tuesday morning, April 9, at about 9:30, another officer took the liberty to again show her the same one. On neither occasion was she able to pick out her attacker from among the group. Regardless, the real deception began that same day when Goolsby sent George White over to Tim's apartment with the objective of taking another photo of Tim under any pretense necessary. "He was the victim of a robbery [on January 19], and since I had talked with him prior to this, I went to his residence to obtain a picture of him," White said. "The reason I told him I wanted [it] was in reference to the robbery."[22]

Parramore and White arrived at 1306 Avenue W and found Tim's parked vehicle, the same one observed during the recent surveillance. They knocked on the door and explained the purpose of the visit—an informant, they said, had come forward, but this person needed to see a current photo of him before proceeding. A trusting soul, Tim invited them inside. He suspected nothing. He thought these guys were here to help him get his valuables back. When Tim willingly agreed to have his picture taken, White snapped two color Polaroids. One copy was too dark, so he destroyed it. But he was able to use the second, which is displayed in position five of State's Exhibit No. 21.[23]

After White put together the photo spread that now included the shot just taken of Tim, he and Nevarez visited Goolsby, on his day off at home, to show him what they were going to present to Michele Murray. Goolsby approved, and at about 2:50 that afternoon, the two officers went out to see the rape victim who came down from her dorm room and met them in the lobby. She commented later that when Nevarez showed her the exhibit, "They asked me if I could pick him out of the photograph spread, if any of those were the man who raped me?" Michele

closely examined the layout. She pointed to the person in position number five and she said, "I think that is him."[24]

Their response, she noted, was, *"Are you positive?"*[25]

There has been much confusion as to whether all six of the
photographs included in State's Exhibit No. 21 were color, and
amazingly, some well-known national publications persist in
perpetuating the falsehood that five of them, with the exception
of Tim Cole's, were black and white. Captain Greg Stevens,
Public Information Officer for the Lubbock Police Department,
clarified that during this period, the sheriff's office had two
color cameras on site, one for its use and a second for the police
department. The same deputy, who took a mug shot on one, repeated the procedure on the other if the arrest was made by a

State's Exhibit No. 21: Lubbock Police Department Photo Spread
—Sources: *Texas v. Cole*, vol. IX, 22;
Exhibit File No. 85-403, 151, 99th District Court, Lubbock

police officer (for an example, refer to Appendix 2). And to remove all doubt, the original color version of State's Exhibit No.
21 remains within the 99th District Court Reporter's Archives.
Furthermore, arguments continue today about the manner in
which the officers arranged and displayed this particular photo
array. The Polaroid that White took shows a direct, frontal view
of Tim, while the other photos are more traditional mug shots —
and in fact, four of the individuals are shown holding booking
identification information. After viewing this exhibit, it is
doubtful that anyone would dispute that "Number 5" requires
a second look, solely because it is so different. Therein lies the
problem. Any law enforcement academy in the land teaches the
basics: when showing an eyewitness a photo for possible identification of a suspect, an officer should never make suggestive
remarks or gestures to obtain the desired result. The question
asked of Michele, "Are you positive?" certainly conjures up
other possibilities when one inquires further. Positive of what?
Was she positive that she thought it was Tim? Or were the officers openly trying to influence her decision? The situation is
controversial and begs for additional discussion. A *USA Today*
report posted on November 26, 2002, notes:

> The problems increase when the police officer or prosecutor
> overseeing a photo spread or line-up knows which participant
> is the real suspect. A witness "can be steered toward making
> the 'right' choice, even if the officer isn't consciously trying" to
> influence the witness, says Ronald Fisher, a psychologist at
> Florida International University in Key Biscayne who helped
> prepare a Justice Department study of suspect IDs in 1999.
> "Tone of voice, verbal cues, even raised eyebrows can let the
> witness know whether he got the answer that police think is
> right."[26]

In any event, Michele responded, "Yes, I am positive that is
him." She had first hesitated "to get a better look," she said. "I
mean I had to look at all of them." Now she held no doubt whatsoever that Timothy Brian Cole raped her, and his picture in the
photo display made a permanent imprint on her memory.
According to Michele, before White and Nevarez took her to the

police station to complete necessary paperwork, including a notarized, signed two-page affidavit detailing the rape that occurred on March 24-25, one or the other wrote "That's Him" to the right side of Tim's photo in position number five. She, however, admitted only to placing her initials right above the officers' added comment, and between their other entries including the date, time, and day of the week.[27]

Based on Michele's identification, however questionably obtained, White and Nevarez hastily prepared a Probable Cause Affidavit, and early on Wednesday morning, April 10, they presented the case to David Hess of the District Attorney's Office, who gave the go-ahead after which Justice of the Peace Blalack signed off on an arrest warrant. About 1:25 that afternoon, Goolsby led the team of White, Nevarez, and Ashmore to Tim's apartment, where they saw him getting into his car. Goolsby and Nevarez confirmed his identity, and they approached and advised him that he was being arrested on charges of aggravated sexual assault, aggravated kidnapping, and aggravated robbery.[28]

Tim could not believe it. "Why me?" he asked. Besides, he had done nothing wrong. Surely, he thought, this was a terrible mistake that would be cleared up shortly. But when Goolsby read him his rights, and Navarez placed handcuffs on his wrists, all within three minutes, the seriousness of the situation began to set in.[29]

The officers took him upstairs, and Goolsby put before him two Consent to Search forms—one for his car and the other for the apartment. From inside, Reggie witnessed the spectacle with shock and dismay. Like his brother, he had no idea of what the police were looking for. But Tim put on the best face possible, and around 1:30 p.m., he signed both forms. No one had anything to hide, so what harm could it do? Champing at the bit, Goolsby entered Tim's bedroom on the lower level, and he inventoried the following as possible evidence: "a man's black jacket, brand name L'Avion, size 44, found in the closet, one ladies' yellow gold ring with stone missing, found in middle desk drawer, [and] one pocket knife with brown/white handles and 3 blades, brand name Craftsman." Nevarez took the second bedroom, where he found "one man's yellow pull-over shirt, brand name Brittania, size small." White's search of Tim's car revealed "one small pocket knife with brown handles with one blade, brand name unknown, found under spare tire in trunk, one package of Zig-Zag roller papers found in front portion of vehicle, one rolled cigarette containing what is believed to be a marijuana cigarette, [and] one empty Winston cigarette package (red and white) found in back floorboard of vehicle." According to Goolsby, "All those items were placed in a plastic bag and handed over to me," and they remained in his custody until he turned everything over to the property room.[30]

Relative to the yellow shirt, there appears to be mix-up as to where police located it during the warranted search of Tim Cole's apartment building. On the witness stand, Reggie Kennard later testified that it was hung up in the garage's storage area, adjacent to Tim's room, while Detective Goolsby's summary reflected it as being found in the second bedroom, the one that belonged to Reggie. If the two spaces are reversed, the site of each inventory item seems logical, and in this respect, one should consider that Goolsby may have been confused while writing this part of his twelve-page report.[31]

With the arrest and search warrants now executed, the officers escorted Tim back to police headquarters. Identification Officer Walter Crimmins stepped in and took two photographs: one of Tim, and the other of his boots. Then he "took full handprints and fingertips." Crimmins anxiously compared Tim's prints with those found at the scene of Trina Barclay's assault, but there was no match. During Goolsby's interrogation that followed, Tim emphatically denied any involvement in the crimes for which he had been arrested, but he volunteered other information relating to his honorable discharge from the Army due to alcohol abuse, his purpose of coming to Lubbock to attend Texas Tech, and his arrival during the first part of January, when he moved in with his brother. But when asked to sign a line-up waiver, he balked. He would not sign anything, he said, until he had a chance to talk to Dennis R. Reeves, the court-appointed Lubbock attorney who represented him on the misdemeanor charges of January 19. Tim received the customary single telephone call, but when he could not make contact, he left a message with the attorney's secretary.[32]

Shortly afterward, Tim was taken to the sheriff's department so that he could be placed in a live line-up. Goolsby stayed behind in order to contact as many victims as possible, and have them come in and possibly name Tim as their assailant. The detective also dialed the Lubbock Rape Crisis Center and requested their aid in the roundup. Within minutes, though, Goolsby joined Nevarez at the county jail, where Tim was booked. In a humiliating experience, detention personnel had him remove his street clothing and change into "jailhouse blues." Tim had yet to sign the waiver, and Detective Goolsby began pressuring him to do so. Once again, the young man asked permission to call his attorney, but as before, he had no luck in locating him.[33]

State's Exhibit No. 5
Photograph of Tim Cole
—Sources: Texas v. Cole, vol. IX, 6;
Exhibit File No. 85-403, 151,
99th District Court, Lubbock

Reggie arrived at the sheriff's office to check on his brother and see if he could help straighten out this dreadful mistake. Goolsby quickly suggested that he might persuade Tim to find another lawyer, and he allowed the two to talk. Reggie found his older brother in a small interview room, visibly shaken, and almost in tears. Surely by this time, each of them knew about the horrific charges levied against Tim, but why would someone point the finger at him, of all people? In a gut-wrenching interview, Reggie Kennard commented that he wanted to call his mother and have her get involved. But Tim stopped him short, he said, because there was no need to upset her at this time. When Tim asked Reggie's opinion about whether he should agree to stand in a live line-up, he strongly advised against it, and urged him to wait. Suddenly, Detective Goolsby strode into the room and repeatedly pressed the matter. To paraphrase Reggie's comments, the officer said, "Go ahead, it can't hurt nothing. It might be all just a big misunderstanding. Go ahead and do the line-up, and it'll be over with." Tim struggled with the decision. Then without uttering a word, he looked somberly toward Reggie as if to ask what he should do. By now, Reggie actually felt that Goolsby might be trying to help. This is what police officers are supposed to do, isn't it? So, he gave in and told his brother to do as the detective requested. Tim gave a half-hearted smile through clinched lips and nodded. Then, at 3:35 p.m., without benefit of legal counsel, he reluctantly affixed his signature to the document that would forever change his life.[34]

Timothy Brian Cole's booking photo, April 10, 1985
— Courtesy Lubbock Police Department

Finally armed with Tim's consent, Goolsby moved quickly to the next step, taking his prisoner to the viewing room, where the line-up, as described below by the detective, occurred within procedural guidelines:

> When we attempt to hold a line-up, we get with the jail captain and advise them of the race, sex, height, and general physical description of the suspect or the person we are going to place in the line-up. And they, in turn, go back to the cells, and by height, and by race, and by obtaining the persons inside these cells who fit the general description of our man, then, they bring them back out to the booking area for our okay.
>
> Then, if they are suitable for the line-up, then we give them cards, giving the suspect his preference of his position in the line-up.
>
> [The line-up is conducted] in a small room, being about six feet wide, about 12 feet long. There is a one-way mirror that the men in the line-up face. They are standing on about a six-inch ledge, and they are asked, one at a time, to approach the window, and to come down off of the ledge, so the victim may more easily see their correct height. And then, if the victim wishes to hear the voice of the suspect, each individual in the line-up [is] given the opportunity to say the same thing over a receiver phone.[35]

That afternoon, the jail captain brought out county inmates: Jarvis Hubbard, Fredrick Johnson, Dexter Pope, and Gilbert Williams. Goolsby asked Tim "what position in the line-up he preferred and he chose position #4." With the selections complete, each of the five men held a card with an identifying number and nervously awaited further orders.[36]

Tim took a deep breath — he hoped and prayed as never before that the hellish nightmare, capped off by this parade of bodies, might soon end. The system, he still believed, would protect him, and at some time in the future, maybe he and Reggie would joke about this occasion. But for the present, he had to get through it somehow without breaking down.

Becky Cannon, Director of the Rape Crisis Center, joined Goolsby, Nevarez, and White in the observation room as, one by one, each of the five line-up participants stepped to the mirror and then back on command. Trina Barclay viewed the group, and after three minutes, she "stated that it looked like # 4 (Tim) but that she could not be sure." Then Michele Murray took her turn. A comparison of Tim's photo taken the previous day, the one she identified, with that of his physical appearance in the live line-up reveals similarities so strikingly comparable in the manner of staging that what happened next seems a foregone conclusion. In a notarized, typed affidavit signed later that Wednesday afternoon, Michele said, "I walked into the room and I immediately saw the person who raped me. The man was holding card #4. I am positive of my identification of this man and there is no doubt in my mind." When asked how long it took to make that determination, she replied emphatically, "About half a second." Although they were not victims, student teacher Laura Shelton and Tech instructor Lisa Osteriech, who recently informed the police about a black man acting suspi-

State's Exhibit No. 4
From left: (1) Dexter Pope, (2) Fredrick Johnson,
(3) Gilbert Williams, (4) Timothy Brian Cole, and (5) Jarvis Hubbard
—Sources: *Texas v. Cole*, vol. IX, 5;
Exhibit File No. 85-403, 151, 99th District Court, Lubbock

ciously as he approached the pair on the Tech campus, viewed the line-up separately, and each said that none of them looked like the fellow who had scared them back on April 3.[37]

Before the guard ordered Hubbard, Johnson, Pope, and Williams, along with Tim, back to the cell block, Identification Officers Walt Crimmins and Jimmie Riemer took a photo of the line-up as it wrapped up at 4:00 p.m. Becky Cannon drove back to her office knowing full well that the Rape Crisis Center would never run short of victims to counsel. Laura Shelton and Lisa Osteriech returned to their normal lives at Texas Tech University, while Trina Barclay continued to try and pick up the pieces of hers. Michele went back to her dorm, emotionally drained by the entire affair. Lubbock police officers reported to departmental headquarters with a great feeling shared by all. This had been a good day for the justice system, they thought, and another bad guy was off the streets and behind bars where he belonged. In one of the last entries contained within his report the following day, Detective Goolsby boldly wrote, "With the arrest of [Timothy Brian Cole], this offense should be shown as CLEARED BY ARREST from the files."[38]

In stark contrast, Tim languished in a cell, and his demeanor began to change. He did not smile as often as he once had, and his eyes did not shine as brightly. He kept wondering why and pondering his fate in new and eerie surroundings that brought to mind terrible visions of things to come. Repeatedly, he recalled Goolsby's comment made early in the day. "Go

Walter Crimmins
— Courtesy Lubbock
Police Department

ahead and do the line-up, and it'll be over with." But one thing was certain: the detective's tactic taught Tim to be very distrustful of anyone in authority whom he previously thought of as a protector.[39]

As Tim prepared to spend a long, restless night behind bars, Lubbock Police Officers Franklin and Stark arrested Jerry Wayne Johnson for "reckless conduct" at 7:50 p.m. They brought him to the county jail, where at 9:37, he was booked. Unbeknownst to Tim, this fellow prisoner had already made a disgraceful impact on his future. But unlike him, Johnson would easily post a bond of $300, be released immediately — and by the next day, all charges were dismissed. Basically, he was held in custody just long enough to create a report and have his mug shot taken. Tim would not be so lucky. He had more torment to bear.[40]

The bad news just kept coming. On Thursday, April 11, Goolsby took the identical photos of Tim and the others and, in the same order as they were shown to Michele Murray, he put

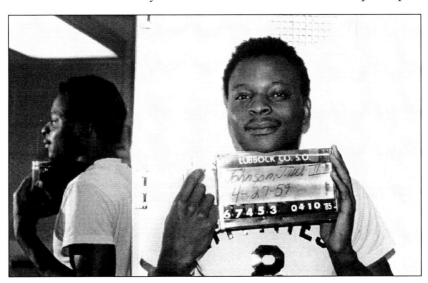

State's Exhibit No. 10
Mug shot of Jerry Wayne Johnson, April 10, 1985
—Sources: *Texas v. Cole*, vol. IX, 11;
Exhibit File No. 85-403, 151,
99th District Court, Lubbock

them inside a new folder, and drove to Brenda Jones's apartment. When he arrived at 10:45 a.m., he asked the young lady to look very carefully at the array and see if she could identify her assailant. Brenda described what followed:

> I immediately picked out picture #5 and said, 'That's him!' I am positive of my identification of this man and he is the same man who tried to get me into his car. I do want to have charges filed against this man for what he did to me and I will be willing to testify against him. I have been told by Det. Goolsby that the person that I picked out in position #5 is Timothy Brian Cole.[41]

It had taken three attempts to get Brenda Jones to make a positive identification from two different photo arrays, and Ronnie Goolsby now had the result he wanted. In no time, he had his witness sign a statement that doubled as an affidavit for an arrest warrant, and by the end of the day, Tim stood charged with a second count of aggravated kidnapping. Since he was already in custody, the Lubbock Sheriff's Office had little to do except attend to the formality of the actual arrest. Unfortunately, the latest charge came at a price, not only to Tim Cole's physical and mental being, but to basic police work. In an extremely tense situation, Brenda Jones saw her assailant no more than ninety seconds, it was 4:30 in the morning, Tim Cole did not own a red car, and his license plates did not match the description supplied by the victim. She could not pick Tim out of the first two photo spreads that were shown to her—and finally, one has to ask: did the police determine whether the young man could provide an alibi? What other evidence did they have? Did the authorities rely solely on the single eyewitness identification before issuing the arrest warrant? Despite everything, the damage was done. With the April 13, 1985, morning edition of *The Lubbock Avalanche-Journal* that carried in bold letters an article titled: **Accused Rapist Charged In Second Abduction**, Tim Cole's credibility gap had widened to a chasm.[42]

It seemed as if none of the fundamentals of good police investigative work really mattered anymore. Detective Goolsby became ever more determined to put this young man away for good, and in the process, he utilized any tool necessary to tie him to as many unsolved crimes as possible.

While the investigation of his brother's alleged criminal activities continued, Reggie called his mother. She dropped everything and flew immediately to Lubbock to be near her oldest son in this dark hour. Goolsby said that he did not become aware of a report completed by the Texas Tech Police Department that described the rape of Velma Chavez until after Michele Murray issued her statement. With the new information, the detective noted that the two cases bore a strong resemblance, so at the direction of David Hess, District Attorney Darnell's first assistant, Goolsby contacted Chavez and asked her to come in and view a new folder that contained the photo array (without the markings) previously shown to Michele Murray. To an outsider, this action might seem completely off-the-wall, because Tim had not yet arrived in Lubbock at the time of Chavez' rape. Still, the young woman said that her attacker looked like him. At this time, Goolsby set up another live line-up, this one on April 12. The officer expanded on the reason why. "Because I had Timothy Cole and Terry Clark in this particular line-up together," he said. "I wanted her to see Tim Cole." But when actually sizing up the two men, she did what she had previously done: she identified Clark.[43]

On April 17, seven days after Tim's arrest that essentially tagged him as the *Tech rapist*, Ruby Session put up as security her real estate, valued at $100,000, and posted a $35,000 bond in order to secure his temporary release. Mike Brown, Tim's defense counsel, strongly advised that his client would be best served by leaving town, and he gladly obliged. He went directly to his apartment, packed a few things, and drove with his mother to the airport, where they boarded a plane bound for Fort Worth. Due to Texas Tech's speedy decision that resulted in both brothers being asked to leave the university, Reggie had no reason to stay around, either, except to drive Tim's car back to the family home.[44]

On the flight out to Lubbock to arrange bail, Ruby said that the plane met with quite a bit of turbulence, and after landing, she relayed that information to Mike Brown. Later in the day as she and Tim prepared to return home, Brown asked Ruby to call him as soon as they got back to Fort Worth, because he did not want to worry needlessly about their safety. So she did. This is when the defense attorney mentioned that another rape had occurred in Lubbock while they were in the air and oddly enough, the victim had picked Tim out of a photo spread, an amazing feat given the physical and time constraints involved.[45]

State's Exhibit No. 7
From left: (1) Gary Howard, (2) Terry Lee Clark,
(3) Timothy Brian Cole, (4) Marshall Baxter, and (5) Charles Wilson
—Sources: *Texas v. Cole*, vol. V, 413; vol. IX, 8;
Exhibit File No. 85-403, 151,
99th District Court, Lubbock

CHAPTER FIVE

THE INTERIM

"A false sense of security is the only kind there is."
— MICHAEL MEADE

With Tim's arrest as the suspected *Tech rapist*, the women-folk of Lubbock could breathe a little easier. But could they, really? People have always known that death and taxes are givens, but actually rape can be added to the list. No place, regardless of size, is totally exempt from such aberrant behavior, and Lubbock is no exception. Detective Ronnie Goolsby confirmed, then underscored, this fact with the following admission. "We have probably, on an average week, about three or four [rapes]. Sometimes in the summer seasons it doubles that."[1]

During the 1980s, census figures put Lubbock as the eighth largest city in Texas, but it had grown from humble beginnings. Located "327 miles northwest of Dallas and 122 miles south of Amarillo," Indians once roamed the region, but when they were pushed out by buffalo hunters, ranchers soon followed, taking advantage of the South Plains grasses to support livestock by the thousands. In 1909, the Santa Fe Railroad extended its line from Plainview, and with it, the city began to change its image as "a treeless, desolate waste of uninhabited solitude." Farmers tapped the Ogallala Aquifer and used its abundant waters to irrigate cash crops consisting mainly of cotton and grain, and by 1980, the city boasted of having "the world's largest cottonseed processing center." Texas Tech University, formed originally by the legislature in 1923 as Texas Technological College, along with Lubbock Christian University, added to the tally of the city's numerous assets, which included museums, a multitude of parks, an orchestra, a ballet, tourist attractions of all sorts, several hospitals, "forty elementary schools, eight junior highs, and five senior highs," Reese Air Force Base, sixty-seven whole- sale outlets, manufacturing plants such as Texas Instruments and Gould's Pumps, "thirteen banks with deposits approaching $1.5 billion," other savings institutions, and at least 250 churches of most denominations whose congregations blocked the sale of spirits until 1972, when liquor by the drink became legal.[2]

But no matter how well a city succeeds in advertising its positive attributes — and contrary to all safeguards implemented by local authorities, wherever and whoever they might be — events do occur that reinforce the supposition that bad people do bad things. The Lubbock Police Department, so recently hopeful that rapes within its jurisdiction might now subside, re- ceived word on July 4, 1985, that another violent sexual assault had taken place. This one had no connection with that of Michele Jean Murray, Jim Bob Darnell argued, because the right man, Timothy Brian Cole, had been arrested for that particular crime. The district attorney said flat out, "There weren't any more so-called Tech rapes." For obvious reasons criminals do not always operate in the same geographic locale, choosing in- stead to move on to better hunting grounds. Therefore, with the change of modus operandi, the brazen behavior may well esca- late. At the very least, that possibility should have been consid- ered.[3]

CHAPTER SIX

ADVERSARIES AND THE BALANCE WHEEL

*"Courts have become nothing more than a chess match,
and the integrity of justice becomes trampled beneath
all of those who play the game."*
— WILLIAM KNOTTS,
A JUVENILE ON ALABAMA'S DEATH ROW

Many scholars and writers from all walks of life compare the courtroom to a game of chess, wherein one player, by a series of skilled and well-planned offensive and defensive maneuvers, eventually places his opponent's King in a position where capture is imminent. And a judge stands by, ready and able to settle disputes when they arise. Most assuredly, this description applies well to the public trial system within the United States as we know it today, in which a defense attorney and a prosecutor spar for jury favor, with the ever-present judge making sure that all toe the mark. In a perfect world, prosecuting attorneys would follow the advice of the great English jurist, Sir William Blackstone, when he said, "All presumptive evidence of felony should be admitted cautiously: for the law holds that it is better that ten guilty persons escape, than that one innocent suffer." Unfortunately, our judicial rules of conduct have grown far beyond such simplicity.[1]

Due to the expected uphill battle that Tim faced in his forth-coming trial, it became apparent to Ruby and Dewitt Session that their son required a seasoned go-getter to act on his behalf. An attorney for Dewitt's family could not take the case, because he specialized in civil law. However, a partner in his firm had known Mike Brown from law school days, and he recom-mended Brown highly. Although Tim's court-appointed repre-sentative, Dennis Reeves, was officially shown in this role until about June 5, 1985, Brown assumed those duties more than a month before he filed a court motion to substitute counsel that effectively transferred Tim's case from the Law Offices of Griffin, Dunn & Reeves to Brown, Harding, Fargason & Brown. Long considered a Lubbock defense powerhouse, the firm had been founded by the well-respected Clifford Wilton Brown.[2]

Cliff Brown had practiced law since his 1948 graduation from the University of Texas School of Law in Austin, and dur-ing his career, he had served as president of the Lubbock County Bar Association, Lubbock County Criminal Defense Lawyer's Association, and Texas Criminal Defense Lawyer's Association. The Session family needed this type of know-how and clout, so Ruby Session flew to Lubbock and talked with the elder Brown's 37-year-old son, Mike, the second Brown on the firm's letterhead. After that conversation, Ruby agreed to hire him. Robert Michael "Mike" Brown grew up in his father's shadow, but he had the reputation of being a good lawyer in his own right, one who went by the book and did the work by the numbers. He carried impressive credentials of his own, having been named by the Lubbock County Bar Association as Outstanding Young Lawyer in both 1976 and 1979.[3]

Around town, word spread that Mike Brown would not face one of the district attorney's subordinates in the *Tech rapist* trial. Instead, he would go up against the man whom the electorate put into office in 1983, to replace "Maximum John" Montford, known "for his aggressive prosecution and the lengthy terms he sought in sentencing." The current D.A., Jim Bob Darnell, born December 24, 1947, seemed to have "special empathy for vic-tims of sex assaults, though he said he knew no one personally who was a victim of such a crime." Additionally, Becky Cannon, the Executive Director of the Rape Crisis Center, urged him to personally try the case and send a strong message to would-be rapists.[4]

Soon after graduating from the Texas Tech School of Law in 1976, Darnell joined the Lubbock District Attorney's Office as assistant, and then served as Montford's top gun from 1979 through 1982. He had come up through the ranks and learned his craft well, taking on and "winning death penalties in the three capital murder cases he tried," and in 1981, the Lubbock County Bar Association presented him with the Outstanding Young Lawyer Award. Yet he was not infallible. There were chinks in his armor from "unsuccessful campaigns against clubs staying open past midnight and pornography sold in the city." On the personal side, however, "he was shy and quiet out of court, irritated with the political side of his job," and "campaign posters advertised him as a 'Prosecutor, not a Politician'." But as

Jim Bob Darnell
—Courtesy 140th District Court, Lubbock

the trial of Tim Cole drew nearer, Darnell found himself in an unusual situation. He now occupied a lame-duck position in county government, because during the previous election, voters ousted him in favor of Travis Ware, who would take office effective January 1, 1987.[5]

For the time being, however, Darnell had at least one more case to prosecute, and he knew that he would have to be on point while plying his trade in the 99th District Courtroom, because Judge Thomas L. Clinton, a 65-year-old veteran, occupied the bench and had since January 1, 1976. "Tom" was born in Durant, Oklahoma on September 7, 1921, but early on, his family moved to Lubbock, where he received a high school education. Afterward, he enrolled at Texas Tech, but World War II interrupted his plans of becoming a member of the legal profession. When hostilities ended, he attended St. Mary's University in San Antonio and obtained a law degree from there in 1951. He moved back to Lubbock, began private practice, and earned the

Judge Thomas L. Clinton, 1921–1993
— Photograph by Allen Studios
Courtesy David Slayton, Lubbock

reputation of being "an intense and capable advocate," which led to his first appointment in 1975 as Judge of the County Court at Law Number Two.[6]

On June 5, 1985, Jim Bob Darnell confidently stood before the grand jury of the 99th Judicial District of Lubbock and presented the State's evidence against Tim Cole, the suspected *Tech rapist*. The district attorney had little to lose, unless he factored in a future judgeship, because this would most probably be the last high profile case in which he was personally involved, given that his term of office would expire on the last day of December 1986. But all rested on one basic premise: whether the twelve members, in their opinion, determined that Darnell and police investigators had accumulated enough evidence — proof, if you will — to warrant a trial. However, such speculation soon became moot. After hearing the testimony of but a single witness, Detective Joe Nevarez, the panel issued a True Bill, formally indicting Tim on one count of aggravated sexual assault, one count of aggravated kidnapping, and one count of aggravated theft. Bura Russell, the jury foreman, signed the document that also left unchanged the original bail amount of $35,000. The following day, Mike Brown, Tim's new attorney, filed with the court a Waiver of Arraignment, which, in effect, entered a plea of not guilty on behalf of his client. On July 18, Darnell announced that he was ready to begin the trial, but the defense counsel was not prepared to go forward. The Docket (see Glossary) set the date for the first proceedings to be held during the week of November 11, but they did not occur, nor did they take place on the revised date, the week of April 28, 1986. Finally on June 11, Brown filed a Defendant's First Motion for Continuance and Waiver of Speedy Trial, which claimed that he, as attorney of record, "has not had sufficient time to prepare for trial."[7]

On August 29, Brown filed a Motion for Exculpatory Evidence (that which is favorable to the defendant) and sent a copy to Darnell's office. The defense counsel followed on September 5 with A Defendant's Motion for Notice of Evidence of Other Crimes. Judge Clinton reset the case for the week of September 8, but this time, at 10:40 on the morning of September 10, 1986, the court convened. It had been almost seventeen months since Tim's release on bond.[8]

During the flight to Lubbock for the trial, Tim expressed concern to Reggie that he might not return to Fort Worth for good reason. So far, according to Mike Brown, the woman who pointed him out in the line-up, held resolute in her identification, and nothing indicated that she would change her mind. Tim turned to his brother, who was scheduled to testify for the defense, and remarked that "they were going to get [me] for something [I] didn't do." Reggie tried his best to reassure him. "Tim, we've got round-trip tickets," he said. "You're coming back. And he looked at me and he smiled and said, 'OK'."[9]

CHAPTER SEVEN

THE TRIAL—DAY ONE

*"But as you sit before the defendant right now,
the law says you must presume him to be innocent
until the State, the government, proves him
to be guilty beyond a reasonable doubt."*[1]
*— JIM BOB DARNELL,
DISTRICT ATTORNEY, TO JURY POOL*

Wednesday — September 10, 1986
Preliminaries

After Clinton called the case to order, Darnell announced that he was set to go. Brown said the defendant was present, but that he could not say they were ready to proceed—an amazing admission considering that he had represented Tim for more than a year and three months. Whether he was geared up or not is certainly a matter that only he can sort out, but regardless, the attorney inserted a barrage of motions clearly intended to establish justification for appeal should Tim be found guilty. Brown's posturing began. He requested a ruling on a Motion to Quash (nullify) the grand jury indictment, because it contained three separate offenses, he argued, that should not be tried in combination. Darnell stiffened and recalled that, two days prior, he had informed both Brown and his co-counsel, John Tabor, that his office would most likely try the aggravated sexual assault and then leave the other two alone. When Brown declared that

80

he had no recollection of any response to the question asked on
two separate occasions, Clinton mentioned a conversation that
he'd had with both Darnell and Brown. The judge looked
Brown sternly in the eye and said, "I advised you that they
would proceed under Count 1, which was the aggravated sexual assault." Again, the defense attorney complained. He did
not remember it quite this way. The seemingly endless tit-for-tat
continued, until the court overruled the defense attorney's motion. Brown countered again, but this time he reversed course.
Now he wanted Clinton to go ahead and try Tim on all three
original counts in one case and attach jeopardy. This way, he
said, the State could not go back and separately retry his client
on each of the remaining counts of aggravated kidnapping and
aggravated robbery. With his patience wearing thin, Judge
Clinton denied this motion as well.[2]

But Brown persisted, because he had other concerns to resolve, specifically with what he viewed as prejudicial evidence.
He said,

> We would move the court to instruct counsel for the State, and
> the witnesses for the State, including Michele Jean Murray,
> and any of the law enforcement officers, to not allude to, re-
> mark about, discuss or in any way present to the jury the fact
> that at the time of the offense alleged in the indictment, . . . Ms.
> Murray was a virgin and had no prior sexual involvement.[3]

Before Judge Clinton ruled on this motion, the defense attorney introduced another. "I ask the court to direct the State to refrain from attempting to allude to or elicit any testimony concerning any other crimes, wrongs, or other acts, or extraneous
offenses (see Glossary) in its case in chief [against Tim Cole]."
Darnell replied that he believed Brown intended to bring in information about other "similar type crimes that were committed
within about a six-month period of time on or around the campus of Texas Tech University."[4]

The district attorney emphasized that unless the crimes
against Velma Chavez, Tana Murphy, Trina Barclay, and
Margaret Russo could be shown to connect directly with that
against Michele Murray, Brown should not refer to them, or

show to the jury an enlarged version of Detective Ronnie Goolsby's chart. Clinton reacted quickly and forged a compromise of sorts. Brown required the court's approval before he delved into details of other rape cases. Darnell would also be held to the same standard before he brought up Murray's virginity, and neither counsel could introduce either of these matters in the jury-selection phase, with one exception. Brown was free to question potential jurors as to whether they had seen newspaper reports or television coverage about the *Tech rapist*. Both defense counsel and prosecutor accepted the rulings.[5]

But Brown had not finished. He added a motion to suppress the State's warrant to obtain blood and saliva samples from his client. For some odd reason, the judge neither wanted to broach this issue, nor even mention the term "warrant to draw blood." He continued to tiptoe around the topic, but when he advised that defense would be given ample opportunity to bring at a more convenient time an objection to the court, Brown relaxed a little. Then the proceedings, which had seemed to drag on painfully, for much longer than the actual forty minutes, in essence came to a close with two brief exchanges. Brown said, "That is all I have, your honor."[6]

Darnell smiled, showing a sense of humor. "I had something, but it slipped my mind," he responded. "It must not have been too important."[7]

Seating of Jury Panel

As potential jurors, an unusually large number for a Wednesday, began filing into the courtroom at 10:55 a.m., Tim Cole, dressed impeccably in a dark suit, white shirt, and tie, sat uneasily behind his attorneys, casting glances at the goings-on inside and thinking about what might happen over the next few days. Since his arrest in April of the previous year, Tim had noticeably aged. And there were other changes as well. He had let his hair grow into a medium, well-trimmed Afro, and he now wore a beard and mustache. But he no longer flashed the smile that in youth he had exhibited so freely. His eyes were much more intense, and his face reflected the effects of months worrying about what would become of him and his family should a jury fail to believe his plea of innocence and grant his plea for justice. Brown and Tabor huddled nearby, poring over names on a master list that numbered fifty, of which only twelve and alternates could remain by the end of the day. Besides, there were other last minute details that needed attending. Before Judge Clinton signaled the beginning of the *voir dire* (questioning) process, Brown approached the bench at the last possible moment and, out of earshot of all spectators, injected two additional motions. His client, he disclosed, elected "to have the Jury assess his punishment in the event of a verdict of guilty," and he submitted an Application for Probation, which stated:

> I, Timothy Brian Cole, defendant in this cause, after being duly sworn, do hereby swear that I have never been convicted of a felony in this or any other state or in the United States, and that I am eligible for probation under the laws of the State of Texas, and that I hereby make application that any sentence given me in this cause, if I am convicted, be probated under Article 42.12, Code of Criminal Procedure.[8]

From left, Tim Cole, Reggie Kennard, and Ruby Lee Session
— Courtesy *The Daily Toreador*, Lubbock

Judge Clinton briefly addressed the prospective jurors before introducing Jim Bob Darnell, and then Mike Brown. With this part of the formality finished, he turned the session over to the district attorney, who quoted law, statute, and scripture, stressing that those jurors selected must be fair and impartial. He wanted to know whether opinions had been formed already after potential jurors read articles in *The Lubbock Avalanche-Journal* or heard reports on radio and television. He said that the grand jury indictment against Mr. Brown's client, in itself did not justify a guilty verdict. Almost ad nauseam, Darnell stressed that a defendant is presumed innocent until found guilty by the evidence presented in court testimony. After naming employees of the Rape Crisis Center, previous rape victims, including Michele Murray, members of the police force, and especially the ones involved in Tim Cole's investigation that led to his arrest, members of his own staff, all those he intended to call as witnesses for the prosecution, and the four partners in Mike Brown's law firm, he then asked if anyone knew any of them. Walter Raymond Lupton, the individual who would become foreman of the jury, raised his hand and acknowledged knowing George White and J. R. Ashmore, both police officers on the case, as well as Derry Harding, one of Brown's associates. Nevertheless, Lupton said that none of these acquaintances would prevent him from rendering a fair and impartial decision. Darnell questioned whether everyone could consider a full range of penalties when deciding guilt of aggravated sexual assault—could they, in other words, sentence Tim Cole to five years' probation, could they give him ninety-nine years plus a $10,000 fine, or anything in between? And finally, he wanted to know whether anyone felt he or she could not serve on a jury for religious reasons.[9]

The district attorney's plan of narrowing down the juror list appeared somewhat scattershot, as evidenced by his phrasing general questions and citing the responsibilities of those selected. By contrast, the defense counsel leaned toward a systematic method of soliciting additional replies on an individual level. And the defense lawyer took more time; after all, his client's future hung in the balance. He inquired about affiliations with Texas Tech. Did those in the jury pool see the composites of the rapist in the newspaper, did they consider *The Lubbock Avalanche-Journal* a credible source of information, and could they offer probation for such an evil crime? He asked those who worked at Tech and had daughters whether they took special precautions to ensure their daughters' safety. He questioned whether they could reserve judgment until all the evidence is presented. He asked whether, if Tim Cole did not testify, they would deem this an admission of guilt. Finally, he harangued the potential jurors about the concept of "reasonable doubt." When discussing "burden of proof," Brown presented a folksy example. "It is like pushing a boulder on a hill, and it is the State's burden to push that boulder up against the presumption of innocence," he said. "It is not enough for the State to push the rock to the top of the hill. They are required to push it to beyond a reasonable doubt."[10]

The questions continued. Would they view the defense attorney harshly if he vigorously cross-examined Michele Murray, the rape victim in this case? And what would their opinion be if he made numerous objections—would they see this as a ploy of common courtroom antics resulting in obstruction of justice, or delay tactics? He advised that it is the State's responsibility to convince the jury by the evidence at hand. And should they convict his client, could they render a sentence that called for probation? Would they consider the full range of punishment? Had they previously served on juries? Did they know the victim, defendant, anyone in his law office, or on the district attorney's staff? Had they been victims of a crime, and finally, was there anything that would prevent them from serving to the best of their ability?[11]

At 5:05 p.m., about six hours after the process began, with a break for lunch and only one fifteen-minute recess, the two—district attorney and defense counsel—struck the few remaining names and marked their final choices. Among the twelve left standing, nine men and three women would ultimately decide the fate of Timothy Brian Cole. Two female alternates rounded out the selections, but within the lot, no African-Americans were represented. For a listing, refer to Appendix 3. Vocations of the jurors ranged widely, and included a sanitarian in the city's health department, a grocery store owner, an insurance salesman, a deputy fire chief, a pathologist with a Master's degree in Biology who worked at Texas Tech, a U.P.S driver, a supervisor with Texas Instruments, and two teachers—one who taught first grade at All Saints Elementary, and another, an industrial technology instructor at Mackenzie Junior High. Most of the jurors were married with children, and two were the parents of students enrolled at Tech.[12]

Judge Clinton impaneled the jury as the afternoon proceedings wound down. He called out the names of the jurors and the alternates, and dismissed the others. He read aloud the indictment, and then he looked at Tim and asked, "How do you plead, guilty or not?"[13]

Tim answered, "Not guilty."[14]

Moving forward, the judge instructed the jurors on the rules governing their behavior during the trial. They should not discuss the events among themselves until time to render a verdict. They would not be allowed to take notes, make contact with the lawyers, witnesses, or participants, try and investigate the case, read about it in newspapers, listen to descriptions on radio or

The Lubbock County Courthouse
—Source: 1988 District Clerk Letterhead

television, or inspect articles or other documents admitted into evidence. He finished by saying that court would be in session early the next morning, but as for Friday, there would be no activity, because he had previous obligations.[15]

As Tim, his family, and his attorneys walked outside, thunderstorms were moving through the area, and as they descended the stairs of the courthouse toward their cars, all felt the effects of the stressful day. Yet they were relieved, thankful that the long-awaited trial had finally begun—and hopeful that it would soon end in acquittal. During the earlier break for lunch, Tim had authorized Darnell's office to take the requested samples of his blood and saliva, and perhaps, he thought, these would be used to convince all doubters, and especially the twelve members of his jury, that he was telling the truth.[16]

CHAPTER EIGHT

THE TRIAL—DAY TWO

*"Did your assailant smoke during the time
you were in the car with him for that
two and a half or three hour period of time?"*[1]
*— JIM BOB DARNELL,
DISTRICT ATTORNEY, TO MICHELE MURRAY*

Thursday — September 11, 1986
Testimony of Witnesses

At 9:00 a.m. in the courtroom, Michele Murray sat next to her mother and behind Jim Bob Darnell and his second chair, Denise Williams. Like Tim, Michele seemed to live in constant twilight, although in the last few months, after having attended several psychological counseling sessions, she seemed much better. It was bad enough to have gone through the police investigation, in which she stripped her spirit to the core, recounting each and every facet of the terrible rape she'd experienced on March 24–25 of the previous year — but now, she had to relive it all, this time in a public forum, with the press, members of the jury, and other interested spectators listening to the most private of details.[2]

Darnell decided to lead with Michele as his principal witness. If he could somehow establish early on that Tim Cole had taken her virginity while committing a *revolting* crime, then most certainly, he thought, the jury would be sympathetic to-

88

ward the testimonies of the remainder of those he put on the witness stand. He and Denise Williams prepped Michele as best they could, but everything boiled down to one reality. However scared, she must be able to withstand a harsh cross-examination intended to undermine her previous statements, including that of identifying Tim as her assailant. As the time for her testimony approached, she began to tremble, and when the district attorney loudly proclaimed, "State will call Michele Murray," she barely heard the call.[3]

Somehow, though, Michele made it to the stand, where she was sworn in, and stated her full name. Immediately problems arose. Judge Clinton could not understand her answer, and he asked her to speak up. She gave her age as twenty-one. She gave her place of residence, and said she was employed as a child care provider for a family who lived in Baytown. She added that she was going to enter the Navy on November 24. Again, the judge interrupted the proceedings as he told Michele to raise her voice. Both Darnell and Clinton reminded her of the importance of speaking up so that everyone could hear her exact words. "Don't get . . . too close to the microphone," the judge cautioned, "because if you do, it will reverberate and it distorts the voice, as well as the recording."[4]

Michele appeared disoriented, but she nevertheless continued. She explained where she lived when the abduction took place, and gave the location of Doak Hall in relation to the St. John's Methodist Church parking lot. Suddenly Mike Brown stood up and asked for permission to approach the bench. He told the judge, "I can't hear anything she is saying." Clinton responded by again scolding Michele and ordering her to sit back from the microphone and speak louder.[5]

At this point, Michele seemed to calm down somewhat, and during the lengthy questioning by the district attorney that followed, she provided particulars. Brown objected to what he described as her narrative testimony, and Judge Clinton sustained. But with the report of the attacker's having taken her to a friend's house, Darnell approached the bench. Brown followed. The district attorney explained how important it was to his case that he be able to present information about Michele's prior sexual activity, specifically the virginity issue. That's when the judge delivered the bombshell. "With reference to testimony relating to her virginity . . . during the course of this transaction," Clinton said, "the court is going to rule that is a part of the *Res Gestae* [the overall event], and is admissible as such."[6]

Brown's face reddened, for this is what he'd feared might happen. The mere suggestion that Michele was a virgin prior to the assault would be like throwing gasoline on an open fire, so of course, he did not want the jury to find out about it. Brown protested vehemently, saying that "the basis of my objection is Rule 412 of the Texas Rules of Criminal Evidence, which specifically excludes this testimony." Time and again, Brown objected. Time and again, Judge Clinton overruled him. The examination resumed, and everything went smoothly until Michele reached the part where she told her assailant that as a virgin, she was saving herself for marriage. The defense counsel could no longer hold his tongue, so once more, he quoted Rule 412. The judge, clearly perturbed by the constant disruptions, responded,

> I am going to instruct you not to be reading out of a lawbook to the jury. When it comes time to give the law to the jury, the court will give the law to the jury. Now, you have your objection. That is what the bench conference was about, and I have made my ruling. You know what that ruling is. It is not necessary for you to interrupt the testimony on that again . . . .[7]

The district attorney asked Michele to describe what her abductor wore. He had on blue jeans, she said, a yellow terry cloth shirt, and beach thongs on his feet. Relative to the shirt, it was "like a Polo [with] a fox or an alligator, or something on it, like a cheap one . . . from K-Mart or something, one of those kind." When Brown advised the judge that he could not hear Michele's answer, Clinton almost lost his composure. He looked at the young lady and said,

> Now, I am going to caution you for the last time. I hate to do this continually, but you—I don't know why you won't keep your voice up. I don't understand that at all. Now you must talk louder than you are talking, and you must. I realize that

you are in court probably for the first time, and it is rough on you to do this, but you must keep your voice up loud. They have to hear you.[8]

Darnell slowly walked back to where Denise Williams sat and picked up a shirt—the one that detectives found in Tim's apartment on the day of the search warrant. He carried it back to the witness stand. With high hopes of obtaining a quick and easy recognition, he spoke to Michele. "I am going to show you what has been marked as State's Exhibit No. 16, and ask you if it looks anything like the [one] that the individual was wearing on the night of the 24th and 25th of March, 1985."[9]

"No, not really," Michele answered instantly, "because that is not terry cloth." After the prosecution's drawn-out attempt at getting the young woman to explain what she considered as terry cloth, most everyone in the courtroom became completely confused, including Jim Bob Darnell, who appeared to have egg on his face after having one of his key pieces of evidence shot down in open court.[10]

Judge Clinton called for a fifteen-minute break. The jury left immediately, but before everyone else followed, he took the opportunity to address two con-

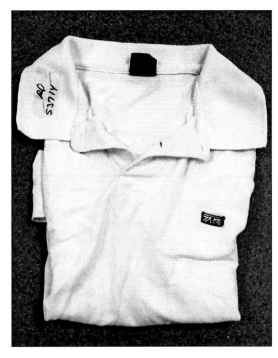

State's Exhibit No. 16
—Photograph by Fred B. McKinley
Sources: *Texas v. Cole*, vol. IX, 17;
Exhibit File No. 85-403, 151,
99th District Court, Lubbock

cerns. First, he chastised both lawyers. They should not, he barked, come to the bench each and every time they wanted to make an objection. Secondly, he looked toward Michele and said, "I am not going to tell you any more to speak up and keep your voice up loud." The dressing-down did not sit well with the young lady, and "she stormed out of the courtroom in tears."[11]

For a while, it appeared that Michele could not continue, but the support she felt from her mother, as well as from various members of the Rape Crisis Center, propped up her confidence. All advised her to be strong and hold her head up high. After all, they reminded her, the worst part—taking the stand—was over. Michele reluctantly agreed to resume her testimony. In short order, the district attorney recovered from his previous setback as well, and he relentlessly demonstrated the power of his office. Michele narrated the details of the rape, the police investigation, and how, by way of police photographs, she had come to identify Tim in the first place. Darnell stressed the fact that Michele had seen her attacker in a well-lighted parking lot for three or four minutes, and he said this was enough time for her to remember what he looked like. Pointing his finger toward Tim, the district attorney asked, "Is that the person that sexually assaulted you on March 24th, 1985?"[12]

Michele answered, "Yes, sir. He is sitting right there, and he is in a blue suit."[13]

The direct accusation made Tim sick to his stomach, and once again he questioned the motives of this person whom he had never laid eyes on until the day before. Mike Brown glanced at the members in the jury box, taking note of the shock on their faces. He certainly knew that Michele Murray had inflicted serious damage to his client. One way or another, he had to shift the momentum.

Darnell touched on the items stolen from Michele: the $2.00, her Timex watch, and small ring. Immediately, as expected, Brown protested. He argued that the theft aspect was related to the aggravated robbery indictment, which had been dropped. Judge Clinton overruled him, though, saying that the theft had to be considered part of the general crime. Michele confirmed that investigators did show her a ring, State's Exhibit No. 18, but it did not belong to her. Furthermore, she could not identify the two knives, labeled as State's Exhibits 19 and 20. The prosecutor spent considerable time on the smoking issue, and how cigarettes were found in Michele's car immediately after the rape occurred. The witness testified that these were left by the person who assaulted her, because she did not smoke, nor did she allow anyone who rode with her to light up.[14]

By the time the district attorney's direct examination moved to a close, Michele had dispensed with most of the key items taken as a result of the search warrant: the yellow shirt, ring, and two knives. So far, there was no direct evidence, other than her identification, that incriminated Tim. Darnell, therefore, closed hard with what he had. He reiterated that Michele did not have consensual sex with her attacker, nor was he her spouse, both crucial elements in the criminal statute. "And [did he]," the district attorney asked, "intentionally and knowingly, by acts and words, place you in fear that death would be imminently inflicted on you if you didn't do as you were told?"[15]

State's Exhibits No. 19 and 20
—Photographs by Fred B. McKinley
Sources: Texas v. Cole, vol. IX, 20, 21;
Exhibit File No. 85-403, 151,
99th District Court, Lubbock

Michele replied, "Yes."[16]

Darnell passed the witness to defense attorney Mike Brown, who began by stating that he had but a few short questions. He asked Michele to focus on an easel, and he had her mark the locations of 15th and 16th Streets, the Shell station, St. John's Methodist Church, Mr. Gatti's Pizza, and where, exactly, she had parked her car on the night of the abduction. Brown then unleashed a series of inquiries plainly calculated to test her memory, during which he hoped to trip up Darnell's star witness. He quickly moved to the subject of lighting at St. John's parking lot, and how on that particular night, she noticed that it had improved substantially. The defense counsel had Michele indicate other details, down to the location of each light pole. He asked her if she knew that another woman had been abducted from the same spot as she. Michele acknowledged that she did. Brown brought up the fact that she had bitten her assailant's right thumb, but she reported that as far as she knew, she had not drawn blood, pierced the skin, or left a scar. Michele explained that since she never actually saw the handle of the knife that her attacker held, she could never make a positive identification of the weapon. The defense attorney questioned her recollection of the events, leveling rapid-fire questions involving everything from the earliest conversation involving the jumper cables, which car belonged to the abductor, whether he was acting strange, and whether he asked her to engage in sex acts after they left the setting where the assault took place. Brown pointed out that she had once described the attacker as between "five feet-eight inches and five feet-ten inches tall," and later as "between five feet-six inches . . . and five feet–eight inches . . . ?" Had she mentioned to the Rape Crisis Center volunteers that the man who assaulted her said that he'd killed other women, and that he was free on probation? Did she repeat that quote to the police? Was the officer whom she met at the hospital from Texas Tech or the Lubbock Police Department? What was the name of the doctor who treated her at the hospital, and what did he look like? Would she be able to recognize him? What did his voice sound like? Was there anything strange about his hands? Relative to the physician, Michele recalled little about him, and in fact, she struggled with answers to most of the questions Mike Brown shot at her. When Judge Clinton realized that the defense counsel's opening statement about brevity had evolved into flat-out contradiction, he broke for lunch.[17]

At 1:15 p.m., Brown continued the cross-examination. Michele said that her attacker smoked during the assault, but she could not remember in which hand he held the cigarettes. She acknowledged that she stood five-feet and three inches—but what about her rapist's exact height? "I just knew he was taller than me," she said. "I was just guessing. I didn't know exactly." Michele explained that during the attack, she suffered no cuts that required stitches. The defense attorney had her describe the appearance of various police officers, and under duress, she finally admitted that she could not remember much about the occasion in which she identified Tim Cole, other than looking at some photos and attending a line-up at the sheriff's office.[18]

"And no one ever told you," Brown asked, "that your rapist might not be in that line-up, did they?"[19]

Michele sharply replied. "I knew that, though," she said. "I mean I knew if I didn't see him, that he wouldn't be there."[20]

The remainder of Brown's time with Michele centered on the rape itself and whether she could provide convincing details that would peg Tim as the guilty party. The young woman explained that, due to the poorly-lit rape scene, she could not describe "the torso, the body, the chest area, the back area, of the man who assaulted [her] that night." Furthermore, she could not recall whether he had a medium build or otherwise. She said he had a small amount of hair on his chest, but she remembered nothing special about his right arm, his back, or whether either had "noticeable scars, marks, or birthmarks." At this time, the defense requested special permission from the judge to allow his client to stand and prepare for a demonstration. Clinton agreed. Darnell must have wondered what the defense counsel was up to.[21]

Brown had Tim remove his coat, tie, and shirt. Noisy discussions broke out all over the courtroom, and Judge Clinton called order. The defense attorney led the defendant to the witness stand, stopped in front of Michele, and asked her to look at "a darkened black birthmark on Mr. Cole's arm, his forearm below the shoulder." After that, he pointed to "the discoloration and scarring on his back." He walked with Tim over to the jury box and repeated very slowly the exhibition so that each member could closely examine the defendant. When Tim put his shirt back on and returned to the defendant's table, Brown turned to Michele and asked her to respond to what he termed as an embarrassing observation. "I want you to describe the male organ of the man who assaulted you." Michele became completely frustrated, so Brown followed up, requesting this time whether her attacker was circumcised or uncircumcised.[22]

"I have no idea what that means," she admitted. Brown shook his head and tried again, but he got the same answer. He gave up and passed the witness.[23]

During redirects (see Glossary), Darnell turned his immediate attention to damage control. "Were you paying any attention to the pimples on the nose of the person that assaulted you," he asked, "or were you making observations of what the person looked like?"[24]

"I was trying to remember what he looked like," Michele replied, "because I knew if I got out of there alive, that I was going to go straight to the police. I was looking at his face."[25]

By now, it had become apparent that the witness could be sarcastic, too. Darnell wanted to know if it took "more than a second to recognize the individual that assaulted [her] on the 24th?" and she snapped, "About half a second."[26]

With his trial proficiency clearly showing, the district attorney piled up serious points with the jury. Now he went for the jugular. "Did you ask the assailant to stand up so you could measure him to see how tall he was?"[27]

"No, I didn't have a ruler handy," she said. No matter how strenuously — or how often — Brown objected to this line of questioning, or "bolstering," as he called it, Judge Clinton overruled him. The defense attorney did win one small skirmish, though, when Darnell tried to slip in the fact that Michele had undergone psychological counseling. The judge stopped this one in its tracks, yet failed to agree with Brown that he should order "a mistrial for the prejudicial question."[28]

Darnell positioned State's Exhibit No. 5 in front of Michele and asked "if this [was] a fair and accurate picture of Timothy Cole, as he appeared in April or March of 1985?"[29]

Brown objected and requested that his reason be heard "outside the presence of the jury."[30]

Clinton agreed. Shortly, the defense attorney made his argument with the judge:

> May it please the court, I object to the admission of State's Exhibit 5, a photograph of the defendant. [T]his photograph was taken as the result of a warrantless search and seizure conducted without the effective consent of my client, but under a ruse and a direct lie from police officers to gain his cooperation in taking this picture.[31]

The district attorney lashed back. "That picture was taken after a warrant had been issued for his arrest."[32]

Over and again, Brown raised objections, but they were repeatedly overruled. Darnell pressed his luck once too often, however, by alleging that Brown, in an attempt to discredit Michele based on her recollection of the emergency room doctor who treated her after the assault, had therefore impugned her character. Clinton ruled that this matter should be decided by the jury. When the panel members returned to their seats, Darnell presented Michele with State's Exhibits No. 5 and No. 21, and requested that she compare the two photographs. He wanted to know if this was "the same person that is seated over there behind Mr. Brown and Mr. Tabor [and] the same person that you saw in the line-up that you immediately identified when you walked into the room on the 10th of April, 1985?"[33]

Michele answered, "Yes," to both questions. Thus, for the second time during her testimony, she identified and pointed to Tim as the person who had attacked her on March 24 and March 25, 1985. At this point, Darnell felt that he had done as much as he could with this witness, so he handed her off to Brown. Consequently, the defense attorney had one more potential opportunity to get in the last word and even the score. Strangely, he chose instead to pass.[34]

Why?

Mike Brown later admitted, "I will grant you that I did not vigorously cross-examine her, as a matter of taste. There is no need to quarrel with a sincere person." Could there have been another reason? Perhaps Brown did not relish leaving an impression with the jury that he was unnecessarily beating up on a helpless rape victim, thereby providing his opponent with more sympathy ammunition than he already had.[35]

Jamie Herrera stepped to center stage and took the oath. As Darnell's second witness, the six-year patrolman briefly recounted how he had made contact with Michele at the Lubbock General Hospital emergency room in the early morning hours of March 25, 1985. He described her condition, the identity of those who accompanied her, and how he came to lift a fingerprint from the cigarette lighter in Michele's car. He also pointed out that a search of the automobile produced two cigarettes, one a butt and the other never smoked. Both were Winstons. Brown's cross-examination contained nothing out of the ordinary, until he asked, "Were you aware that another woman had been abducted from the parking lot at St. John's Methodist Church on an earlier occasion?"[36]

Without thinking, Herrera said, "I believe there had been several." By his swift answer, the officer opened the door that the defense hoped for, and Brown took full advantage. Expanded testimony might flesh out his contention—one he'd held all along—that other rapes with similar characteristics had occurred in the area, and that fact itself could lead to a finding of reasonable doubt, followed by full vindication of his client.[37]

The district attorney objected, and he asked for a conference. Complying, the judge sent the jury from the courtroom. Darnell explained,

> Your honor, I made an oral motion *In Liminie* (see Glossary) yesterday concerning him going into other offenses, and the court ruled that if he was going to go [there], he would approach the bench and take it up with the court outside the presence of the jury, because of the fact that we are trying this case and not all other cases where the victim is not involved.[38]

Clinton listened intently, but he was not convinced. Since

the defense attorney had not so far sought out specific details, he rationalized, there was nothing wrong with this type of questioning. The judge ordered the return of the jury. While Darnell cringed, Brown took this unexpected break and ran with it. He asked Herrera whether, while serving in the line of duty, he had received information about the following cases:

- A woman being abducted on the parking lot of Lubbock General Hospital in December of 1984?
- The abduction and rape of a Texas Tech student from the dormitory parking lot on Sunday, January 13, 1985?
- The abduction and rape of a woman from the St. John's parking lot on Friday, February 1, 1985?
- The abduction and rape of a woman on Avenue Q on Sunday, February 3rd, 1985?[39]

The officer responded with either, "I don't recall," or "I don't recall none of them dates."[40]

Reading from his report, Herrera testified that Michele never said anything about her attacker's being circumcised, or whether he had birthmarks, scars, or further discoloration on his back. She only told the officer that "she . . . bit him on the thumb." When Brown passed the witness, Darnell closed by asking very general questions about the St. John's parking lot, and the lighting conditions on the night of Michele Murray's assault. He also made the argument that only she, aside from the rapist, "saw what happened to her on the . . . 24th and 25th of March of 1985 . . . ."[41]

Jennifer Rosson, a volunteer with the Rape Crisis Center, took the stand next. Darnell led her to testify as to the condition of Michele Murray when she checked into Lubbock General after her rape, to the description that she gave of her attacker, and to the various samples taken and medical tests performed by emergency room staff. By and large, Rosson emphasized that Michele was in shock after the ordeal, and that she was scared to death. Mike Brown had the witness go over Michele's report, the one in which she provided a description of her rapist whom she had recalled as much shorter than Tim. Michele also said that her attacker had smoky breath. Rosson listed the superficial bodily injuries that the young woman sustained, but as to whether the attacker ejaculated or not, Jennifer said, "[Michele] didn't really know, but she said there was fluid between her legs."[42]

Jim Bob Darnell called his last witness of the day. Detective Joe Nevarez confirmed that he had taken Michele's report on March 27, 1985, and the officer recounted how he and Michele retraced the events of the night of the attack. However, after failing to locate the rape site, the two returned to the police station, where they jointly prepared a composite of the assailant, shown previously as Exhibit No. 3. Nevarez said he participated in the surveillance of April 7, 1985, and he also explained the occasions on which he showed Michele a photo spread that included Tim's picture, and the time that he, along with other officers, arrested Tim at his home on April 10, 1985. Nevarez was also present during the execution of the search warrant and the line-up in which Michele identified Tim as her assailant.[43]

Darnell showed Nevarez a picture of Tim's right hand, and he identified it as the one taken the day of the arrest. The photo was introduced as State's Exhibit No. 6. "Did you make any observation," the district attorney asked, "of anything unusual about the thumb of Timothy Brian Cole on the 10th of April?"[44]

"Well, there appears to be some type of a scar or wound there on the thumb," Nevarez answered, "there by the joint, the first joint ... from the fingernail."[45]

Strangely, the district attorney did not continue his line of questioning about the injury to Tim's thumb, but instead returned his attention to the yellow shirt, the one he had tried to get Michele to identify as belonging to her attacker.

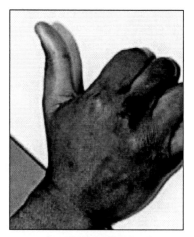

State's Exhibit No. 6
— Courtesy Lubbock County District Attorney
Sources: *Texas v. Cole*, vol. IX, 7; Exhibit File No. 85-403, 151, 99th District Court, Lubbock

He asked the detective if he ever showed this garment to the rape victim. "No," Nevarez said, "I didn't show her the shirt, but I believe Detective Goolsby done that." When he said he remembered nothing special about the defendant, Darnell took the position that if a trained detective such as Nevarez never noticed "any tattoos or scars, or marks, or birthmarks on [Tim's] person," why would Michele be held to a higher benchmark?[46]

During cross-examination, Brown validated the point that Tim not only voluntarily consented to the search warrant, but also he in no way interfered with the proceedings. In recounting this, Brown hoped to convince the jury that his client, an innocent man, had nothing to hide. He then picked apart two pieces of evidence. Nevarez admitted that the ring discovered while conducting the search did not belong to Michele, and no one ever recovered her gold Timex watch. Brown also referred to the black jacket and yellow pull-over shirt, but he was never able to get the detective to name the exact spot from which both items were retrieved. He closed, over Darnell's objections, with his recently-laid *modus operandi* argument. "During those early months of 1985 and the late months of 1984," Brown asked, "did law enforcement officers begin investigating several rapes and abductions that had occurred near the Texas Tech neighborhood?" When Nevarez confirmed this, the defense attorney then quizzed him about specific crimes and dates, being careful not to mention names. Nevarez acknowledged that Goolsby assembled "information about similarities between this offense and other offenses." Just before Judge Clinton called for an overnight recess, Brown got the detective to admit that the common features among the rapes that had occurred between December 1984 and March 25, 1985, had prompted the surveillance that ensnared his client.[47]

At the end of day two, Darnell had cause to be cautiously optimistic. His chief witness, despite a shaky start, had managed to hold on and deliver devastating testimony by pointing directly, not once but twice, to Tim Cole as her attacker. This was substantiated by a veteran Lubbock police officer with almost eighteen years on the job. With relative ease, the district attorney had managed to get into the record the premise that Michele had been a virgin prior to the assault.

What about her contradictions in describing the rapist's height? This probably mattered little to the jury, given what Michele had been through. Plus, a Rape Crisis Center volunteer had done a good job collaborating her statements, including how she'd feared for her life, and subsequently suffered profound shock, realizing she could have died.

But Brown had scored some successes, too. So far, no actual evidence taken from Michele's automobile or as a result of the search warrant carried out at Tim's apartment linked the defendant to the crime. He had also made substantial progress at establishing reasonable doubt. The opposition's witnesses, Officer Herrera first and then Detective Nevarez, had allowed him to introduce information about other rapes with similar characteristics that had occurred in the same general vicinity. Too, both Herrera and Jennifer Rosson permitted the defense to drive home the point that Michele Murray's rapist smoked.

As an asthmatic, Tim Cole did not smoke.

CHAPTER NINE

THE TRIAL—DAY THREE

"And your statement to him that you needed
his photograph because of the robbery investigation
was not true, was it?"[1]
— MIKE BROWN TO GEORGE WHITE

Monday — September 15, 1986
Testimony of Witnesses

During the previous evening's weather report, forecasters had said it would be cloudy and humid all day, with rain expected by early afternoon. Tim woke up to the gray morning, put on a dark blue suit with a white shirt and blue tie, and sat down to breakfast with his family. Of course they talked about the trial, and everyone tried to stay optimistic. But Tim himself had a nagging, bad feeling.

When they arrived at the courthouse shortly before 9:00 a.m., Mike Brown reiterated that, all things considered, the district attorney had thus far failed to prove his case. But privately, Brown worried about Michele Murray's testimony, especially about how jurors had reacted to her. He asked himself whether he had done enough to cause them to doubt Michele's eyewitness identification.[2]

The resumption of Nevarez' testimony did not occur as planned. The officer's appearance was delayed so that he could be with his extremely ill father who was undergoing surgery. So

103

with the jury retired, Darnell next called George White who explained "the circumstances under which [he] went to the residence of Timothy Brian Cole to obtain a photograph of him."
White readily admitted to the ruse, and that he had lied when
he told Tim that he needed to snap the picture (the one in position number 5, State's Exhibit No. 21) in connection with his previous robbery investigation. But before the judge brought back
in the jury, the district attorney emphasized:

> As far as the testimony that I plan to elicit from [White], your
> honor, is the testimony to the effect that this is the photograph
> that he obtained from Timothy Brian Cole, and I am not going
> to go into anything beyond that, other than the fact that the
> photograph he took is the photograph of Timothy Brian Cole,
> this defendant, and that this is the picture in State's Exhibit
> No. 21 that was put in the photograph spread.

With the stipulation that Darnell would refrain from character-
izing his client as the defendant, or the suspect in the robbery
case, Brown agreed, and Judge Clinton accepted.[3]

The detective explained in open court how and when he became involved in the Michele Murray rape case investigation,
and he also provided comprehensive details about the surveillance activities in which Officer Bagby drew out Tim Cole. In
addition, he discussed the photograph that he took of Tim, and
the circumstances under which he and Detective Nevarez had
showed it to Michele, who used it to make her identification.
Before Darnell completed his direct examination, though, he
had White identify all items that he personally seized while
searching Tim's brown Buick. The list included a small pocket
knife, the Zig-Zag rolling papers, the marijuana cigarette, and
the empty Winston package, the last an apparent attempt to link
it with Herrera's preceding testimony about finding Winstons
inside Michele Murray's vehicle.[4]

As he approached the witness, Brown accentuated the fact
that rapes with similar M.O.s had occurred around the Texas
Tech area, and White verified that both Tim Cole and Terry
Clark were in the same line-up in which Velma Chavez identified the latter as the man who had assaulted her. And White

admitted there was no crime in the fact that Tim had held a conversation with Officer Bagby during the stakeout. When the defense finished with the witness, Darnell walked to the bench and argued that "Mr. Brown has opened the door, as far as identification goes, by bringing up another victim, Velma [Chavez], and bringing up another suspect, Terry Clark . . . ." Mike Brown grinned in agreement. With Judge Clinton's ruling in favor of the defense, Brown had finally succeeded in obtaining what he had wanted all along: there would be no further restrictions to his asking direct questions related to similar crimes for which his client was being tried.[5]

Darnell's examination of Rosanna Bagby dealt with her participation in the stakeout, but when Brown's turn came around, he let the cat out of the bag by bringing up the time Bagby ar-

State's Exhibit No. 15
—Photograph by Fred B. McKinley
Sources: Texas v. Cole, vol. IX, 16;
Exhibit File No. 85-403, 151,
99th District Court, Lubbock

rested his client for carrying a firearm. *Better now*, he thought, *than have Jim Bob do it later.* The defense attorney then adroitly pointed out that such a charge is classified as a misdemeanor, and he followed up swiftly, getting Bagby to admit that, to the best of her knowledge, Tim had never before been convicted of any felony, anywhere. Period.[6]

Brown felt the tide shifting in his favor, so he turned his attention to the reason surveillance activities were conducted in a specific area — "because the victim in this case and one other victim had been abducted from the St. John's parking lot . . . ?" Bagby replied, "I believe so, yes, sir."[7]

The defense methodically compared the similarity of these two rapes by floating a number of questions intended to lay the foundation that would ultimately substantiate his client's innocence.

- And were the descriptions of those assailants in both cases relatively similar?
- They were both black males, were they not?
- And the M.O. in each of those cases were very similar, were they not?
- In each case, a white female was abducted from the parking lot, isn't that so?
- And it was a week-end night when this happened to each one of these people, was it not?
- In each of the cases, the assailant displayed a pocket knife, isn't that correct?
- And in each of those cases, the assailant robbed the victim after the sexual occurrence, isn't that correct?

The patrol officer answered in the affirmative to most, and to the rest, she claimed that she did not know. Finally, the defense counsel offered that "in both of those cases, the assailant did not have an automobile . . . ," leaving the members of the jury to ponder why Tim Cole, if he were the *Tech rapist*, would approach Rosanna Bagby in his car, especially in such a public area as near the intersection of 14th Street and University Avenue on a Sunday night?[8]

Just as Mike Brown suspected, Darnell could not steer clear of a golden opportunity. He asked Bagby to dredge up the time when she "responded to a call at approximately 6:00 . . . in the morning [January of 1985] to the Alamo Motel on Idalou Road." Besides going through Tim's robbery report and his subsequent arrest for unlawfully carrying a weapon, the district attorney, through his witness, described the shady reputation of the motel by its use as a base for those involved in the sale of illegal drugs. And without a definite mention of Tim's arrest on the marijuana charge, Darnell implied, why would the defendant be way over on the east side of town at such an early hour, given that he lived so near the Tech campus? He allowed jurors to draw their own conclusions.[9]

The defense questioned the relevance, but Darnell took issue, claiming that he only added to what opposing counsel had already brought up. Out of the presence of the jury, the district attorney exclaimed, "He has attempted to show that [his client] is a person of good character who has never been in trouble and has never done anything wrong in his life."[10]

"And I believe that this is one of the things that shows that he is not a good person, that he runs around the wrong places, and that he does things of an unlawful nature . . . ." After several minutes of hearing grounds and rebuttals, Judge Clinton ruled in favor of the prosecution.[11]

Rosanna Bagby's place on the stand was immediately filled by Ronnie Goolsby, who repeated the reasons for — and how his team carried out — various surveillance activities. He also characterized the investigation that culminated in the arrest of Tim Cole. During his direct examination, Darnell introduced several exhibits, including State's No. 49, the marijuana cigarette found in the young man's automobile. At this, Brown stopped the proceedings. "I object to Exhibit 49 as being irrelevant to this case," he said, "and its prejudicial value outweighs its probative value . . . I ask that it be excluded." Judge Clinton agreed.[12]

Much of the questioning remained fairly routine, until Mike Brown stepped forward. He used the chart prepared by Goolsby and had him review line by line, item for item, each of the five rapes — Velma Chavez, Tana Murphy, Trina Barclay, Margaret

Russo, and Michele Murray—attributed to the *Tech rapist*. The defense attorney outlined the traits shared by each crime, among them the day of the week, time of the offense, excuse to gain access to the victim, type weapon used, place of occurrence, description of the assailant, property taken, sex acts per-

State's Exhibit No. 49
—Photograph by Fred B. McKinley
Sources: *Texas v. Cole*, vol. IX, 54;
Exhibit File No. 85-403, 151,
99th District Court, Lubbock

formed, and the suspect's remarks, especially the vulgar language used. Aimed at showing how easy it was to confuse the two, Brown said that at one time Velma Chavez erroneously identified Tim Cole as her assailant, but recanted shortly thereafter, and named Terry Clark. When the defense revealed that fingerprints taken from Michele's car did not match those of his client, Darnell fired back that Ronnie Goolsby could not testify to this because he was not a fingerprint expert. Although Brown tried to rephrase the question several times, each met with a stern objection from the prosecutor, who wanted to plug this hole and fast! The defense attorney eventually retreated — he would try it again, with a future witness.[13]

Mike Brown asked the detective if a man named Jerry Wayne Johnson was "the subject of an investigation for [a] rape committed approximately September 27th, 1985." When Goolsby answered, "Yes," Jim Bob Darnell asked to approach the bench. He had fought tooth and nail to prevent the defense from developing testimony in this direction, but with the jury retired, the judge allowed the questioning to continue. Brown pounded his fist "on the desk claiming that Jerry Wayne Johnson was just as likely to have committed the crime as Timothy Cole." Goolsby also admitted that Johnson had been arrested in connection with another rape that occurred on July 4, and in addition, he had "been indicted for capital murder of a woman whose body was found outside the city limits." After the detective agreed with Brown's conclusion that there were "some similarities between the M.O. involving Jerry Wayne Johnson and the M.O. involving the offense against Michele Jean Murray," Darnell offered a stunning retort. "Are we going to try every rape that occurs in Lubbock County over a six-month or a one-year period of time involving black males?"[14]

Brown argued successfully that he merely wanted to establish information about the two rapes that Johnson was charged with to show that this type of crime had continued in Lubbock long after Tim Cole had been arrested, released on bond, and returned to Fort Worth. Throughout the trial, the defense attorney seemed intent on painting Johnson as the *Tech rapist*, so when had he arrived at this opinion? In an interview conducted on

August 24, 2009, former Police Chief Tom Nichols said that while his department worked to make the case against Tim Cole, no one, including Mike Brown or any of his associates, called him personally to raise red flags, nor suggest that perhaps another, more probable, suspect should be investigated. Nichols said that nothing like this ever happened—that is, until the case went south.[15]

The judge ordered the return of the jury, and testimony resumed. Goolsby acknowledged that the rapes of July 4 and September 27, 1985, had, in fact, occurred after Tim Cole's release, and he disclosed he knew personally that the Texas Tech Police Department had all along suspected Johnson to be the *Tech rapist*. Goolsby expanded on the confusion caused by Barclay's erroneous identification of Tim, but he said it did not really matter, because his department had ruled Tim out as a suspect. When Brown referred to the Margaret Russo assault, Goolsby said that he had also suspected Tim in that case, but that he had eventually eliminated him from this one as well. He did not say, though, how he reached this conclusion. After her rape, Russo moved to Amarillo, and then to Colorado, where she went by the name of Margaret Sanford. On August 30, 1985, Chief Nichols and Goolsby sent a joint letter to Detective T. L. Thompson of the Colorado Springs Police Department, in which they enclosed a photo spread of six black males—the identical photos and set-up by which Michele Murray had identified Tim. The letter offered alarming details:

> The suspect that already has been filed on in our city for Aggravated Sexual Assault is placed in position #5 in the picture spread and is the same suspect we believe that committed the aggravated sexual assault with Margaret [Russo-Sanford], due to the time of the day, area of attack, MO being the same prior to attack, during attack, and after attack, and because our series of sexual assaults have ceased after the arrest of this suspect, known as "The Tech Rapist"[16]

Detective Thompson telephoned Margaret and asked her to come in. She did, and on September 9, she looked everything over. "The photo I chose was no. 5," she said. "When I looked at the picture, if his hair was longer, I could be more sure." Apart from the result, the wording of the request submitted by Chief Nichols and Detective Goolsby raises dire questions. Why would they alert the Colorado Springs police that Tim's photo occupied a specific position? And in light of Goolsby's contradictory trial testimony, why did they say that the series of rapes in Lubbock had ceased after his arrest?[17]

During redirects, Darnell pursued a line of questioning that might appear to some people as blatant, unsubstantiated smear tactics. He asked, "You suspected [Tim Cole] in rapes that occurred after he was out on bond, did you not?" Goolsby answered in the affirmative, and Darnell followed up. "And you confirmed that he was in Fort Worth at the time, did you not?"[18]

The detective replied with a mind-bending disclosure. "I talked with Mr. Brown and he told me that he [his client] was in Fort Worth. It was not confirmed, though."[19]

The latter response begs the question: if Goolsby suspected Tim Cole of other crimes, why would he not take the time and find out exactly where the young man was when the subsequent rapes occurred? Before he finished with Goolsby, however, the district attorney quickly pointed out that the detective did not really believe that Tim had committed the two rapes on which Jerry Wayne Johnson was charged. Given this, why did the defense counsel refuse to question Goolsby about the specific crimes that he suspected Tim Cole might have been involved in after his release on bond? Instead of allowing the jury to hear additional testimony that might have refuted that of the detective, Brown let the matter drop, and Judge Clinton excused the witness.[20]

Darnell recalled Jennifer Rosson briefly for the purpose of introducing the clothing that Michele wore on the night of her abduction and rape, along with various slides containing medical samples. Next, the district attorney called his last witness of the day—Jimmie Riemer, who admitted that he possessed no evidence whatsoever that connected Tim Cole, or any other person for that matter, with the Murray case. Instead, the twenty-eight-year veteran identification officer with the Lubbock Police Department gave confusing testimony, in which he discussed his extensive experience in reading fingerprints, and the fact that he personally destroyed those received from Michele Murray's cigarette lighter because "they were found to have no I.D. value." Riemer exited the witness stand, and Judge Clinton called an overnight recess.[21]

THE TRIAL—DAY FOUR

"The evidence in this case raises the . . . prospect
that one Jerry Wayne Johnson was the
assailant of [Michele Jean Murray] . . . ."[1]
— MIKE BROWN

Tuesday — September 16, 1986
Testimony of Witnesses

After Judge Clinton seated the jury for the morning proceedings, Darnell called his first witness of the day, Leon Henry, who testified that he had installed the extra lighting at the St. John's Methodist parking lot prior to Michele Murray's rape. John Roosevelt Hubbard, a microbiologist with the city's health department, followed. He talked about having obtained various medical samples from Tim Cole on September 10 and having turned everything over to Steve Holmes, an investigator with the district attorney's office. Brown questioned Hubbard at great length, and in the process probably baffled almost everyone in the courtroom, including the jurors, about antigens, antibodies, and how a person might be excluded as a crime suspect due to an explicit blood type.[2]

When Judge Clinton excused Hubbard, Holmes took the stand and merely restated that he had executed "a search warrant for the taking of blood and saliva samples from one Timothy Brian Cole." Then he said, "I took them directly to the laboratory, Region 5 Laboratory of the Texas Department of Public Safety here in Lubbock."[3]

One of the most controversial aspects of the trial involved James Martin "Jim" Thomas, a supervising chemist with the DPS laboratory, whom Darnell tapped as an expert witness to testify as to whether analyses of various samples might prove undeniably that Tim Cole raped Michele Murray. Almost immediately, Mike Brown began the process that ended with an objection to Thomas's being on the stand in the first place. Because Warren R. Snyder, one of Thomas's employees, actually performed the tests, Brown maintained that he should be the person to answer questions, rather than his supervisor—and furthermore, he said that if Thomas continued, his answers would represent nothing more than hearsay. Judge Clinton did not see it this way, and he overruled Brown.[4]

Darnell resumed questioning, putting before the jury the relative tests performed on spermatozoa, seminal fluid, foreign pubic hair, and the like. Brown objected again "for reasons previously stated on state and federal constitutional grounds and hearsay," but as before, he was overruled. Thomas continued with a long-winded, tortuous presentation that only a trained clinician might understand, much less the twelve jurors sitting in judgment of Tim Cole. Did any of the tests run on Tim's hair, saliva, and blood actually determine who raped Michele Murray? Thomas could not confirm anything by the hair samples, he said, except that Murray's rapist was Negroid. What about the others? Unfortunately, the DPS chemist resorted to the tried and true method widely used by so-called expert witnesses, in collusion with many "good ol' boy" prosecutors. Thomas could neither point to Tim Cole as the guilty party, nor could he exclude him, so the question remained one for the jury to sort out.[5]

Brown made it known to the court that he intended to call Officer Roberto Garcia, "who would [testify] in regard to a fingerprint that was lifted from the door handle [and rear view mirror] of a car belonging to Trina [Barclay], who was a rape victim, but not in this case." Judge Clinton ordered the jury from the courtroom while the two attorneys bickered over the validity of the proposal. As expected, Jim Bob Darnell raised several objections, but Brown persisted by stressing the similarities of the rapes of Michele Murray and Barclay. When the defense counsel lost the dispute, Brown announced plans to enter the testimony of both Garcia and Walter Crimmins through a Bill of Exception (see Glossary), evidently intended for use in a future appeal. Judge Clinton called the jury back in to advise them that the State had rested its case, and that its members would have to retire yet once more, so that other matters could be attended.[6]

Mike Brown called Garcia to take the stand, after which he presented the basic facts of the Trina Barclay case, including the mention that Trina had been abducted from the St. John's Methodist parking lot, just as Michele had. When the officer said, "I recovered two latent prints taken off the inside door handles of the victim's car, and some latent prints off the rearview mirror inside the victim's car," Brown stopped. He turned to Judge Clinton and reiterated that he wanted "to again use this testimony to show that these fingerprints recovered in the [Barclay] case were compared to the known prints of Timothy Cole and found not to match . . . ."[7]

The defense then called upon Walt Crimmins of the Identification Division of the Lubbock Police Department to confirm his credentials, experience, and the fact that he personally compared the fingerprints to those of Tim Cole, without finding a match. When the short testimony ended, Mike Brown said, "That completes my bill, your honor." Judge Clinton called the jury members back in and promptly dismissed them for the lunch recess.[8]

Shortly before 1:00 p.m., Brown reviewed his notes and made ready to present his side of the case. It was crunch time. He hoped that he had done enough so far, but *there is always doubt as to any verdict*, he thought. And what about the witnesses for the defense? They were few, and besides, would the jury believe them? Brown had cautioned those who would give an alibi for Tim's whereabouts on the night of March 24 and the early morning hours of March 25, 1985, to do nothing except tell the truth. As the hour for the afternoon events drew nearer, brother, Reggie Kennard, and his mother, Ruby Lee Session, tried to assure Tim that the ordeal would be over soon, and that every-thing would turn out in his favor.

Tim walked into the courtroom and took his usual seat. Texas Tech Detective Supervisor Jay Parchman became the first witness for the defense. Brown's questioning resulted in his ad-mission that at one time he suspected Jerry Wayne Johnson in the Tana Murphy case, even though she picked Terry Lee Clark as her assailant. And in the Chavez case, the detective said that he wished Johnson had been in the line-up conducted on April 12, 1985 — the one in which Terry Clark and Tim Cole were both present. Obviously with this testimony, the defense wanted to show that Parchman strongly suspected Johnson to be the *Tech rapist*, so why didn't the Lubbock Police Department pursue the same logic?[9]

When Judge Clinton excused Detective Parchman, Brown called four witnesses in a row who he hoped would convince the jury that, on the night of March 24 through at least 4:00 the next morning, Tim Cole remained in his apartment, and there-fore he could be guilty of neither the abduction nor the rape of Michele Jean Murray. Marlo Jones, Tim's friend who worked at Mr. Gatti's Pizza, said that on Sunday, March 24, he was on the job until 10:00 or 10:30 p.m. After quitting time, he went over to Tim's apartment, and he did not leave until 2:30 the next morn-ing. All the while, Marlo said, Tim studied. Asked how he re-membered this date, the witness explained that he sent his brother a birthday card around the same time.[10]

As soon as Darnell began to question Jones, he challenged the young man's credibility head-on. "Have you ever told any-body at the police department about this?" Much to the amaze-ment of the jury, Marlo said no. While trying to keep up with the quick-paced questions, Marlo stumbled badly, and he became confused as to what day March 24 fell on. The district attorney hammered away at which dates the young man actually remem-bered, and why. Furthermore, Darnell raised doubts as to whether Jones could recall anything at all, because he, too, might have been impaired from too much drinking at the party held at Tim's apartment.[11]

Reggie Kennard followed, and he seemed much better prepared. He vouched for the fact that Tim had finally gotten a job that started on Saturday, March 23, 1985, and that his brother entered this information on a calendar kept in their apartment. And, too, Reggie said that he saw Tim after he got off work that night, and that he never left home the next day and through the following Monday morning. Regarding the visitors who came by on Sunday night, Reggie testified that when Jackie Boswell and Leslie Thompson left about 4:00 a.m. on Monday, Tim still sat at the kitchen table. During the cross-examination, Darnell asked Reggie why he couldn't remember the specific dates of March 6, 1985 (the Texas Tech Library affair), and April 7, 1985 (Tim's sting operation), yet he vividly recalled March 24–25, 1985. However, when the D.A. explained what had happened on these two previous dates, Reggie had no problem explaining where and what he had been doing.[12]

During redirects, Reggie discussed the items that police officers took while conducting the search warrant. He had bought a ring that he saw advertised on television, but when it arrived and he gave it to his girlfriend, the stone fell out. So he went to Zales Jewelry and bought a higher quality replacement. The ring that the detectives took, he said, was the one without the stone, as turned out to be the case. As for the black jacket, Reggie said that it belonged to him. But what about the yellow shirt, on which the district attorney concentrated so much in earlier testimony? For that, Reggie provided a simple explanation. As a favor to their landlady, he and Tim had moved out some furniture and other items from another property that she owned across the street and placed everything in their downstairs storage area. The yellow shirt represented part of the inventory. When Mike Brown finally brought up the question of whether Tim smoked or not, Reggie insisted that his brother did not, nor had he ever smoked, because he long suffered with asthma.[13]

Leslie Thompson, who had traveled from San Bernardino, California for the trial, followed Reggie on the stand. Mike Brown did his best to have her explain to the jury that she could provide an ironclad alibi for Tim during the time of Michele Murray's rape, but throughout Darnell's cross-examination, everything fell apart. Thompson admitted that she never told

State's Exhibit No. 17
— Photograph by Fred B. McKinley
Sources: *Texas v. Cole*, vol. IX, 18;
Exhibit File No. 85-403, 151,
99th District Court, Lubbock

anyone until the previous week about her presence at Tim's apartment. Unfortunately, the next witness for the defense did not fare any better. Although Jackie Boswell confirmed Tim's alibi, she also said that she had previously told no one, including the police, that Tim could not be guilty. When Darnell asked what had prompted her to connect the dates and the events of March 24–25, 1985, she mentioned that Reggie called her about three weeks prior. She said, "He asked me did I remember a night that he and Mike [Cates] were over there, that they had been drinking and Mike had gotten very intoxicated, and when I replied, he told me that was the night the events had happened."[14]

The proverbial state of affairs, best described as being "between a rock and a hard place," now looked Mike Brown squarely in the face. Although giving their best, the testimony of the last four witnesses had exposed some of the fatal weaknesses of his case. Brown knew that the jury would certainly wonder why until just recently, two of those he called upon were never asked to offer vital information to aid an ongoing police investigation. Besides, it might appear to the nine men and three women on the panel that all were not to be trusted when it came to remembering actual dates, because on balance, they had faltered. Moreover, Darnell had done a pretty good job instilling doubt as to whether any of Brown's witnesses were even sober on that night and morning of March 24–25, 1985 — sober enough anyway to be reliable. Mike Cates and Quincy Johnson, another two who could have backed up Tim's alibi, were so inebriated during the time frame that Mike Brown dared not enter their names on his final witness list. What would the defense attorney do now? He put Michele Murray's convincing testimony on one side of the scale, and his case thus far on the other. The results clearly pointed to a huge advantage for the State and Jim Bob Darnell, so there was no other choice, the defense attorney believed, but to put his client on the stand.

Mike Brown asked and received permission to approach the bench. He alerted the judge of his decision, but before Clinton permitted the swearing-in, he directed the jury to retire, after which he advised Tim of his constitutional rights. Tim said he understood that under the Fifth Amendment, he could not "be compelled to give testimony that might tend to incriminate [him] in any way in a criminal offense." However, Judge Clinton stressed that, once Tim agreed to testify, he would have to answer each and every question regardless.[15]

Before allowing the defendant to take the stand on his own behalf, Clinton ordered the jury back in. Tim raised his right hand, took the oath, and settled into the witness chair, searching hard for any friendly face in the crowded courtroom. Dewitt Session, his stepfather now retired, had stayed back in Fort Worth to be with the younger children, but Karen, Tim's sister, attended all of the trial proceedings. As for Ruby and Reggie, both had been called as witnesses for the defense, so they were sequestered and had to wait it out in the witness room. Tim felt relieved to know that his entire family would stand beside him despite the outcome, and in fact, they supported his decision to turn down a plea bargain offered by the district attorney the day before the trial began, which would have set him free on probation—if only he admitted guilt. Standing firm on principle, Tim said that he would rather go to jail for something he did not do than have the stigma of sex offender attached to his name.[16]

As Timothy Brian Cole awaited the first question, most people in attendance, save a few, really knew how he would react. But those who expected that a hardened, arrogant, and cocky individual with a bad attitude would finally reveal his true colors were sorely disappointed. What they saw instead was a young man with values, who had been taught at the outset to give respect, and one who prefaced his answers with "Yes, sir" and "No, sir." Such personality traits do not occur by sheer accident or as a result of brief witness preparation on how to best testify. They result from family upbringing.

Brown established the names of Tim's parents, his roommates, along with the number of siblings, his relationship with Reggie Kennard, the date in 1985 that he'd arrived in Lubbock, his enrollment at Texas Tech, and where he lived. Furthermore, Tim explained that he first went to work for the Elephant Restaurant on March 23, 1985, and he specifically marked this date on the calendar that hung in his kitchen. He continued with how he hurt his right thumb while washing and stacking dishes, where he was on March 24–25, and who was with him. He emphatically denied that he took part in the rape of Michele Jean Murray.[17]

Jim Bob Darnell started his questioning—some say badgering—about the calendar and when the defendant made certain entries. Tim explained that he left it in his apartment back in April 1985, and when he was released on bail and left town, his attorney retrieved the instrument and kept it in his possession. During the relatively short cross-examination, the district attorney systematically named Tim's numerous employers from January 1983 until January 1985, a move apparently aimed at showing the jury that he must be untrustworthy, and therefore incapable of holding a steady job. He listed Tim's arrest at the Alamo Pool Hall on January 19, 1985, his run-in with Texas Tech Police on March 6, 1985, and finally, the fateful evening of April 7, 1985, when he became the only man to approach Rosanna Bagby during the sting operation. Darnell then focused his interest back to the calendar issue, questioning why the defendant chose to mark the importance of some dates while ignoring others, and whether, after consulting with his brother, he wrote out what would become his official story line. "No sir," Tim replied, "I did not sit down and write it out."[18]

The district attorney attempted to defame Tim's purpose for stopping to talk with Officer Bagby on that night, and he scoffed at the idea that the young man hurt his thumb while on the job. Answering directly to the injury, Tim said, "It is the truth." Darnell then centered on the gathering at Tim's apartment, the one that occurred on March 24-25, 1985. Smelling blood, the prosecutor asked how many times he and his roommates threw such parties—on thirty or more occasions—and whether the guests usually remained until the wee hours of the mornings "while you were studying and going to school?"[19]

Before he was done with the witness, however, the district attorney succumbed to the temptation of getting in one last dig. He ridiculed Tim's study habits that included staying up all night. "When did you sleep?" he asked.[20]

Tim provided a telling reply. "When Reggie and Quincy were not at home."[21]

During Tim's testimony, neither Brown nor Darnell questioned him about whether he smoked cigarettes, a critical point that even *The Lubbock Avalanche-Evening Journal* picked up on. Without benefit of their respective commentary, maybe Brown did not want to draw further attention to the fact that Tim did smoke marijuana, and Darnell wanted nothing to tarnish the detective's finding of an empty Winston cigarette package in the defendant's automobile.[22]

For his last witness, Mike Brown called Tim's mother, Ruby Session, a fifteen-year teacher with the Forth Worth Independent School District, to substantiate previous statements that her son "had never been convicted of any offense by a court of the United States," and that ever since bail was granted back on April 17, 1985, Tim had lived with her in Fort Worth. During his direct examination, Darnell inquired, "Was it a normal habit of his to stay up all night?"[23]

"Not at home," Ruby answered gently. "I was not here in Lubbock at the time, but Reggie did call me several times and tell me, 'Mother, Tim needs to go to bed. He is studying too hard.'"[24]

After her brief testimony, Judge Clinton directed the witness to stand down, and soon thereafter, both Darnell and Brown advised the court of their intention to rest and close. Before he called an overnight recess, Clinton spoke to the jurors, "Please be back in the jury room at [nine] o'clock in the morning, and we will be ready at that time to read the charge to you, and the argument to you . . . ."[25]

CHAPTER ELEVEN

THE TRIAL—DAY FIVE

*"If identification isn't enough to convict someone,
then we will have to turn 90 percent of our
prison inmates loose."*[1]
– JIM BOB DARNELL

Wednesday – September 17, 1986

Prior to the start of the daily affairs, Judge Clinton provided copies of his Charge of the Court on Guilt or Innocence (see Appendix 5) to opposing counsel. Darnell accepted everything at face value, but Brown sternly objected to the wording found in Item 9. Delving into the finer points of legalese, the defense attorney argued unsuccessfully that the statement regarding the issue of Tim's misdemeanor arrests for unlawfully carrying a weapon and possession of marijuana should read "that you [the jury] cannot consider such testimony for any purpose in this case," which completely eliminated the original addendum "tending to show guilt or innocence of the offense charged in the indictment." Brown said he raised the matter simply because of the judge's own "opinion that there is a disputed issue of material fact concerning the possession of marijuana, based upon the victim's statement that her assailant smoked constantly, and the defense testimony is that the defendant does not smoke because of asthma." Therefore, the defense argued

123

that any disputed issue of material fact "should be limited to the purpose for which it was admitted and for no other . . . ."[2]

After losing the first round, Brown tried yet again. He objected "as a whole because nowhere therein does the Court charge on the affirmative defense of mistaken identity raised by the evidence in this case." Michele Jean Murray, he said, erred in her identification of Tim; furthermore, the defense attorney recognized the possibility that Jerry Wayne Johnson actually committed her rape. Judge Clinton overruled Brown on all points, but before he ordered the jury to return to the courtroom, each attorney agreed to the introduction of State's Exhibit No. 30 into evidence, representing Michele's jumpsuit top, the one worn on March 24–25, 1985.[3]

The jury was seated, and after the judge read aloud the Court's Charge on Guilt or Innocence, he turned to Jim Bob Darnell to begin the State's opening argument. The district attorney stood, walked toward the jurors, and paused briefly. At first he spoke softly, but as he continued, the level and tone of his voice intensified. Adhering to the spirit of Judge Clinton's recent instructions, Darnell forcibly reiterated that since the rapes of Velma Chavez, Tana Murphy, Trina Barclay, and Margaret Russo had nothing to do with the case being tried, they should not be considered. Michele Jean Murray's identification of Tim Cole was enough, he said repeatedly. Besides, the description she provided of her assailant had remained consistent throughout the investigation, not to mention the composite that she helped create. Darnell accentuated the significance of Rosanna Bagby's testimony and derided that of Tim's witnesses, who were not, in his opinion, believable because they never wrote anything down. Instead, he suggested, put your faith in police officers who offered testimony based on written investigative reports that contained all pertinent details — no guesswork required.[4]

The district attorney then delivered a string of stinging jibes. Relative to the claim that the defendant did not smoke, what about the Winston cigarette package found in Tim's automobile? And didn't the police find, after searching Michele's Oldsmobile, "Winston cigarettes in the car, one smoked and one unsmoked?" What about the "studious young man that we have over here, that is so diligent in his labors to get an education, where was he at 6:00 a.m. on the morning of January 19th, 1985? He was at the Alamo Motel. I guess he was buying some books." After the sarcasm, Darnell then pointed out that Tim was actually arrested during that occasion on the weapon and possessing marijuana charges.[5]

He also discussed Tim's run-in with Texas Tech police on March 6, 1985, which, taken together with the Lubbock police sting operation of April 7 that same year, reflects a personality completely opposite of the picture portrayed by the defense and the defendant's family. The district attorney praised Detective Ronnie Goolsby, specifically his comparing the various rapes and then setting up the intelligence-gathering activities in the area around St. John's Methodist Church that resulted in luring the only man who took the bait. Finally, the D.A. explained to the jury the reason for waiting until the trial began before obtaining blood, hair, and saliva samples from Tim Cole. These particular requests, Darnell admitted, were issued more than a year ago. "That is a pretty big risk, ladies and gentlemen," he said, "unless somebody felt for sure that the person that was being tried was the right person." He continued by saying that, even though none of the tests proved beyond a reasonable doubt that the defendant did the crime, neither could the results rule him out as the guilty party. "Put aside what I would call 'rabbit trails' and look at the case of Michele Murray and ask yourselves, do you have any doubt in your mind that Timothy Cole is the person that did what the person did to her that night?" He ended with, "I ask you to find him guilty."[6]

For his part, Mike Brown hinged his argument to the concept that Michele Murray honestly misidentified his client, and he backed up his contention with a platitude. "Experience teaches us," he said, "that even our heartfelt perception of the eye is very susceptible to mistake." He cautioned the jurors to take into account that Michele had expressed uncertainty the first time she saw Tim's picture in the photo spread. He reminded them that on the witness stand, Michele had admitted that she guessed at the height of her assailant, which was noticeably less than Tim's measurement of six feet. Furthermore, Michele had detected none of the discolorations so obvious on his client's back, not to mention that she totally overlooked his birthmark. The jury should also consider that, because Tim Cole had nothing to hide, he had cooperated fully with all investigative requests, including the warrants to search his house and car, and that even after all this, nothing tied him to any crime. Plus, at one time or another during the investigation, there had been two others—Terry Clark and Jerry Wayne Johnson—whom the police thought to be the *Tech rapist*. Brown asked who had committed the rapes that took place after Tim was released on bond and left town? And what about Darnell's questioning of his witnesses' credibility? "Please believe them," Brown begged the jury. "Their alibi should give rise to reasonable doubt that Timothy Cole was the rapist."[7]

In closing, the defense attorney pointed to the convoluted testimony of Jim Thomas, Darnell's scientific expert. "We contend that the evidence in this case is inconclusive," Brown said. "There are reasons to doubt, and we ask you to return a verdict of not guilty."[8]

The district attorney walked to the jury box to deliver the last of his rebuttals, the first of which contradicted Brown's comments on why Michele recalled some features of her assailant, but not others. "Is that person going to be embracing that individual and remembering everything about that person's back when they are being sexually assaulted and their soul is being taken from them?" When Michele began to cry after hearing the prosecutor's remark, she received solace from her mother, who extended an arm around her daughter's shoulder. Darnell could not have been more pleased with the sight, and perhaps when rendering a verdict, the jury would be even more sympathetic toward the victim. Speaking to the jury members, the district attorney said that, putting everything else aside, Michele's identification of Tim Cole as her assailant should be all that mattered when they met to make a decision.[9]

CHAPTER TWELVE

THE VERDICTS

"The only time I got worried during verdict
deliberation was when I got sick."[1]
— JIM BOB DARNELL

Wednesday — September 17, 1986 (continued)

By the time that Jim Bob Darnell completed his closing argument and Judge Clinton instructed the jury to retire and consider its verdict, it was five minutes 'til 10:00 in the morning. Tim watched closely as, one by one, each of the twelve jurors filed from the courtroom, most appearing as solemn as the duty they were now expected to perform. *Surely*, he thought, *someone on the panel will believe me.*

After an hour and a half, no decision had yet been reached. At 11:34, Clinton advised the panel to break for lunch, and to reconvene at about 1:00 p.m. Sometime in the early afternoon, the bailiff delivered a message to the judge. The jurors wanted more information "about Cole's giving police consent to search his car and residence during his arrest [on] April 10, 1985."[2]

With the trial now in its fifth day, nerves were strained as people waited in the corridors, in the courtroom, and on the courthouse steps. They tried not stare at the clock as 3:00, then 4:00, and now 5:00 p.m. passed. Given how long they were taking, some folks thought the jury might end in deadlock, but twenty-seven minutes later — after about six hours of deliberation — the foreman, Walter Raymond Lupton, sent notice that the verdict was in.[3]

Spectators and reporters hurried in to hear the decision. Jim Bob Darnell took a seat alongside Denise Williams at the prosecutor's table, and on the opposite side, Mike Brown smiled encouragement to his client. Ruby Session and her two other children in attendance, Karen and Reggie Kennard, appeared ashen, their eyes fixated on Tim, expecting the worst, but hoping for a miracle. Even if they lost this one, the defense attorney told the family, they always had the appeals process to fall back on. Michele Jean Murray, who had waited so long for closure, clutched her mother's hand.

After Judge Clinton glanced at the sheet of paper, he read aloud the unanimous decision. "We, the jury, find from the evidence beyond a reasonable doubt that the defendant is guilty of the offense of aggravated sexual assault as charged in the indictment."[4]

But before the judge could finish his statement and take on the remaining business of the day, the 99th District courtroom erupted with sounds of joy from those who supported Michele on the one hand, and on the other, gasps and cries of disapproval from others who interpreted the verdict as nothing more than a sham. Michele, herself, shouted out, "Thank you," as she grinned and embraced her mother, while Becky Cannon and other Rape Crisis Center personnel, who sat nearby, offered congratulations to Jim Bob Darnell and Denise Williams. Tim didn't say anything, but he couldn't hide his pain and disappointment.[5]

Judge Clinton called for immediate restoration of order. When the quiet returned, he asked Mike Brown if he wished to poll individual jurors, to which the dejected defense attorney replied no. After all, this would only serve to prolong the agony of Tim and the members of his family, who were stunned by a ruling they were incapable of understanding.[6]

With the verdict marked as accepted, Clinton explained in detail to the jury about how the second part of the trial, that of the punishment phase, would be conducted. And before calling it a day, he spoke to Tim directly. "All right," he said, "I will allow you to remain on the bond you are on, and we will be recessed until [nine] o'clock in the morning."[7]

Jim Hansen, who covered the case for KCBD–TV, commented on the verdict. "Hearing the whole trial from beginning to end, of course I was just a reporter, not a juror," he said, "but I left the thing totally convinced justice had been done and that they had the right guy."[8]

Denise Williams quickly escorted Michele from the courtroom, but both soon returned to find Jim Bob Darnell, who once said, "This is the most bizarre case I have been involved in [during] the last 10 years," still at the table placing files and paperwork into his briefcase. Michele hugged both the prosecutor and his co-counsel, declaring that she wanted to thank them again "for all you've done for me." [9]

But for Timothy Brian Cole, there was no such elation. As he got into his attorney's car, the dam finally broke, and the tears that he had so carefully held back in public could be contained no longer.[10]

"Of course, he was scared and he was emotional," Brown said of his client. "He struck me as so very young, and out of his element. An easy mark, I thought."[11]

That night in the hotel room and with his family close at hand, Tim fell to the floor, grief-stricken. Ruby Session kneeled down and cradled her oldest son in her arms. "Why [do] they do this to me, mother?" Tim asked. "I don't even know that girl!"[12]

But Ruby had no answers for him.

Thursday — September 18, 1986
The Final Day

By the time Tim, Ruby, Reggie, and Karen arrived at the courthouse on the morning of September 18, 1986, to begin the sixth day of the trial, the previous night's anguish had diminished somewhat. Tim now exhibited more of a positive attitude—more positive about the possibility of receiving a lighter sentence, if ten years in jail can be considered light. And too, he might also be eligible for probation, but for now, all speculation would have to wait. The jurors, the same ones who pronounced him guilty the day before, had yet to meet and determine his ultimate punishment. Tim raised his right hand and flashed an all's-well signal toward a camera crew. "I'm holding up OK, considering I didn't do it," he told waiting reporters. "I feel sorry for the girl, but I didn't do it." He went on to explain that "he was under much pressure while he was a student at Tech because he was dating a 'white chick' and because of his arrest at the Alamo Motel in early 1985."[13]

"He doesn't fit the description you people have on him," Ruby added. "The victim claimed the assailant had hair on his chest but [Tim] doesn't."[14]

Before excusing himself and walking away, Tim released pent-up frustrations. "I think the judge pressured the jury into a decision," he said. "They're trying to throw the book at me."[15]

During the 10:00 a.m. recess, Mike Brown had to take care of a piece of urgent business—he had gotten wind of something that might further damage the outcome. Supposedly, some "good ol' boy" prosecutors of the day regularly resorted to any means to discredit a witness for the defense, and if what Brown had heard contained a shred of truth, Jim Bob Darnell planned on indicting Reggie Kennard for conspiracy as part of a rape scheme headed up by none other than Tim Cole. This way, during his summation, the prosecutor could hammer home the point that even the brother, also a witness for the defendant, was himself under indictment, thereby totally negating the validity of his testimony. However implausible, Mike Brown dared not risk the possibility that Darnell might be serious. The defense attorney walked into the witness room and ordered Reggie to leave the courthouse immediately, go down the street to his office, and knock on the back door. "My secretary is waiting to put you on a plane to Fort Worth," he said. "Get in the back seat of my car, lie down, and she'll take you to the airport." So that is exactly what happened—all before Darnell's alleged plot could materialize. According to Ruby Session, the rumors must have been true, because investigators called her home several times asking where Reggie was. Nothing ever came of it, because the calls eventually stopped.[16]

With court back in session, but before the jury made its way in, Judge Clinton heard objections brought by Mike Brown: the defense attorney disagreed with portions of the Court's Charge on Punishment (see Appendix 6). The first centered on "evidence of extraneous offenses" and the second concerned "the sentence or punishment to be imposed." As substitutions and amendments, Brown recommended the following alternatives:

1. You are further instructed that if there is any evidence before you in this case tending to show that the defendant committed offenses other than the offenses alleged against the defendant in the indictment, you cannot consider said testimony for any purpose in reaching your verdict on punishment.
2. From time to time during the trial of this case, I [Judge Clinton] have orally instructed you to disregard certain evidence, testimony, questions, answers, or comments by the parties, witnesses or attorneys. I again admonish you that you shall not consider for any purpose in your deliberations on punishment, nor allude to, refer to, nor discuss any matter which I have previously orally instructed you to disregard.

He might well have saved his breath, because it took no time at all for Judge Clinton to overrule what the defense attorney considered well-thought-out arguments.[17]

The judge ordered the jury to take a seat, and then he turned to Jim Bob Darnell who called Eddie Lee Huckabee, a sergeant with the Texas Tech Police Department, to provide testimony on what he thought of the defendant. Huckabee explained that he had known Timothy Brian Cole since the fall of 1979, when Tim was a student at Tech the first time.[18]

"I would say his reputation was bad," the officer said, "based on my knowledge." The prosecution requested no further clarification.[19]

Mike Brown chose not to ask any questions of this witness. Obviously he wanted no part of bringing out unnecessary details that might further blemish the jury's perception of his client's character. With Huckabee's departure from the stand, Darnell called Becky Cannon, who had been Director of the Lubbock Rape Crisis Center since March 1975. Relying on her experiences as a former probation officer in two Texas counties,

Lubbock County and Crosby County, and another in Marion, Indiana, she argued strongly against extending probation to any person convicted of rape charges. Cannon explained her reasoning. "Recidivism for sexual assault offenders and rapists would be extremely high," she said, "anywhere from the low seventies to the low ninety per cent [sic]."[20]

With Cannon's testimony now on record, both Jim Bob Darnell and Mike Brown called no additional witnesses. After Judge Clinton read the Court's Charge on Punishment to the jury, he turned to the district attorney and directed him to begin his argument.[21]

Darnell opened with, "I don't sound too good this morning. I guess some bug jumped down my throat, and I apologize for that." In spite of how he felt, though, the district attorney came out swinging on all fronts. He immediately called upon the jury to consider either a ninety-nine-year or life penalty based on Tim's actions as a dangerous person, and he challenged them to "think about the mental anguish and the amount of suffering that young lady has gone through and will go through for the rest of her life, because of that man right here . . . ."[22]

Without calling names, the district attorney pronounced the witnesses for the defense—Marlo Jones, Jackie Boswell, Leslie Thompson, and Reggie Kennard, Tim's own brother—guilty of perjury. "What type of people do that sort of thing?" he asked, and "What type of person was [Tim Cole] on March 24th and 25th of 1985, that would do the things that he did to a young 20-year-old girl?"[23]

As Mike Brown stepped up to deliver the final argument of the defense, he faced a dilemma, in that he could ill afford to alienate the twelve individuals who already believed his client guilty of a despicable crime. Therefore he had no choice but to appear tentative, expressing "a great fear on my part, in this case, that the things that I say to you will be taken lightly, possibly laughed at." He maintained that during the trial he had neither intended to lessen the severity of Michele Murray's emotional state nor play down her suffering, which would last indefinitely, regardless of whether she required hospital care following her attack. He called for the jurors to be compassionate when rendering judgment on his client, and he quoted the late Louis Brandeis, Associate Justice of the U.S. Supreme Court. "The character of a society's justice is measured not by how it treats its best citizens, but by how it treats its worst." The defense attorney described crime as "a youthful phenomenon," and that therefore the jurors should take into account Tim Cole's age and the fact that he must have hope and purpose in life. Finally, with his allotted twenty minutes about to expire, Brown made one last push—a plea that his client deserved a consideration of probation and "a sentence not exceeding ten years in the Texas Department of Corrections."[24]

Jim Bob Darnell used his seven minutes of rebuttal to rip apart the previous statements made by the defense. "If we are to consider compassion and caring for [Tim Cole]," he asked contemptuously, "are we to say: 'Thank you for sparing the life of Michele Murray?'" And furthermore, as an adult, the defendant is expected "to respect the law, respect the rights of others, and if we violate those laws, we are going to be punished for them." He closed with, "It is like I said yesterday, and I will say it again today, Timothy Cole took . . . her dignity, her peace of mind and her soul, and all I ask of you is to give him a punishment that he deserves."[25]

Before he called a recess, Judge Clinton delivered a 165-word directive to the jurors about being mindful of others when smoking in the jury room. As Tim Cole sat and listened, he must have wondered why the judge spent so much time voicing concern about those who would meet shortly and determine his sentence, especially when considering that Mike Brown rarely touched on the issue of his non-smoking, which, if given proper attention, might have altered the course of the trial.[26]

At 9:59 a.m., the jurors met to decide the conditions of punishment, but without making a decision, they broke for lunch ninety minutes later. At 1:00 p.m, the members reconvened, and deliberations lasted until 3:00 that afternoon, when Lupton advised Judge Clinton that the jury had arrived at a unanimous verdict. With all the disruption in the courtroom created by the latest announcement, the judge called for order. And then he read the decision, which had taken about three and a half hours to reach. "We, the jury, having found the defendant, Timothy Brian Cole, guilty of the offense of aggravated sexual assault, assess his punishment at confinement in the Texas Department of Corrections for a period of 25 years."[27]

As before, Mike Brown did not ask for a poll of the jury. He was noticeably upset by the judgment as Clinton accepted the verdict, quickly thanked, and then discharged the men and women who'd served on the panel, and appeared ready to get on with other matters. After requesting Tim to stand, the judge asked, "Do you have anything at this time to say before the court assesses your sentence?"[28]

In light of all that had transpired since his arrest on April 10, 1985, what could the young man say, but "I didn't do it, your honor."[29]

Judge Clinton restated the length of Tim's prison term, explained his right to an appeal through specific procedures, and advised him that he would "not be transported to the Texas Department of Corrections before such time as those motions are filed and heard." Mike Brown notified Judge Clinton that his client intended to appeal, and with this, the trial ended. Tim appeared stone-faced, lifeless. As he had always in troubled times, he looked toward his mother for guidance, but this time there was nothing Ruby could do for him. She was inconsolable as a deputy placed handcuffs on her son. And as Tim was being led away, she tried not to think about what might happen to him next.[30]

After they were discharged, the jurors didn't wait around to talk with reporters. However, other participants in the trial spoke freely. "It's been very difficult for [Michele]," observed Becky Cannon, Director of the Rape Crisis Center, "and it's still not over." On behalf of the victim and her family, Cannon complimented Darnell on a job well done. She said she could find no fault with the outcome, especially since Tim Cole would not be able to gain release on an appeal bond.[31]

Neither counsel criticized the jury. There were times, the district attorney admitted, that the defense's introduction of certain testimony, which brought out "several other rapes occurring before and after the case on trial," caused him to worry about the eventual verdict. Mike Brown simply repeated his long-held opinion that Michele Murray had misidentified his client, but he added, "We got our chance."[32]

For the time being, however, the charge of kidnapping Brenda Jones remained on the books. But Jim Bob Darnell eventually dismissed this matter, because with Tim's conviction on the Murray rape, he had gotten what he wanted.[33]

CHAPTER THIRTEEN

A Meaningless Victory

*"There are those who look at things the way they are, and ask why . . .
I dream of things that never were, and ask why not?"*
– ROBERT FRANCIS KENNEDY

Keeping to his promise to carry on the fight to free his client, on October 13, 1986, Mike Brown petitioned Judge Clinton for a new trial on the basis of five points:

1. The Trial Court erred in overruling the Defendant's Motion to Quash the Indictment.
2. The Trial Court erred in permitting the State to elect to prosecute Count 1 of the multi-count indictment, alleging aggravated sexual assault, when the rule of lenity [see Glossary] required the State to proceed only on the allegation of aggravated kidnapping contained within Count 2 of the indictment.
3. The Trial Court erred in excluding the evidence contained within the Defendant's Bill of Exception.
4. The Trial Court erred in admitting hearsay evidence concerning the results of chemical tests performed by an absent Department of Public Safety chemist.
5. The Trial Court erred in failing and refusing to give a limiting charge on extraneous offenses in the Court's Charge on Punishment.[1]

When the judge reviewed this motion, he denied it immediately. There was, however, another problem — one of money. Paying for a defense attorney had taken its toll on the Session family's savings, and Tim's current financial picture was paltry, considering that his personal assets — never much to begin with — had dwindled to less than $300, and he had debts that now exceeded $4,000, made up entirely of legal fees owed to Mike Brown's law firm. In order to continue the appeals process, something had to be done to ease the situation, so Brown sat down with his client, and they decided to take the next practical step: declare Tim indigent and apply for a court-appointed attorney. This would ensure that Brown's future legal bills would be paid by the County of Lubbock. On October 15, the defense attorney followed through on this motion, and on the same day, he filed with the 99th District Court a Notice of Appeal that announced his intention to take Tim's case to a higher level. Before Judge Clinton approved the request on December 3 and then ordered Mike Brown, as the duly-named counsel, "to appeal to the Court of Appeals for the Seventh Supreme Judicial District of Texas, Amarillo, Texas," Tim was transferred from a holding cell in the county jail to the Texas Department of Corrections' Ferguson Unit at Midway, Texas, about twenty miles northwest of Huntsville.[2]

The Ferguson Unit had been designed primarily as a prison work farm, but it had another more ominous name. Inmates called it the "Gladiator Unit," where some say that beatings occurred daily. Tim tried to remain positive about prison life in letters to his family, but behind the scenes, conditions were grim. His asthma attacks were serious enough to require medical attention, and his mother worried. "Sometimes I'd have nightmares, because he was sick," Ruby said. "I thought about him being down there in the dust and the dirt, and they tried to have him go work in the fields. He wasn't able to do that."[3]

A few months after Tim's transfer, Ruby, Reggie, and Dewitt went to see him, but only two of them were allowed a "first contact visit."[4]

"He came out, he was smiling, he was upbeat, and he told me what it was like in there," Reggie remarked. "He said,

'You know, I came here a man and I'm going to leave here a man.'"[5]

By January of the next year, Tim had already begun to seek a reduced sentence, even perhaps probation, on his own, however shaky his legal argument. On the fifteenth of that month, he directed a letter to Judge Clinton in which he pointed out that the jury in his case did not find that he used "a deadly weapon, therefore the defendant prays that the aggravated be dropped and that the court rule in the defendant's favor." Upon receipt, the judge took no action other than to have his court coordinator forward Tim's letter to his attorney.[6]

Mike Brown's appeal documents to the Seventh Supreme Judicial District of Texas, sitting in Amarillo, went out from the 99th District Court of Lubbock in early February 1987, and it contained four points of alleged error:

1. Excluding evidence contained in his bill of exception;
2. Admitting hearsay evidence concerning the results of chemical tests performed by an absent Department of Public Safety chemist;
3. Failing and refusing to give a limited charge on extraneous offenses in its charge on punishment; and
4. In admitting evidence of the victim's past sexual behavior, in violation of Rule 412, Texas Rules of Criminal Evidence.[7]

Justice John T. Boyd wrote the opinion of the court, and on August 17, 1987, he released the findings that affirmed all of Thomas L. Clinton's prior rulings.[8]

On the first point, Justice Boyd said that even though the rapes of Michele Murray and Trina Barclay were indeed similar, fingerprint evidence in the latter could not be considered, due to the lack of testimony about it in the original trial.[9]

Regarding the admissibility of the chemical tests on which James Martin Thomas, a supervisor with the DPS lab, testified instead of his employee, Warren R. Snyder, who actually conducted the tests, the court declared such testimony as legal under the Business Records Act as an exception to the hearsay rule.[10]

Relative to the third point, the court determined that since Mike Brown introduced information about other rapes with comparable characteristics "as a matter of trial strategy," he could not ask for "a limiting instruction at the punishment phase of the trial."[11]

And finally, to the fourth point, the court held that Michele Murray's virginity represented such an overriding issue in the case that it had to be considered.[12]

When Mike Brown received his copy of the decision, he asked for a rehearing, but the court on September 14 refused to grant his request.[13]

Brown next filed an appeal with a higher venue. Eventually, the Court of Criminal Appeals in Austin agreed to hear it, but restricted arguments to the legality of admitting the chemical tests and the testimony of James Martin Thomas. On November 14, 1990, a decision was reached. In the majority opinion, Justice White said that, as a full-time chemist with the Department of Public Safety, Snyder was considered a law enforcement employee, and as such, his supervisor could not legally testify in his place as he did. Therefore, the chemical tests should not have been introduced into evidence. Tim Cole had won his first victory—well, sort of. Even though the Austin court reversed a previous ruling, it refused to order a new trial and simply remanded the matter to Amarillo.[14]

CHAPTER FOURTEEN

THE REPEAT OFFENDER

"I think I know what caused me to rape the two girls . . .
I had some issues at the time I didn't know,
but I discovered over the years what they were, and I corrected them."[1]
— *JERRY WAYNE JOHNSON*

Throughout the night that followed his sentencing hearing, Tim Cole bitterly struggled with the reality of his life as he sat inside a holding cell directly across from one occupied by a fellow named Jerry Wayne Johnson, a former student at Estacado High School in Lubbock. Already a career criminal by age twenty-seven, Johnson, nicknamed "Duck," awaited his own trial on two brutal rapes that had occurred on July 4 and September 27, 1985. Elliott Blackburn, a reporter with *The Lubbock Avalanche-Journal*, conducted an interview with the convicted felon who admitted straight-up that he listened in as Tim cried and then conveyed to his other four or five cellmates that he had been falsely accused.[2]

But who is this man — this Jerry Wayne Johnson — believed earlier to be the *Tech rapist* by Jay Parchman of the Texas Tech Police Department and Mike Brown, Tim's defense attorney? Born on April 27, 1959, to Jonell Johnson, "[he] grew up on Lubbock's east side, in a home with a small café along the train tracks and across the pasture from a cottonseed plant," and according to one of his victims, he led a troubled life, stating that

140

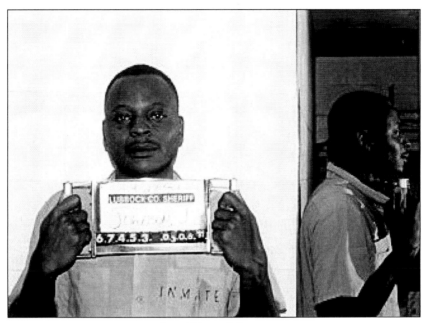

Jerry Wayne Johnson

—Courtesy Lubbock County
District Attorney

he was forced to watch his own sister being raped and then killed. After high school, Johnson held several jobs, but by the end of 1984, perhaps even sooner, he had found the one thing in which he excelled—crime.[3]

According to police reports, at about 11:41 p.m. on November 24, 1984, Della Warner, a twenty-three-year-old black female, said that Johnson showed up at her house, located at 3311 East 17th Street in Lubbock, and gained entry using the pretense that he came to tell her that her brother had been in an automobile accident. When Della found out otherwise, she told Johnson he should leave. At this time, he "pulled a small, blue-steel revolver out from underneath his jacket" and forced the young woman into one of the bedrooms where he had vaginal sex with her. Before he left, he warned her "that if she called the police, she would be dead by Friday."[4]

However, Della immediately made the call. She also agreed to press charges, provide a statement, and submit to a rape examination. At 12:30 a.m. on November 25, dispatchers sent Officer C. L. Graham to Johnson's house located at 3316 East 17th. It seems that two of Della's brothers and a brother-in-law had visited him and issued some threats about killing him for their relative's rape, so he wanted to come in and set the record straight. Graham took him to the station, where he gave a statement that completely contradicted that of his alleged rape victim. He denied owning a gun, but admitted having known Della his entire life. In fact, he said, she was a former girlfriend with whom he had sex about four times since high school. This current charge of rape was completely false, he argued. Sure they'd had intercourse, but it had been consensual. Detective Ronnie Goolsby witnessed statements made by both the victim and the suspect.[5]

In order to get a better feel for who was telling the truth, both parties took polygraph tests—Della on November 27, and Johnson two days later. The examiner determined that the young woman proved deceptive, while her alleged assailant "was being truthful when he denied raping this victim." But with verification by the DPS Lab that Della had experienced sex on that particular night, the Lubbock District Attorney's Office presented its findings to a grand jury in its January 1985 term—but citing insufficient evidence to indict Jerry Wayne Johnson, the panel promptly issued a "No Bill," after which the police had no alternative but to drop the charges against him.[6]

On July 4th of the same year, Johnson again found himself in the spotlight. Rebecca "Becky" Parker, a white female, aged twenty, had gone to a party on East Broadway, and she prepared to leave with Johnny Ramos, a nineteen-year-old friend. A black man whom both later identified as Johnson approached the young Mexican male and offered him money to take him to his house where he had a drug stash. Ramos agreed, and when they arrived, Johnson invited the couple to come inside. Ramos did, but Parker refused—she stayed in the car. When it became apparent to Johnny that Johnson had no drugs, he started to walk out. Before he could, Duck offered to pay another $5.00 for a ride back to the party. On the way, though, he suddenly reached from the backseat, placed a rope around Ramos's neck, and started to choke him.[7]

Ramos managed to stop the car, and Johnson ordered the couple to get out, threatening their lives if they tried anything. The three—Jerry Wayne with the abductees in tow—walked across the schoolyard of Martin Elementary, and then to a cotton field. Johnson made Ramos lie face down in one of the rows, and then he had Becky lie on top of her friend, with both parties back to back. And with the young woman still in this position, Duck raped her. After Parker dressed and walked away, Duck told Johnny to call her back. "He wanted me to go and tell that white girl he wanted her to do it with him one more time," Ramos said, "and if she did not want to he was going to kill both of us."[8]

Becky felt that she had no choice but to comply. At this moment, Duck directed the Mexican to bring his car nearer to where they were. "And by that time," Duck concluded, "[I will] be through." Instead, Johnny telephoned the police. When an officer arrived at the school, he saw Parker running out of the cotton field, disheveled, crying, and hysterical, still carrying a white rope, and exhibiting signs of burns around her neck.[9]

Lubbock police began canvassing the neighborhood around 3000 East Broadway, and finally located a witness, the host of the party, who confirmed that Parker and Ramos left with a person named Jerry Johnson. When Officers Carter and Bulls caught up with the suspect, he lied about his name. Duck claimed to be Wayne Wilson, who lived on 16th Street, but a quick check of his driver's license provided the correct identification. He was arrested on the spot, and on the way to be booked, he denied the rape and kidnapping charges, admitting only that "he left the party with a 'Mexican guy' and a 'white chick.'"[10]

Each of the victims arrived at the police station on July 5 and looked at a photo spread in which Johnson occupied position number 5. It took Becky no more than a few seconds to point out Duck as her assailant, and even though Ramos thought Johnson to be the one, he said that he could not be positive. Unfortunately, though, our criminal justice system does not always protect innocents, and Jerry Wayne Johnson was released on bond until his case was brought to trial.[11]

On September 10, Herbert Brink made a frantic telephone call to the police station. He wanted to file a missing person's report. He had last seen his daughter, Mary Louise Smith, a white female, age thirty-two, at about 5:30 on the previous Monday afternoon, as she left for her job selling insurance and collecting premiums door to door. Mr. Brink worried that Mary might have been a victim of foul play, especially when he realized that she had anywhere from $600 to $1,200 on her person. Added to that, Mary's debit route included the east side, an area that she feared to work after dark.[12]

No one had to wait long, however, to locate Mary. At 6:25 p.m. on Tuesday, two teenagers, Curtis and Robert Phipps, happened upon her car, a 1974 Ford LTD, parked in an open field near 700 North Zenith. When their closer inspection revealed a body lying facedown about twenty yards away, the boys ran to the George Woods Community Center, where a worker, Betty Jean Robinson, alerted police of their grisly discovery. First responders noted that Smith was fully clothed, and although her blue skirt "was pulled up around the hips," she did not appear to have been raped. Detective Ronnie Goolsby's report of September 11 indicated that the victim showed signs of strangulation, and that she "had suffered several blows to the head with an unknown object . . . due to the face being covered in blood, with apparent swelling to the eyes . . . ."[13]

Mr. Brink's son-in-law, Mike Knotts, had already retraced the victim's steps of Monday, to each and every household address provided by the local Commonwealth Life Insurance office, and he learned that the last verified call occurred at 6:30 p.m. Detectives Billy Hudgens and George White also went back over Mary's stops, but they found that she had been at 3307 East 15th as late as 8:00 p.m. Ironically, one of the collections should have been from Jonell Johnson, Jerry Wayne's mother, at 3317 E. 17th, but neither Jonell nor any of her relatives living in the same house remembered seeing Mary on the day she disappeared. Another contact, however, a man named Fred McClin, said that he saw the victim's car parked a long while across the street at 3305 East 15th, where Jerry Wayne Johnson stayed with an aunt.[14]

Detectives began talking among themselves, and due to their previous common experiences with Duck, they soon determined that he should be considered a person of strong interest in Mrs. Smith's murder. Hudgens and White, accompanied by Jackie Peoples, a Texas Ranger, went to Johnson's house, but he wasn't home. They finally tracked him down while he walked along the 3300 block of East Broadway. Jerry Wayne was prepared for their visit, he insisted, because he had seen the detectives in the neighborhood the previous day. But before he could reach them, they drove off. He said he wanted to tell them that no insurance person had come to his house on the night of the murder, and besides, he did not personally know the woman. Perhaps their informant mistook his wife's car, a brown 1979 Oldsmobile Cutlass, for the one that belonged to the victim.[15]

Johnson claimed as an alibi that he watched a Dallas Cowboys game on television during the night in question. Investigators followed one lead after another, conducting numerous interviews, and checking every possible suspect, down to the victim's ex-husband, Jesse Smith—but all pointed back to Jerry Wayne. Earl Harris, whom Johnson said visited him on September 9, explained that he also saw a dark colored Ford parked in front of Duck's house, one that matched the description of the murder victim's car.[16]

While the investigation continued, Johnson remained free on bond, and able to run the streets with reckless abandon. Once called a scumbag by a local reporter, he soon would justify the title by further demonstrating just how much a danger to society he had become. At a little before 2:00 a.m. on Friday, September 27, 1985, Jaime Herrera, the same officer who first interviewed Michele Murray at Lubbock General Hospital, received a call to investigate a traffic accident at 3520 East 13th Street. When he arrived at the scene, Herrera found a maroon and white Mercury Cougar smashed against a fence and its driver outside "swaying from side to side," with "blood-shot eyes" and slurred speech. In a drunken stupor, Jerry Wayne Johnson became more verbally abusive by the minute, venting his hatred toward all Mexicans and at Herrera, specifically, because he shared the same ethnicity.[17]

After Johnson refused a field sobriety test, Herrera searched his car and found a steak knife, three marijuana joints, and an open beer container, enough to justify an arrest for D.W.I. and drug possession. By 2:50 a.m. Johnson once more landed in jail, but he did not stay put for long, because shortly before 5:00 p.m. the same day, he made his way inside Estacado High School. He told two custodians, Rosia Lee Taylor and Robert Earl Moore, "I am looking for my sister."[18]

Taylor first saw him, "a tall, slender black man with short hair," wearing dirty brown pants and a blue shirt, maybe a uniform, as he walked into a men's bathroom that she was cleaning. "I could smell alcohol and his speech was blurred [sic], and I couldn't understand what he was saying most of the time," the school worker told investigators. "I wondered why he was in at this time of the afternoon because I knew the doors were usually locked by [then]."[19]

Irrespective of his strange behavior, Taylor tried to help the man. They walked toward the band room, then toward the gym, and along the way, they met a few students, but no one knew where the fellow's sister was. Taylor recalled seeing him exit the building by the front door at 5:30 p.m., but before he left, his verbiage may have provided a clue as to his real purpose for being there. "He asked me if I was married, and when I told him that I was," Rosia explained, "he said he wouldn't bother me since I was probably a good woman."[20]

Moore also said that he had seen a man, whom he knew only as Duck, wandering around. And he, too, saw Duck leave the premises. However, both Taylor and Moore were mistaken in their assumptions. Jerry Wayne Johnson never actually left the immediate area, because about twenty minutes later, he approached Tina Martin, a fifteen-year-old white student, in the hallway. He told her that he was a watchman. The young woman, who had stayed late for ROTC practice, sold him some M&M candies for a class project. After she gave him some change, Duck announced that he had to lock up, so she had to go. Tina followed the command, and when outside, she waited

on her parents for a ride home. Out of the blue, Johnson grabbed
the girl, put "a knife to her throat and advised her to come with
him or else he would stab her in the heart." In a strange twist,
Tina's father arrived to pick up his daughter at the same time
Duck was forcing her to walk with him to the teachers' parking
lot.[21]

Tina's dad did not recognize her, he said, "Because her head
was down and the guy had his arm around her neck."[22]

Johnson ordered Tina to close her eyes and lie on the floorboard of "a maroon-over-white Mercury Cougar," and then he
drove to a cotton field, the entire time threatening her with
death if she cried out for help. There, Johnson savagely raped
the teenager, and afterward he let her out of the car close to
Idalou Road and told her to start walking—but not before taking between $11.00 and $15.00 from her. Duck's car was running
close to empty, he claimed, and he needed money for a fill-up.
A short time later, he returned, drove up beside her, and had
her get back in the car.[23]

Tina recalled, "On the way back, he did use some profane
language."[24]

"I am a very sick man or I wouldn't have done this," the assailant declared. "I have never done anything like this before."
He drove around for a while, then stopped, and put Tina out
once more, this time near the high school baseball field. Before
taking off, though, Johnson added a final insult, saying that "he
had lots of cousins at Estacado and that it would be stupid to go
to court because all her friends would be there and laugh and
say she wasn't a virgin now." Shaking and in shock, Tina made
her way on foot to a friend's house, and within minutes, her parents arrived and took her to Lubbock General Hospital, where
she met two representatives of the Rape Crisis Center.[25]

On the following Thursday, October 3, the two school custodians, Taylor and Moore, visited the office of Mr. Carrol
Thomas, the principal of Estacado High School, and identified
Jerry Wayne Johnson as the person they had seen in the building on September 27. Both picked out his photograph that appeared on page 136 of the *1977 Matadors* student annual. But
Thomas did not stop here. He more or less took matters into his

own hands. Without waiting for police action, the next after-noon he called Miss Martin in and showed to her pages 136 and 137 of the same yearbook, but he carefully concealed all names. "I looked at the pictures and I saw the man that forced me into his car and who took me out to the cotton field and raped me," Tina said. "I am positive of this."[26]

Mr. Thomas talked the matter over with Gib Weaver, Assistant Superintendent for Secondary Schools, who tele-phoned Juvenile Officer E. A. Rendleman and explained the cir-cumstances. On Tuesday, October 8, Rendleman brought Tina to the police station, where she met Detective Nevarez, who asked her once more to identify Johnson from the school annual. After she did, Nevarez obtained an arrest warrant for aggra-vated kidnapping, aggravated sexual assault, and aggravated robbery. Officers drove to Johnson's house, but he was not there, so they began searching for his 1977 Cougar, which they found parked at 800 Idalou. Before 10:00 that same night, Johnson was handcuffed, booked, and placed behind bars — never again to prey on the women of Lubbock.[27]

With his latest arrest, jailhouse tips began to roll in, and one, in particular, looked promising. After county inmate Lucious Weatherspoon provided details to police about an unrelated case, a burglary of a highway patrolman's residence, he asked Sergeant Doyle Nelson if he could help out further. The officer inquired whether Weatherspoon knew anything about the re-cent murder of a white woman [Mary Smith], and when the in-mate said that he did not, supposedly the two worked out a deal with no promises attached. Johnson was placed in the same cell as Weatherspoon, and Lucious agreed to pass on any informa-tion that might implicate Duck in the crime. On Sunday, October 13, Duck allegedly confessed to his cellmate. Police were ecstatic, for a while at least, but they were let down the next day when Weatherspoon failed a polygraph examination, and from their standpoint, matters only got worse when the murder suspect passed one given to him. Even though detec-tives continued to feel that the case had merit, Duck was never convicted of this offense.[28]

With Jerry Wayne Johnson's being found guilty of the

aggravated rapes of Parker and Martin, he began serving a life sentence plus ninety-nine years at the Daniel Unit, located in Snyder, some ninety-three miles southeast of Lubbock. He is still there today.[29]

Meanwhile, Tim Cole marked time at various prison locations, including Coffield and Michael, both at Tennessee Colony, 135 miles southeast of Fort Worth, and Clements in Amarillo. And for a while, he was sent to the Rusk State Hospital, a facility that treats psychiatric patients. In between, he was in and out of prison hospitals, where he received treatment for various medical problems, including his asthma condition. Yet, he never divulged to those closest to him the true extent of his pain, choosing instead to focus the content of his letters and conversations on more positive subjects. "Tim always assured his family he was fine, and quickly turned to how things were going with school or work," his brother Cory said.[30]

Ruby Session explained what Tim did with his limited funds. "He invested money while he was in prison," she said. "And he donated money to worthy causes." She went on to discuss his enrollment at Elkins Institute of Dallas, and how in 1989, he completed a correspondence course that earned him a certificate in Small Business Entrepreneurship. But there were times, she said, that the system fought against her son. She gave as an example the time his Westlaw Library books were stolen. Tim complained and wanted restitution from the facility. Surely by accident, Ruby said that a note was attached to one of Tim's letters sent to her. The comment was, "He can't prove a thing, so don't pay him a dime."[31]

CHAPTER FIFTEEN

An Unlikely Ally

"Reformation of my convicted behavior began
when I started seeking to clear Tim . . . ."[1]
– JERRY WAYNE JOHNSON

By the spring of 1993, Tim Cole had been behind bars for more than six years, but even so, he clung to the possibility that he might be granted a new trial. After all, the Court of Criminal Appeals in Austin previously ruled that the original trial judge, Thomas L. Clinton, had violated the hearsay rule by allowing James Martin Thomas, a DPS supervising chemist, to take the witness stand and present evidence on tests conducted by a subordinate. But on March 29, 1993, the finality of a fourteen-page opinion shut down all hope for Tim. Justice John T. Boyd, of the Court of Appeals for the Seventh District of Texas at Amarillo, affirmed Tim's verdict by writing, "We have determined that since all of the test results were inconclusive, the jury probably placed little, if any, emphasis on Thomas'[s] testimony in making their determination." There would be no retrial, ever.[2]

While Jerry Wayne Johnson remained in prison, according to his comments, he agonized over Tim Cole's conviction, but he fully expected Mike Brown's appeal to be successful. When this did not occur, Johnson implemented Plan B. But why would such a matter weigh so heavily on his shoulders? He had no vested interest in this case—or did he? Without question, he

150

made no attempt to contact authorities until the statute of limitations expired on Michele Jean Murray's rape, but on February 3, 1995, he prepared a petition which reflected that copies were also mailed to the District Attorney's Office and Mike Brown. Within the document, Johnson never actually named Tim Cole; yet, he did admit to committing a crime for which one of Mike Brown's clients received blame, conviction, and incarceration. Furthermore, he wished to have a court-appointed attorney walk him through the process and protect his interests. He sent the paperwork to the Lubbock courthouse, and on February 6, someone in the office of Jean Anne Stratton, District Clerk, marked it as received, affixed the cause number as 95-550, 214, and assigned it to the 137th District Court.[3]

"My initial goal was to free this man," Johnson said later, "because I knew this man was innocent."[4]

Cause Number 95-550, 214 identified the petition as a civil matter, not a criminal one as it should have been. Whether this played into the delay will never be known, but regardless, Johnson claims that he never received a response from anyone. So after a year, he said that he "wrote a letter to Lubbock Justice of the Peace Jim Hansen to complain about the matter being ignored." When no reply came, Johnson, by his own admission, did nothing. He waited four more years before taking the next step.[5]

During the interim, prison life exacted an enormous toll on Timothy Brian Cole, and his asthma worsened. In effect, he had become a broken man, as evidenced by what is assumed to be the last photo of him, taken on April 12, 1999, by the Texas Department of Corrections. Amazingly, after all the heartbreaks and disappointments, the continual trips to the hospital to treat his medical condition, and yes, the brutality he endured, Tim still smiled! But prison has a way of changing an individual, and there is no doubt that it changed Tim Cole. During his thirteen years of incarceration, however, only four minor disciplinary reports, obtained through an open records request, are contained in his file. These offenses occurred between January 30 and May 1, 1993, and the most serious on April 5 involved his tearing off the covers of two law books and destroying some of the inside

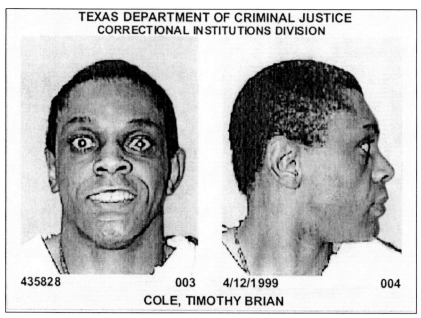

Timothy Brian Cole
— Courtesy Texas Department of Criminal Justice,
Correctional Institutions Division

pages, perhaps triggered by complete frustration and the loss of faith in a judicial system that had recently denied his final appeal.[6]

The parole board offered probation, but in order to gain his release, Tim would have to do something that cut across the grain of his character. Not only would he have to admit that he raped Michele Jean Murray, but also he would have to declare remorse. Given these requirements, he refused. "I would rather spend all twenty-five years living in prison as a convicted rapist," he explained to his mother, "than to come out and live in the free world as a registered sex offender, all for a crime I did not commit."[7]

As the years dragged by, he began to withdraw further and further, as, reportedly, "he refused to see his nieces and nephews while in prison." And when his stepfather, Dewitt

Session, died on February 4, 1996, Tim chose to skip the funeral, because he did not want to bear the humiliation of appearing in public "shackled and under guard." Too, he was troubled that life would pass him by before he had the opportunity to realize his dreams, considering that September 2011 — the end of a twenty-five year sentence — looked a long way off. In a letter to his mother, Tim wrote, "I don't have anything but a lot of time to think about it, just think about it, 24 hours a day, seven days a week. How soon it will be over and life starts anew. Don't worry. I'll be fine."[8]

In spite of what he did or did not do in life, it seems that from the very start, the deck was stacked against Tim, and unfortunately, destiny was about to deal the cruelest hand yet. At age thirty-nine, Timothy Brian Cole lost the ultimate battle, when on December 2, 1999, he "died of respiratory failure," brought on by a severe asthma attack. In the end, the human spirit can sustain a failing body for just so long. However, other factors may have contributed to his death as well, including a loss of will to go on. Who can say for sure? No one knows how a lengthy jail term might affect a person, especially when that person is asthmatic.[9]

At 8:02 p.m., the events of Tim's tragic death were recorded under the authority of Captain David Driskell of the Darrington Unit, located at Rosharon, south of Houston. The report is displayed below:

> On December 02, 1999 at approximately 1540 hours [3:40 p.m.] offender Timothy Brian Cole #435828 was being escorted to the unit infirmary due to complaining of chest pains. As he arrived at the exit door of B-Line cellblock offender Cole informed Officer Good that he felt as if he was going to passout [sic]. At this time offender Cole began falling and Officer Good assisted him to the floor. Officer Good contacted the Medical Dept. who arrived on B-Line moments later. Offender Cole was placed on the strecher [sic] and immediately taken to the unit infirmary emergency room where medical staff began administring [sic] CPR. At approximately 1613 hours [4:13 p.m.] offender Cole was pronounced dead by Dr. Dinh. Internal Affairs was contacted and arrived in the E/R room

prior to the death announcement. At approximately 1700 hrs. [5:00 p.m.] the next of kin has not been contacted at this time. Baker Funeral arrived on the unit and transported the body to TDCJ Hospital Galveston at approximately 1805 hrs. [6:05 p.m.].[10]

When the prison chaplain put in a call to Tim's mother, there was no answer. The next day, he tried again, and this time, Kevin, another of Tim's brothers, picked up the telephone. As the family gathered, Ruby could do little but reminisce about things that she wished she could change, particularly the day that Tim left for Lubbock to meet with Mike Brown about his upcoming trial. "That . . . Sunday, I didn't, we didn't fix dinner," she said. "We ate Kentucky Fried Chicken. And I regret that to this day. My child never sat down at the table and had another meal at this house."[11]

At this juncture, Jerry Wayne Johnson said that he was not aware of Tim Cole's death, but in any case, he continued trying to confess, although on a cautious note, being careful not to reveal Tim's name. On June 13, 2000, he wrote to Judge Cecil

Timothy Brian Cole's marker and resting place
Mount Olivet Cemetery, Fort Worth

—Courtesy Ancestry.com

Puryear of the 137th District Court and complained about not
hearing anything about his original request back in 1995. By
now, he was even more puzzled, and he began to suspect a conspiracy. Johnson said, "It appears there may be a concerted effort by those interested to leave the matter unacted upon so that
the sure negative publicity never occurs." He added:

> Judge its [sic] hard to amagine [sic] attorney Mike Brown has
> made [no] attempt to contact me to start the process of getting
> the information to finally prove his client was in fact innocent
> but wrongfully convicted. It is more hard to amagine [sic]
> when you look at the documented fact that Mike Brown
> sought to show at the mans [sic] trial that I committed the
> crime.[12]

What transpired during the months in between remains a
mystery, but on January 12, 2001, Judge J. Blair Cherry, Jr. of the
72nd District Court "ordered without necessity of a hearing that
the relief requested in the petition herein is hereby denied."[13]

Soon though, Johnson's quest received an indirect, but
much-welcomed push from the state legislature. Although
"Senate Bill 3 took effect on April 5, 2001, and immediately provided Texas prison inmates the opportunity to request DNA
testing of biological evidence retained by the State after trial," it
is indeed regrettable that it came too late to help Timothy Brian
Cole overturn his prior conviction and walk out of prison fully
vindicated. Other inmates were more fortunate. As for Johnson,
he claims that he took full advantage of the new provisions in
May 2002 and then again in October, in which he allegedly admitted to Murray's rape. But in so doing, he incorporated allegations that DPS Lab personnel produced bogus test data in the
Cole case, and he asserted that the same thing might well have
occurred in his.[14]

Through 2006, Johnson, who had received "his high school
equivalency and paralegal certification by correspondence"
while in the penitentiary, kept busy submitting one grievance
after another about "faked serology results" to various
statewide agencies, as well as Lubbock entities, including the
West Texas Innocence Project (now the Innocence Project of

Texas) and *The Lubbock Avalanche-Journal*. None of his admissions or complaints made any real impact — that is, until May 11, 2007, when he laid everything on the line by writing to Tim Cole, who he thought by now would be out on parole.

> Dear Mr. Cole:
>   I hope this letter reached you. My name is Jerry Wayne Johnson. I'm presently a Texas prisoner.
>   You may recall my name from your 1986 rape trial in Lubbock. Your Lubbock attorney, Mike Brown, tried to show I committed the rape.
>   I have been trying to locate you since 1995 to tell you I wish to confess I did in fact commit the rape Lubbock wrongly convicted you of. It is very possible that through a written confession from me and DNA testing you can finally have your name cleared of the rape and be removed from being a parolee, registered sex offender and to received [sic] compensation for the time you were wrongly incarcerated.
>   If this letter reaches you, please contact me by writing so that we can arrange to take the steps to get the process started. Whatever it takes, I will do it.[15]

In a few days, Rodney Kennard walked to his mother's mailbox in Fort Worth and retrieved the letter directed to his deceased brother of over seven years. At first, he believed it nothing more than a morbid prank, but as he began to read on, his attitude soon changed. Within minutes, the entire family became swept up in a state of jubilation. Finally now, they thought, Tim's exoneration had a real possibility of succeeding. "My husband left this earth with the same prayer that I've had all these years, that one day, maybe somebody would own up to it," Ruby said. "Now that's what this said in this boy's letter."[16]

In no time, information about Johnson's written confession made its way to *The Lubbock Avalanche-Journal* and to the Innocence Project of Texas — and when the story hit the streets and other media outlets picked up on it, all hell seemed to break loose. Lubbock found itself mired in controversy, and Jerry Wayne Johnson finally learned of Timothy Brian Cole's death when he read about it in a newspaper article. Elliott Blackburn, the reporter, showed up to talk with him, and during their frank discussion, Johnson vividly narrated the details of the rape that were so strikingly similar to those included in the victim's original statement, the account appeared to be legitimate. When asked why he chose Murray as his target, he responded that she "just happened to be the first to pull into that cold church parking lot in March 1985."[17]

But what of this jailhouse confession? Such are all too frequent, attorneys warn us, and most don't pan out. District Attorney Matthew D. Powell offered up his opinion. "If one innocent person is put in the pen, that's a travesty of justice," he said. "We also remember that a jury, [twelve] citizens of Lubbock County, looked at this and made a decision that he was guilty. For us to overturn, to get into the purview of the jury, it's going to take a lot for us to do something different."[18]

Jerry Wayne Johnson
— Reprint courtesy of
The Lubbock Avalanche-Journal

Jeff Blackburn, the organization's chief counsel, added, "Inmates have flooded the Innocence Project with claims in the wake of exonerations in Dallas and other cities, and investigators must move slowly and carefully to root out false cases."[19]

Meanwhile, the student volunteers of the Innocence Project, under the supervision of Natalie Roetzel, began to reconstruct the crime and determine how Tim Cole had become convicted of it. And likewise, they visited Jerry Wayne Johnson and obtained a signed confession. Regardless of their plans, however, everything boiled down to one test — DNA. With increased news coverage about Johnson's letter, Powell softened his previous position considerably. Now he promised to do everything possible to prove the validity of the Snyder inmate's story. He assigned George White, then an investigator in his department, to head up the effort, but it had yet to be determined whether any of Michele's clothing or samples contained DNA left behind by the perpetrator. Besides, in a case of this age, the evidence file could have by now been completely destroyed.[20]

"I really and truly hope that there is something over there [Lubbock County Courthouse] to resolve the question," White said. Remarkably, he got his wish, the first part anyway: the evidence file remained intact.[21]

After Tim's death, Ruby Session said many times that her son wanted three things: "exoneration, vindication and a pardon from the governor." But even she knew that this would be hard, if not impossible, to get. There had never been record of a

Natalie Roetzel
— Courtesy the Innocence
Project of Texas

Jeff Blackburn
— Courtesy the Innocence
Project of Texas

posthumous exoneration in the Lone Star State, so every step would be taken in uncharted territory. Jeff Blackburn realized, too, that it would be a slow and tedious process. The Texas court system, he said, was set up to try and convict those guilty of crimes — not to set them free. Even if DNA could prove Tim's innocence, Lubbock judges might shy away from taking on such a hot issue, especially now that Jim Bob Darnell was sitting on the bench of the 140th District Court. For months, nothing much happened. The wheels of justice turn slowly, and members of the Session family began to doubt a positive result. But they kept trying.[22]

"I know he's deceased," Tim's brother Cory said. "That's why it's just more and more important to us. Everybody wants to hear about someone who got out of prison and they're moving on with their lives. Well, we want to hear about someone who didn't deserve to go to prison."[23]

Through the years, Jerry Wayne Johnson has made many allegations of racial bias, phony test results, incompetent defense lawyers, and prosecutorial misconduct. Once he even charged a district judge with potential "misuse of official information."

George M. White
— Courtesy Lubbock County
District Attorney

For this reason, it is often hard to tell fact from fiction in his rants. As an example, he asserts that on January 9, 2008, George White and Todd Smith, both investigators with the Lubbock County District Attorney's Office, visited with him about the Cole case. "They attempted to intimidate me to back off by threatening to offend my future parole possibilities," Johnson said. It seems that the investigators wanted all of Johnson's correspondence that named "officials and people dating back to 1995" that were involved in his efforts to free

Tim. When Johnson refused, the two left. But three months later, they returned—and this time Johnson allowed them to take a specimen for DNA testing.[24]

On May 19, 2008, word came down:

> The Texas Department of Public Safety informed the Lubbock County District Attorney's Office that it had tested known biological samples from Michele Mallin [Michele Murray's married name], Mr. Cole, and Mr. Johnson. After extensive DNA testing, the agency concluded that the sperm cells left by Ms. Mallin's assailant belonged to Mr. Johnson and not to Mr. Cole. The report, which stated that 'to a reasonable degree of scientific certainty, Johnson is the source of the DNA on the sperm cell fraction from stain two from the panties.'

George White advised Michele of the findings on May 21, and on Friday, May 23, Jeff Blackburn delivered news to the Session family that one of Tim's last three wishes—vindication—had been granted at last. Jerry Wayne Johnson did not get his notice until sometime in June.[25]

CHAPTER SIXTEEN

UNCHARTED GROUND

"We've already found moral redemption.
Now we need legal redemption."[1]
– JEFF BLACKBURN

With the DNA analysis out of the way, folks wondered what action District Attorney Powell would take next. Would he go forward with the initiative of clearing Timothy Brian Cole's name? Not so fast, he cautioned. "[My] office has already done much more than the law required," he bragged. "Now [I'm] leery of setting the precedent for an unprecedented legal problem."[2]

Jeff Blackburn is a tenacious trial lawyer with the mentality of a pit bull and the legal expertise and experience to back up his rhetoric. None of Powell's remarks made any sense to him, and frankly, as chief counsel for the Innocence Project of Texas, he did not want to face the Session family with a half-hearted excuse. "If we're going to live in a society where the court system operates in a fair way, then it's got to do it across the board," he urged. "They have a right to have a court of record tell them that their son was innocent."[3]

Blackburn, along with Natalie Roetzel, the project's executive director, knew that part of Powell's argument rang true — after death, no one in Texas had ever been exonerated — and in fact, through DNA analysis, no one in the entire nation had.

161

"The normal way an inmate seeks exoneration," Roetzel said, "is by filing an application for writ of habeas corpus under Article 11.07 of the Texas Code of Criminal Procedure, or by filing a motion for forensic DNA testing under Chapter 64 of the same code. He's [Cole] obviously not available to file either."[4]

So how would they proceed? While Blackburn searched the statutes, innovation held the key. The answer revealed itself in Article 52.01 of the Code of Criminal Procedure, wherein he found an old provision, which "allows any district judge of the State of Texas to hear such a petition" through a

Matthew D. Powell,
Lubbock County District Attorney
— Reprint courtesy of
The Lubbock Avalanche-Journal

Court of Inquiry. On June 26, 2008, the Innocence Project took its case to the 99th District Court, filing a motion asking it "to request the Presiding Judge of the 7th Administrative Judicial District to appoint a district judge to commence a Court of Inquiry . . . ."[5]

Experts from all over weighed in on the subject, both pro and con, and as strange as it might seem, an unforeseen source — Jerry Wayne Johnson — filed his own motion in opposition. If at the conclusion, he argued, a Court of Inquiry found him to be the guilty party in Murray's rape, he could not be charged with the crime because the statute of limitations had expired. The district court, therefore, had no legal authority to grant the petitioners' relief. Since 1995, Johnson had professed that he wanted to clear Tim Cole's name, but now with exoneration in sight, he fought the legal action to make it happen.[6]

His resistance, in any case, became moot when, on August 5, the Lubbock court announced its refusal to hear the proposition.

The Honorable Charles Baird
—Courtesy 299th District Court

Though disappointed, Jeff Blackburn pointed out, "I'm still enough of a believer in the court system, even in Texas, to think that somewhere, someplace, there's a judge who's willing to say what's right is right and what's wrong is wrong." And then he threw down the challenge. "We will go to every single district judge until we find one that thinks something ought to be done here."[7]

He next turned to the state capital in Austin and specifically to Judge Charles Baird of the 299th District Court in and for Travis County, Texas. Judge Baird agreed to look at the evidence, which he found met the criteria, and he then set the dates of February 5 and 6, 2009, for the formal hearing. Representing the Session family were Blackburn and Barry Scheck of the Innocence Project based out of New York. During the two-day affair, numerous parties took the stand, among them Michele Murray Mallin, Jerry Wayne Johnson, Michael Logan Ware, Gary Wells, Ph.D., and members of the Session family. No representatives from the Lubbock District Attorney's Office were present, nor were Judge Jim Bob Darnell, the prosecutor in Tim Cole's trial, or Mike Brown, Tim's original defense attorney.[8]

Ware, the Special Fields Bureau Chief of the Dallas County District Attorney's Office, "testified . . . on the causes and consequences of wrongful convictions in Texas," and Dr. Wells discussed the inherent problems in the area of eyewitness identification. Afterward, the latter "analyzed this case and applied his scientific understanding to the facts presented." As a Distinguished Professor of Psychology at Iowa State University, Wells is an acknowledged expert in the field of eyewitness iden-

tification, and as such has written, published, spoken, and testified widely on the subject. During any eyewitness investigation,
he fully understands "that people make mistakes," but this does
not mean that we should trash the entire process, only that the
results "be treated—like blood, fingerprints, and fiber evidence—as trace evidence, subject to contamination, deteriora-
tion, and corruption." For a detailed explanation of "The
Problem of False Eyewitness Identification" in the Tim Cole
case, refer to Appendix 7.[9]

Michele Mallin, however, became the focal point of the hearing as she recalled the crime, the police investigation, and how
she misidentified Tim Cole. Johnson, who attended as a result of
a subpoena issued by Jeff Blackburn, admitted his guilt, and for
the first time since March 25, 1985, the assailant and his victim
came face to face. After Johnson's testimony, Judge Baird gave
Michele permission to speak to the man whom she had not seen

Ruby Lee Session at exoneration hearing
—Photo copyright Jana Birchum, 2009

in almost twenty-four years. She pulled no punches. "What you did to me, you had no right to do," she said. "You've got no right to do that to any woman. I am the one with the power now, buddy."[10]

It had taken awhile, but on April 7, twenty-four years to the date of the sting operation that erroneously named Tim as the *Tech rapist*, the Session family's wait paid off as Judge Baird issued a summary of his findings and recommendations. In a scathing indictment of the Lubbock Police Department, he declared Tim Cole innocent of all charges. "I find that Timothy Cole's reputation was wrongly injured, that his reputation must be restored, and that his good name must be vindicated," the judge said. "I find that Timothy Cole shall be and is hereby exonerated."[11]

The report also found fault with the way officers displayed the photo spread, how they conducted the line-up and "con-

Michele Murray Mallin at exoneration hearing
—Photo copyright Jana Birchum, 2009

sciously ignored" critical pieces of evidence, and their failure to accurately record in written reports the initial hesitation on Michele's part and the exact words she spoke during the identification session. Apart from all the shortcomings of the investigation, it seemed impossible to reconcile the fact that so many people turned a deaf ear to Jerry Wayne Johnson, who had tried unsuccessfully for so long to get someone—anyone—to take seriously his confession.[12]

How had it all happened? Judge Baird provided the simple answer—tunnel vision. "It is plain from the record that once the Lubbock police fixed their sights on Tim Cole," he wrote, "all other avenues of investigation were blocked off. To them, it became more of a matter of justifying their arrest than finding out the truth."[13]

Judge Baird did not stop here. He criticized officials and various courts for not looking into Tim Cole's repeated claims of being falsely convicted, and then he tossed the entire matter into the lap of the Texas Legislature, admonishing its members to take corrective action to ensure that no other such miscarriages of justice recur.[14]

Finally, someone had drawn a line in the sand. Finally, someone had done the right thing! The second of Tim's wishes had now been granted, but with a stipulation. In order for Judge Baird's ruling to become official, "it will take action from either Texas Governor Rick Perry, or the state's highest criminal court."[15]

Meanwhile, others joined the fight, not only paying tribute to Tim Cole and his family, but also authoring legislation designed to help others who were wrongfully convicted obtain additional benefits that would allow for assimilation into society once more. State Representative Marc Veasey (D-Fort Worth) and State Senator Robert Duncan (R-Lubbock) sponsored joint resolutions honoring Tim that were read in both houses of the Texas Legislature. Then, Senators Duncan and Rodney Ellis (D-Houston) introduced SB 2014 in the Texas Senate, while in the Texas House of Representatives, Rafael Anchia (D-Dallas) and several others authored HB 1736. When combined, both pieces of legislation became known as the Tim Cole Act, which on May

19, 2009, went to the Texas chief executive. When Governor Perry signed it into law eight days later, his office issued a press release. "While we cannot give back the time lost to those wrongfully convicted who have spent time in prison, or their families," the governor said, "this new law is a significant step for justice by increasing compensation for the innocent."[16]

The Tim Cole Act increases "lump-sum payments from $50,000 to $80,000 for every year of confinement and grants an annuity to provide a life-time of income. Exonerees [also] get 120 hours of paid tuition at a career center or public college." By accepting a settlement, however, "they give up their right to sue the State. And they will lose the money if they are convicted of another felony."[17]

Also as part of the task to determine why Texas leads the nation in wrongful convictions "overturned by DNA testing with 36 exonerations, including 29 that involved eyewitness misidentification," Senator Ellis and State Representative Ruth Jones McClendon (D-San Antonio) introduced bills that would overhaul the way criminal investigations are handled, and especially how eyewitness testimony is obtained and then applied to the case at hand. Ellis summed up the discontent shared by many. He said,

> Enough is enough. Day after day, week after week, we learn of more innocent Texans who have had their lives torn from them in tragic error. It is time for Texas to create an Innocence Commission to launch in-depth investigations each time an innocent person is wrongfully convicted, review what went wrong in these cases, why, and spell out the changes necessary to ensure these injustices are not repeated.

The legislation, though watered down from its original version, passed and became law on September 1, 2009, creating the Timothy Cole Advisory Panel on Wrongful Convictions, which held its first meeting on October 13, 2009. It is much too early, however, to determine what future impact the panel will have in its attempt to force police, prosecutors, and judges to correct many long-overdue errors in the way they do business.[18]

On December 2, 2009, the ten-year anniversary of Tim's

death, a $100,000 scholarship in his memory was created at the Texas Tech School of Law. "Four attorneys, Kevin Glasheen, Noe Valles, Chad Indemer, and Jeff Blackburn, director of The Innocence Project, contributed to the scholarship," said Assistant Dean Kay Fletcher. "It's in recognition of the hard work that they have done . . . towards the exoneration of those wrongfully convicted."[19]

During the presentation ceremonies, Glasheen stated, "We wanted to create this scholarship not only in honor of Tim, but [also] to help students work towards justice."[20]

"Our movement has a safer and better home at Tech than anywhere else," Blackburn added. "I've never been prouder to be connected to this school than today."[21]

The endeavor to restore Tim's name has been fraught with delays and challenges. Even though the Texas Legislative Council, a research organization for lawmakers, determined that his pardon might be completely legal, others resisted for a specific reason: "a decades-old attorney general's opinion that precludes posthumous pardons." Subsequently, Governor Perry made the initial decision that he must await a constitutional amendment to provide the necessary authority.[22]

For those who called for a more immediate resolution, this choice proved totally unacceptable in that it would have tacked endless years onto a process that had taken much too long already. So other avenues were explored. Responding to requests by Senator Ellis, Texas Attorney General Greg Abbot ruled on January 7, 2010, that his predecessor's prior opinion is out of step with "modern United States Supreme Court decisions," and that the State's chief executive can, after all, issue a posthumous pardon. As he had previously promised, Governor Perry took quick action. "I have spoken with Tim Cole's mother about this good news, which finally gives his family the opportunity to officially clear his name," he said. "I hope the Board of Pardons and Paroles will act swiftly in sending a recommendation to my desk so that justice can finally be served."[23]

After the Board of Pardons and Paroles reacted positively, Governor Perry kept his part of the bargain on March 1, 2010. Unfortunately, a surgical procedure prevented Ruby Session from attending the Austin ceremony and the signing of her son's posthumous pardon; subsequently, the governor promised to personally deliver the document to her at a future date.[24]

With the affixed signature on the long-sought-after pardon, the governor's office issued a press release. "I have been looking forward to the day I could tell Tim Cole's mother that her son's name has been cleared for a crime he did not commit," Perry said. "The State of Texas cannot give back the time he spent in prison away from his loved ones, but today I was finally able to tell her we have cleared his name, and hope this brings a measure of peace to his family." With that, Timothy Brian Cole became part of Texas history.[25]

STATE OF TEXAS

Proclamation

by the

Governor of the State of Texas

PROCLAMATION NO. 2010-00001   DPS # TX02724961

TO ALL TO WHOM THESE PRESENTS MAY COME:

WHEREAS, Timothy Brian Cole, TDCJ# 435828, D.O.B. July 1, 1960, was sentenced in the 99th Judicial District Court of Lubbock County, Texas, on September 22, 1986, to serve a twenty-five year sentence in the Texas Department of Criminal Justice for the offense of Aggravated Sexual Assault, Cause No. 85-403,151.

WHEREAS, Timothy Brian Cole died while in the Texas Department of Criminal Justice on December 2, 1999.

AND WHEREAS, on the basis of new DNA testing obtained in 2008, after his death, there was a determination of Timothy Brian Cole's actual innocence in Cause No. 85-403,151.

AND WHEREAS, the Lubbock County Criminal District Attorney, Matthew D. Powell, joined with Dale Holton, Chief of Police for the City of Lubbock, in supporting a posthumous Full Pardon for Innocence.

AND WHEREAS, the Board of Pardons and Paroles unanimously has recommended a posthumous Full Pardon for Innocence.

NOW, THEREFORE, I, RICK PERRY, Governor of the State of Texas, by virtue of the authority vested in me under the Constitution and laws of this State, and acting upon the recommendation of the Texas Board of Pardons and Paroles, do hereby grant unto the said Timothy Brian Cole posthumously:

Tim Cole's Posthumous Pardon
— Courtesy the Innocence Project of Texas

A FULL PARDON FOR INNOCENCE ON THE OFFENSE ABOVE SET OUT IN CAUSE NO. 85-403,151, in the 99th Judicial District Court of Lubbock County, Texas.

I HEREBY DIRECT that a copy of this proclamation be filed in the office of the Secretary of State.

By the Governor

IN TESTIMONY WHEREOF, I have heretofore signed my name and caused the Seal of the State of Texas to be impressed hereon, this the 1st day of March, 2010.

Rick Perry
Rick Perry
Governor

ATTEST:

Secretary of State

PROCLAMATION NO. 2010-00001   DPS # TX02724961   PAGE 2

EPILOGUE

*"It is from numberless diverse acts of courage and belief
that human history is shaped. Each time a man stands up
for an ideal, or acts to improve the lot of others,
or strikes out against injustice, he sends forth
a tiny ripple of hope."*
— ROBERT FRANCIS KENNEDY

In an endeavor to afford the major participants in the Tim
Cole case an opportunity to add commentary, the author re-
quested interviews with Michele Murray Mallin, Judge Jim Bob
Darnell, Mike Brown, and the Lubbock Police Department. Only
one, the Lubbock Police Department, chose to respond. Captain
Gregory Stevens, Public Information Officer, said:

> It is not so much that the Tim Cole investigation, commen-
> surate with the standards of 1985, would not stand today;
> rather, Mr. Cole would have been excluded as a suspect in all
> likelihood in a similar current investigation because of the ad-
> vent of DNA technology and its widespread usage in such in-
> vestigations throughout more recent years.
>
> Unfortunately, the police department cannot go back and
> change the outcome of the 1985 investigation which ultimately
> led to Tim Cole's conviction; however, it is clearly apparent
> that the involved detectives acted in good faith in their efforts
> and on behalf of the victim in their investigation.
>
> Criminal investigations have improved vastly throughout
> the history of law enforcement in America. Detectives ar-

guably conducted more proficient investigations in the 1980s than they did in the 1960s, and likewise accomplish more proficient investigations today than in the 1980s. Better education, advances in technology, more modern investigative equipment and enhancements in training all have contributed to this progression, and it stands to reason that we will be doing even better in the 2020s and beyond.[1]

Current research indicates that the man who raped Velma Chavez, Tana Murphy, Trina Barclay, and Margaret Russo has never been identified, and long before the statute of limitations expired, it appears that the police gave up trying to find him. During Tim Cole's trial, Jim Bob Darnell asked Detective Ronnie Goolsby if the same person committed all of these crimes. "I still don't know, based on the identification or non-identification by the victims," Goolsby answered helplessly. "I still am not — well, I just don't know."[2]

Certainly by now, given the eye-opening results of the Michele Murray case, it would seem that the Lubbock District Attorney might order the comparison of Jerry Wayne Johnson's DNA and fingerprints with various medical samples and other evidence contained in each of these four victim's files, if for no other reason than to rule him out as a suspect.

Therefore, after all is said and written, we still face the original question. Was justice served? Perhaps it has, depending on whose version and its interpretation, but one should first consider the times in which Tim Cole was arrested, tried, and convicted. In darker days, such a young man might well have met his end at the hands of a vicious lynch mob, intent on dispensing with the formalities of a trial, and as Captain Stevens outlined above, with the capabilities of contemporary science, namely DNA sequencing, the investigation would probably have never reached the stage where the district attorney sought an indictment.

It is fairly easy to criticize others long after the fact, and to lay blame on many, including Michele Jean Murray, for misidentifying Tim as her assailant. Or fault the Lubbock Police Department, especially Detective Ronnie Goolsby and his team for pushing too hard and too fast the perception that Tim was the *Tech rapist*, for never permitting Michele to see Jerry Wayne Johnson in a line-up, and for employing questionable tactics in the eyewitness investigation. Jim Bob Darnell must be scolded for possibly disregarding obvious signs that pointed to Tim's innocence, and Robert Michael "Mike" Brown for seemingly failing to follow up on key issues. Culpability also extends to Judge Thomas L. Clinton for allowing improper testimony, and to the jurors who arrived at a guilty verdict based exclusively, apparently, on Michele's eyewitness identification. Later, various courts of appeal failed to interpret the law properly. And finally, society as a whole shares the burden, because of ingrained social prejudices.

Jerry Wayne Johnson himself expressed an opinion during a 2007 interview. "When I read in the report [newspaper article] that Mr. Cole had died in prison in 1999," he said, "I cried and felt double guilty, even though I know the system's at fault."[3]

Given the last revealing words of Johnson's observation, it is apparent that by adding a caveat, he has yet to accept complete, personal accountability for his actions that produced a terrible effect: Tim Cole died while serving the thirteenth year for a crime that he did not commit, exacerbated by conditions within a penal system that some say ignored his chronic asthma condition. And regardless of how he spins the end result, Jerry Wayne Johnson neglects to establish himself as the root cause for any "system" failure. He deserves credit, however, because without his admission on May 11, 2007, the offensive thrust required for proving Tim's innocence might never have gained a foothold.

Questions about the original case investigation linger, especially when one considers the impact that eyewitness testimony had on the guilty verdict. Even today, Michele Murray Mallin says she believed that the police had more evidence than her say-so, but of course, we now know they did not. When jurors hear a victim relate from the witness stand the details of a crime, and then see that same individual point directly to his or her assailant as the guilty party, experts like Dr. Gary Wells tell us that such visual and auditory responses displace all others as the most crucial when rendering a final decision. Therefore, law enforcement must take additional steps to ensure as closely as humanly possible that the process remains impartial and untainted.

With benefit of hindsight, this case seems clear, but back in the day when Lubbock police made the arrest, and the district attorney decided to prosecute, things were not as straightforward. Without hesitation, Jim Bob Darnell relied on what he chose as the linchpin—the testimony of the rape victim—and under direction of the long-standing *Law and Order* axiom "That's for the jury to decide," he proceeded to trial. Many police departments and prosecutors nationwide have probably utilized similar methodology; why else would there be so many ongoing exonerations?

Tim Cole was no saint; few people are. Admittedly, Tim made many mistakes along the way, particularly with the abuse of alcohol, the use of marijuana, and unlawfully carrying a firearm, but he was still a good person, deep down where it counted. Recrimination is a hard and bitter pill to swallow, and in truth, probably every man and woman in the Lubbock courtroom, where he was convicted, would change something in their past if provided the opportunity.

There is no question that Tim suffered long and needlessly, but while attempting to pass judgment, we must consider that authorities of that day and age did not have the ability to apply 21st-century forensic techniques to 20th-century crimes. And so the debate goes on.

As for Tim's family, they continue with a remarkable display of strength and unity to search for answers. On September 25, 2009, Jeff Blackburn, acting on their behalf, filed a civil suit in the 99th District Court of Lubbock, "seeking to depose Lubbock officers who investigated the case and looking for any records of evidence kept in a string of other, related rapes at the time." "This is not a harbinger of a lawsuit," Blackburn explained. "This is just an effort to complete the process that has already started." Since then, though, attorneys for the city have succeeded in removing the case from state to federal jurisdiction, and the legal fight continues.[4]

Do the Session family members harbor animosity? Not really. Working closely with the Innocence Project of Texas, Cory has become a viable force in the legislative hallways of Texas and Washington and on the speaking circuit, standing up for the rights of the falsely accused. Ruby, for her part, met personally with Michele Murray Mallin, and after a tearful exchange, they embraced. While this experience helped both parties heal somewhat, unfortunately for Michele, she can't quite put behind her the error in mistaken identity. She explained:

> I still feel guilty. I'll always feel guilty about it because, I mean, my testimony sent a man to prison, and he ended up dying there. Even though I know I did everything I could in my heart of hearts to do the right thing, still that happened. But I know the police are responsible and the D.A., too, because they knew things I didn't know.[5]

Michele Murray Mallin and Ruby Lee Session, September 19, 2008
—Reprint courtesy of the *Fort Worth Star-Telegram*

And during a trip to Lubbock, the family had the opportunity to sit down with Judge Jim Bob Darnell, and afterward, they came away with some sense of comfort. While not completely forgiving him for his role in sending Tim to prison, they did at last understand his compassion and the sorrow that he felt after learning that Jerry Wayne Johnson actually committed the crime. After being advised of Tim's innocence, Judge Darnell made several statements to the press, but in the most poignant, he said, "My feeling was, that someone had just kicked me in the stomach. I wish we could undo it, but we can't."[6]

In an interview conducted on January 24, 2010, Ruby had nothing but kind words for Mike Brown, Tim's defense attorney. "Given the circumstances," she said, "he did the best job possible." However, she thought carefully before answering how she felt about Jerry Wayne Johnson. "He's no hero," she said, "but he could have done two things: died before coming forward, or kept quiet. I'm glad that he did neither."[7]

And in an on-camera interview held on September 1, 2009, Ruby praised Tim as a soldier for justice. "I will never get over it," she said, "but I have to go on."[8]

Such is the moral fiber of the matriarch and her children in their campaign to complete a mission begun many years ago. They have persevered, and they have prevailed. Allies such as Jeff Blackburn, Natalie Roetzel, and members of their staff at the Innocence Project of Texas, the Innocence Project based out of New York, Kevin Glasheen, Senators Ellis and Duncan, and Representatives Anchia, McClendon, and Veasey, along with various other legislators and judges, have been invaluable. In addition, countless other dedicated individuals and organizations, combined with Cory's lobbying, have marshaled the necessary grit and determination to stay the course.

~ ~ ~

Through years of adversity, Ruby Session has remained steadfast at the helm of her close-knit family, which has made it a point to congregate and make the short drive to Mount Olivet

Cemetery, so that they could keep Tim advised of progress made on his behalf. For those fortunate enough to attend one of these visits, it is truly an emotional and memorable experience. On Friday, March 19, 2010, at a news conference held at the Omni Hotel in downtown Fort Worth, Governor Perry fulfilled his promise to Ruby and personally delivered Tim's pardon to her. Later in the afternoon, she, along with several members of the family, a press contingent, and other interested parties, made a trip to the cemetery. On this most solemn occasion, with the framed pardon document in hand, Ruby stood once more at the gravesite of her son. This time, though, she could say, without reservation, "Tim, the final victory is yours."[9]

Governor Perry's Press Conference, March 19, 2010
From left: Governor Rick Perry, State Representative Marc Veasey, Ruby Session, Cory Session, Reggie Kennard, Kevin Kennard, and Sean Session
—Courtesy the Texas Governor's Office

Appendix 1

In order to explain why, at different times, within various police reports and trial transcripts, a particular police officer might be referred to as a detective in one instance, and as a sergeant, corporal, or patrolman in another, the author requested clarification.

Captain Greg Stevens, Public Information Officer for the Lubbock Police Department (GStevens@mail.ci.lubbock.tx.us), by way of e-mail to the author on September 4, 2009, drew a clear distinction between "rank" and "assignment" structures, each a separate entity within the department.

Rank Structure of the Lubbock Police Department

Chief
Assistant Chief
Captain
Lieutenant
Sergeant
Corporal
Officer (formerly Patrolman)

Assignment Structure of the Lubbock Police Department

An officer or corporal may apply for an opening in the Detective Division, and the selected candidate is then transferred from the Patrol Division. While their "rank" remains officer or corporal, they are referred to as "detective" and sometimes "investigator" in reports, on the witness stand, etc. The Detective Division also has two captains, three lieutenants, and several sergeants, who command and supervise their operations as do captains, lieutenants, and sergeants in the Patrol Division who supervise the day-to-day uniform patrol functions of their respective departments.

The Lubbock Police Department has three "divisions," each commanded by an Assistant Chief of Police. The Patrol Division represents one, the Detective Division the second, and the Administration Division the third.

APPENDIX 2

In order to demonstrate the two-color camera approach discussed in Chapter 4, the booking photos shown below were taken one after the other, the first for the sheriff's files and the second for police records.

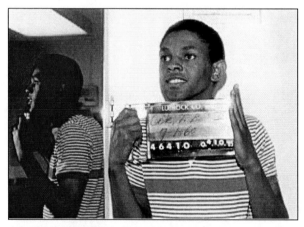

Timothy Cole's booking photo, April 10, 1985. Taken with Lubbock Sheriff's Office camera.
—Courtesy Lubbock County District Attorney

Timothy Cole's booking photo, April 10, 1985. Taken with Lubbock Police Department's camera.
—Courtesy Lubbock Police Department

APPENDIX 3

The following Jury Selection List, filed with Wayne Lecroy, the 99th District Clerk of Court, on September 10, 1986, is included in the master file titled Texas v. Cole, located at the Lubbock District Clerk's Office.

Case Number 85-403, 151
The State of Texas vs. Timothy Brian Cole

Listing of Jurors

Balderas, Jose Gerardo
Crawford, Dennis H.
Davis, Garland Clinton
Goldwater, Gale Wesley
Lupton, Walter Raymond–*Foreman*
Meitzen, Gloria Janet
Moore, Opal Ruth
Price, Lanny Mack
Roberts, Michael Eldwon
Santiago, Yglario Garcia, Sr.
Tenorio, Ronnie Gene
Vogel, Mary Montgomery

Mowrey, Kathy Doylene*
Smith, Patsy Jo*

*Alternates

APPENDIX 4

The following represents a listing of the documentary evidence detailed within the Chronological Index, Texas v. Cole, volume IX. When mentioning the victim, the referral is to Michele Jean Murray. Exhibit numbers that begin with "S" pertain to those introduced by the State's prosecutor, Jim Bob Darnell, and those that begin with "D" point to those offered by the defendant's attorney, Mike Brown.

Exhibit	Description
S-1	Diagram
S-2	Map of City of Lubbock
S-3	Composite drawing
S-4	Photo of line-up
S-5	Photo of defendant—Timothy Cole
S-6	Photo of defendant's hand
S-7	Photo of line-up
S-8	Photo from Sheriff's Department
S-9	Photo of T. L. Clark
S-10	Photo of Jerry Wayne Johnson
S-11	Not identified, nor referred to
S-12	Not identified, nor referred to
S-13	Not identified, nor referred to
S-14	Envelope containing cigarette butts
S-15	Winston cigarette package
S-16	Shirt
S-17	Black jacket
S-18	Ring
S-19	Knife
S-20	Knife
S-21	Photo of six black males in line-up
S-22	Photo spread
S-23	Statement given March 27, 1985

S-24	Calendar
S-25	Report of Jennifer Rosson
S-26	Consent to search Cole's automobile
S-27	Consent to search Cole's house
S-28	Line-up waiver
S-29	Chart prepared by Det. Goolsby
S-30	Victim's warm-up top
S-31	Victim's warm-up bottoms
S-32	Victim's underwear
S-33	Victim's bra
S-34	Not identified, nor referred to
S-35	Not identified, nor referred to
S-36	Clippings from victim
S-37	Combings from victim's pubic hair
S-38	Vaginal washing from victim
S-39	Perineal washing from victim
S-40	Swabs taken from victim
S-41	Sample slides from victim's vagina
S-42A	Victim's blood samples
S-42B	Victim's blood samples
S-43	Blood sample
S-44	Hair from defendant's head
S-45	Body hair of defendant
S-46A	Tube-Sample of defendant's pubic hair
S-46B	Slide-Sample of defendant's pubic hair
S-47	Sample of defendant's saliva
S-48	Sample of defendant's saliva
S-49	Marijuana cigarette
S-50	Original reports of lab results
S-51	Composite by Tana [Murphy]
S-52	Composite by Velma [Chavez]-withdrawn
S-53	Same as S-52 with changes
S-54	Offense report re: Trina [Barclay]
D-1	Summary of complainant's testimony
D-2	Chart prepared by Detective Goolsby
D-3	Enlargement of D-2
D-4	Kitchen calendar from Cole's residence

APPENDIX 5

The following represents a transcription of Judge Thomas L. Clinton's Charge to the Jury (Charge of the Court on Guilt or Innocence). Because it became a critical element in Timothy Brian Cole's appeal, the text is displayed in its entirety. The author has made every attempt to retain the integrity of the original document.

No. 85-403, 151

THE STATE OF TEXAS	§	IN THE 99TH DISTRICT COURT
VS.	§	OF
TIMOTHY BRIAN COLE	§	LUBBOCK COUNTY, TEXAS

<u>CHARGE OF THE COURT</u>

MEMBERS OF THE JURY:

The defendant, TIMOTHY BRIAN COLE, stands charged by indictment with the offense of aggravated sexual assault, alleged to have been committed in Lubbock County, Texas, on or about the 25th day of March, 1985. To this charge the defendant has pleaded not guilty.

You are instructed that you will consider only the guilt or innocence of the defendant from the evidence admitted before you and from the law as given to you in charge by the Court.

You are instructed that the law applicable to this case is as follows:

1.

Our law provides that a person commits the offense of sexual assault if he intentionally and knowingly causes the penetration of the vagina of another person who is not the spouse of the actor by any means, without that person's consent.

Such assault is without the other person's consent if the actor compels the other person to submit or participate by threatening to use force against the other person, and the other person believes that the actor has the present ability to execute the threat.

2.

A person commits aggravated sexual assault if the person commits sexual assault, as defined above, and by acts and words such person places the victim in fear that death will be imminently inflicted on any person.

3.

A person acts intentionally, or with intent, with respect to the nature of his conduct or to a result of his conduct when it is his conscious objective or desire to engage in the conduct or cause the result.

A person acts knowingly, or with knowledge, with respect to the nature of his conduct or to circumstances surrounding his conduct when he is aware of the nature of his conduct or that the circumstances exist. A person acts knowingly, or with knowledge, with respect to a result of his conduct when he is aware that his conduct is reasonably certain to cause the result.

"Spouse" means a person who is legally married to another, except that persons married to each other are not treated as spouses if they do not reside together or if there is an action pending between them for dissolution of the marriage or for separate maintenance.

4.

Now bearing in mind the foregoing instructions, if you believe from the evidence beyond a reasonable doubt that on or about the 25th day of March, 1985, in the County of Lubbock and State of Texas, as alleged in the indictment, the defendant, TIMOTHY BRIAN COLE, did then and there intentionally and knowingly by threatening to use force against Michele Jean Murray cause the penetration of the vagina of the said Michele Jean Murray, a person not the spouse of the said TIMOTHY BRIAN COLE, by the sexual organ of the said TIMOTHY BRIAN COLE, without the consent of the said Michele Jean Murray, and the said Michele Jean Murray did then and there believe the said TIMOTHY BRIAN COLE had the present ability to execute said threat, and the said TIMOTHY BRIAN COLE did then and there intentionally and knowingly by acts and words place the said Michele Jean Murray in fear that death would be imminently inflicted on the said Michele Jean Murray, you will find the defendant guilty of the offense of aggravated sexual assault and so say by your verdict.

Unless you so find from the evidence beyond a reasonable doubt, or if you have a reasonable doubt thereof, you will find the defendant not guilty.

5.

Sexual assault may be prosecuted in the county in which it is committed, in the county in which the victim is abducted, or in any county through or into which the victim is transported in the course of the abduction and sexual assault.

"Preponderance of the evidence" means the greater weight and degree of credible testimony or evidence introduced before you and admitted as evidence in this case.

Now bearing in mind the foregoing instructions, if you believe from the evidence beyond a reasonable doubt that the defendant committed the act alleged committed on Michele Jean Murray, as hereinbefore set out, you must further find by a preponderance of the evidence that defendant, TIMOTHY BRIAN COLE, abducted the victim, Michele Jean Murray, in Lubbock County, Texas, at the time of the commission of the offense charged before you could return a verdict of guilty if you so find. If you do not so believe, you shall by your verdict say "not guilty."

6.

Evidence has been introduced in this case as to what is known as an alibi, that is, that if the offense was committed, as alleged, the defendant was, at the time of the commission thereof, at another and different place from that at which such offense was committed, and therefore was not and could not have been the person who committed the same. Now, if you believe this evidence or if you have a reasonable doubt thereof as to the presence of the defendant at the place where the offense was committed, if an offense was committed, at the time of the commission thereof, then you will find the defendant not guilty.

7.

From time to time during the trial of this case I have orally instructed you to disregard certain evidence, testimony, questions, answers or comments by the parties or witnesses. I again admonish you that you shall not consider for any purpose in your deliberations, nor allude to, refer to nor discuss any matter which I have previously orally instructed you to disregard.

8.

You are further instructed that if there is any evidence before you in this case tending to show that the defendant or any other person committed offenses other than the offense alleged against the defendant in the indictment, you cannot consider said testimony for any purpose unless you find and believe, beyond a reasonable doubt, that the defendant committed such other offenses, if any were committed, and if you find and believe beyond a reasonable doubt from such testimony that other offenses were committed, you may then consider the same in determining the identity of the assailant in this case, and for no other purpose.

9.

You are further instructed that if there is any evidence before you in this case tending to show that the defendant committed the misdemeanor offense of unlawfully carrying a weapon or misdemeanor possession of marijuana, you cannot consider said testimony for any purpose in this case, tending to show guilt or innocence of the offense charged in the indictment.

10.

You are further instructed that the defendant has offered testimony that he did not commit the offense as charged in the indictment and had no connection therewith; now, therefore, if you so believe or if the same causes you to have a reasonable doubt of the guilt of the defendant, you shall acquit the defendant and say by your verdict not guilty.

11.

In your deliberations you will consider this Charge as a whole. You are instructed that the indictment in this case is of itself a mere accusation or charge against the defendant, and is not any evidence of the defendant's guilt; and no juror in this case should permit himself/herself to be to any extent influenced against the defendant because of or on account of said indictment.

12.

You are charged that it is only from the witness stand that the jury is permitted to receive evidence regarding the case, and no juror is permitted to communicate to any other juror anything he/she may have heard regarding the case from any source other than the witness stand.

13.

In deliberating on the cause you are not to refer to or discuss any matter or issue not in evidence before you; nor talk about this case to anyone not of your jury; and after the reading of this Charge you shall not separate from each other until you have reached a verdict.

14.

Your verdict, if any, will be by unanimous vote.

15.

All persons are presumed to be innocent and no person may be convicted of an offense unless each element of the offense is proved beyond a reasonable doubt. The fact that a person has been arrested, confined, or indicted for, or otherwise charged with, the offense gives rise to no inference of guilt at his trial.

16.

In all criminal cases the burden of proof is upon the State. The defendant is presumed to be innocent until his guilt is established by legal and competent evidence beyond a reasonable doubt; and if you have a reasonable doubt as to the defendant's guilt, you will acquit him and say by your verdict "not guilty."

17.

When the Jury wishes to communicate with the Court, it shall so notify the Bailiff, who shall inform the Court thereof. Any communication relative to the cause must be written, prepared by the Foreman, and shall be submitted to the Court through the Bailiff.

18.

You are the exclusive judges of the facts proven, of the credibility of the witnesses and of the weight to be given to their testimony, but you are bound to receive the law from the Court, which is herein given you, and be governed thereby.

19.

After argument of counsel, you will retire and select one of your members as your Foreman. It is his/her duty to preside at your deliberations and to vote with you in arriving at a verdict. Your verdict, if any, must be unanimous, and after you have arrived at your verdict, you may use one of the forms attached hereto by having your Foreman sign his/her name to the particular form that conforms to your verdict.

The above and foregoing is the Charge in this case, and the same is hereby signed and certified by the Court, this the 16th day of September , 1986.

<u>Original signed by Thomas L. Clinton</u>
JUDGE PRESIDING

APPENDIX 6

The following represents a transcription of Judge Thomas L. Clinton's Charge to the Jury relative to the punishment phase. Because it became a critical element in Timothy Brian Cole's appeal, the text is displayed in its entirety. The author has made every effort to retain the integrity of the original document.

No. 85-403, 151

THE STATE OF TEXAS	§	IN THE 99TH DISTRICT COURT
VS.	§	OF
TIMOTHY BRIAN COLE	§	LUBBOCK COUNTY, TEXAS

COURT'S CHARGE ON PUNISHMENT

MEMBERS OF THE JURY:

The defendant, TIMOTHY BRIAN COLE, has been found guilty by you of the offense of aggravated sexual assault. The punishment authorized for this offense is by confinement in the Texas Department of Corrections for life or for a period of not more than ninety-nine (99) years or less than five (5) years, and the jury, in its discretion, may, if it chooses, assess a fine in any amount not to exceed $10,000, in addition to confinement in the penitentiary.

It now becomes your duty to set the punishment which will be assessed against this defendant.

The defendant has filed his sworn motion for probation herein alleging that he has never before been convicted of a felony in this State or any other State.

Our law provides that where the jury finds the defendant guilty and assesses the punishment at imprisonment in the Texas Department of Corrections for any term of years not more than ten years, and the jury further finds that the defendant has never been convicted of a felony in this State or in any other State, the jury may cause the imposition of sentence to be suspended and the defendant to be placed on probation under supervision of the Court during his good behavior.

You are further instructed that the probation period that may be recommended by the jury may be less than or greater than the term of punishment assessed by the jury as long as the period is for a term of years authorized for the offense for which you have found the defendant guilty, and the term of punishment does not exceed ten years.

Now if you believe from the evidence that the defendant has never before been convicted of a felony in this State or any other State, and if you assess the punishment of defendant at confinement in the Texas Department of Corrections for a term of not more than ten years, then you may recommend probation for the defendant and the period that he shall serve such probation. Whether you do or do not recommend probation of defendant and the period that he shall serve such probation is a matter that rest solely within the sound discretion of the jury.

As you consider recommendation of probation, you are instructed that our law provides that the Court, in granting probation, may impose the following conditions:

That the probationer:

a.   Commit no offense against the laws of this State or of any other State or of the United States;

b.   avoid injurious or vicious habits;

c.   avoid persons or places of disreputable or harmful character;

d.   report to the probation officer as directed by the court or probation department;

e.   permit the probation officer to visit him at his home or elsewhere;

f.   work faithfully at suitable employment as far as possible;

g.   remain within a specified place;

h.   pay his fine, if one be assessed, and all court costs, whether a fine be assessed or not, in one or several sums and make restitution or reparation in any sum that the court shall determine;

i.   support his dependents;

j.   pay an Adult Probation Fee not to exceed $40 per month;

k.   participate, for a time specified by the court and subject to the same conditions imposed on community-service probationers by Art. 42.12, Secs. 10A(c), (d), (g) and (h), of the Texas Code of Criminal Procedure, in any community-based program, including a community-service work program designated by the court;

l.   reimburse the county in which the prosecution was instituted for compensation paid to appointed counsel for defending him in the case, if counsel was appointed;

m.   remain under custodial supervision in a community-based facility, obey all rules and regulations of such facility, and pay a percentage of his income to the facility for room and board;

n.   pay a percentage of his income to his dependents for their support while under custodial supervision in the community-based facility; and

o.   pay a percentage of his income to the victim of the offense, if any, to compensate the victim for any property damage or medical expenses sustained by the victim as a direct result of the commission of the offense.

You are instructed that you should not attempt to arrive at the punishment to be assessed by a ballot as to the amount of punishment each juror is in favor of assessing, and then dividing the total of same by the number of twelve, the number of jurors in this case, or by lot or chance, or by any other methods save and except a fair consideration of the evidence.

During your deliberations you are not to discuss or consider the possible actions of the Board of Pardons and Paroles or how long this defendant will be required to serve the punishment which you assess.

Our law provides that a defendant may testify in his own behalf if he elects so to do. This, however, is a privilege accorded a defendant; and, in the event he elects not to testify, that fact cannot be taken as a circumstance against him.

In this case, the defendant has elected not to testify; and you are instructed that you cannot and must not refer or allude to that fact throughout your deliberations or take it into consideration for any purpose whatsoever as a circumstance against him, nor will you refer to or discuss any matter not before you in evidence.

You are further instructed that in considering your verdict regarding assessment of punishment, you may take into consideration all of the evidence admitted before you under this charge and of the previous charge wherein you found the defendant guilty, and you must not receive or consider, refer to or discuss any other matter or testimony.

Your verdict, if any, will be by unanimous vote.

After argument of counsel you will retire and consider your verdict, and after you have arrived at your verdict, if any, you may use one of the forms attached hereto by having your Foreman sign his/her name to the particular form that conforms to your verdict.

The above and foregoing is the Court's Charge on Punishment in this case, and the same is hereby signed and certified by the Court this the 17th day of September , A.D. 1986.

<u>Original signed by Thomas L. Clinton</u>
JUDGE PRESIDING

APPENDIX 7

*The following represents a transcription of Section 3A of Judge
Charles Baird's Order and Opinion of the Court, April 7, 2009, that deals
with the problem of false eyewitness identification. The author has made
every effort to retain the integrity of the original document.*

There is no excuse for the way in which the Lubbock police got
Michelle [sic] Mallin to identify Tim Cole in this case. The procedures they employed were suggestive, improper, and unfair.

It is apparent that there were no rules, policies, or procedures
in place forbidding them from doing what they did. This is a problem that exists throughout Texas and begs for a statewide solution.

Laws can and should be passed mandating the use of fair practices in eyewitness identification procedures.

At a minimum, these laws should require police officers to
fully inform the witness, in writing, that:

1. The perpetrator may or may not be in the line-up or array;
2. The witness does not have to make an identification;
3. The investigation will continue regardless of whether the
   witness identifies someone.

They should also require that line-ups not be suggestive and
mandate the full recording and documentation of the entire procedure from start to finish.

A statute requiring the use of these common-sense practices
would go a long way toward preventing another injustice like the
one done to Tim Cole and countless others. The Court calls upon
the elected representatives of the people of this state to pass such a
statute as soon as possible.

ENDNOTES

Abbreviations

Texas Birth Index Ancestry.com. *Texas Birth Index, 1903–1997* [database on-line]. Provo, UT, USA: The Generations Network, Inc., 2005. Original data: Texas. *Texas Birth Index, 1903-1997.* Texas: Texas Department of State Health Services. Microfiche [accessed July 29, 2009].

Texas v. Cole *The State of Texas v. Timothy Brian Cole*, 99th Judicial District Court case number 85-403, 151, trial transcripts, 9 vols. (Lubbock: Lubbock County District Clerk, 1986).

Acknowledgments
   1. Chuck Lanehart, "Bobby Rogers," Lubbock Criminal Defense Lawyers Association, http://lcdla.org/2007/08/07/bobby-rogers/ [accessed August 30, 2009] (quotation).
   2. Innocence Project of Texas, http://ipoftexas.org/about-us/ [accessed October 10, 2009] (quotations).

Introduction
   1. "Justice," def. 1, *The Random House College Dictionary*, 1968; *Frazier v. U.S.*, 419 F.2d 1161, 1176 (D.C. 1969) (quotation).
   2. "Rape," *New York Times Online*, http://health.nytimes.com/health/guides/ specialtopic/rape/overview.html?inline=nyt-classifier [accessed July 19, 2009].
   3. Texas Crime Rates 1960–2008, http://www.disastercenter.com/crime/txcrime.htm [accessed November 17, 2009].
   4. *Cox Broadcasting Corp. v. Cohn*, 420 U.S. 469 (1975), http://laws.findlaw.com/us/420/469.html [accessed November 17, 2009].
   5. "Texas Tech University Fall Enrollment by Ethnicity since 1985," Texas

Tech University, http://www.irim.ttu.edu/HistoryData.php [accessed July 24, 2009]; Elliott Blackburn, "Hope Deferred Series," part 1 of 3, *The Lubbock Avalanche-Journal*, June 28, 2008, http://www.lubbockonline.com/stories/062808/loc_296894153.shtml [accessed July 30, 2009] (quotation); *The University Daily*, Feb. 15, 1985. The latter source devoted two full pages of that day's paper detailing tactics to be used in rape prevention.

6. "Timothy Cole Exonerated 24 Years Later," KCBD.com, http://www.kcbd.com/Global/story.asp?S=9804937 [accessed November 12, 2009]; Kent Hance, "Adding Tech Students Will Bring Big Bucks into Lubbock Economy," *The Lubbock Avalanche-Journal*, Aug. 6, 2008, http://www.lubbockonline.com/stories/080608/col_314238701.shtml [accessed August 11, 2009] (quotation); *The University Daily*, Mar. 7, 1985. The latter source describes "the rape of a 21-year-old Lubbock Christian College student who was abducted Tuesday afternoon [Mar. 5, 1985] from the Texas Tech campus." Since the suspect was described as "a white or Asian Indian man," this particular crime was not considered to be the work of the *Tech rapist*.

Chapter One / The Beginning

1. *Fort Worth Star-Telegram*, Dec. 7, 1999; *Texas Birth Index*; "Brenham, Texas," *Handbook of Texas Online*, http://www.tshaonline.org/handbook/online/articles/BB/heb11.html [accessed July 29, 2009] (quotation); Ruby Lee Session, interview with author, Jan. 24, 2010, Fort Worth, Texas.

2. *Texas Birth Index*; Session, interview with author, Jan. 24, 2010.

3. Ibid.

4. Session, interview with author, Jan. 24, 2010; Texas v. Cole, vol. VI, 752–753; Elliott Blackburn, "Hope Deferred Series," part 2 of 3, *The Lubbock Avalanche-Journal*, June 29, 2008, http://www.lubbockonline.com/stories/062908/loc_297196667.shtml [accessed July 30, 2009] (quotation).

5. Blackburn, "Hope Deferred," part 2 (quotation); *Texas v. Cole*, vol. VI, 765.

6. Session, interview with author, Jan. 24, 2010.

7. Ibid.; Blackburn, "Hope Deferred," part 2 (quotations).

8. Session, interview with author, Jan. 24, 2010; Blackburn, "Hope Deferred," part 2 (quotation); Elliott Blackburn, "Hope Deferred Series," part 1 of 3, *The Lubbock Avalanche-Journal*, June 28, 2008, http://www.lubbockonline.com/stories/062808/loc_296894153.shtml [accessed July 30, 2009]; "Gerald Myers, Director of Athletics Biography," Texas Tech University, http://www. irim.ttu.edu/SACSFocusReport /PDF/GeraldMyersBio.pdf [accessed August 5, 2009]; Timothy L. Hendricks, Senior Business Assistant, Office of the Registrar, Texas Tech University, Lubbock, Texas (timothy.hendricks@ttu.edu), e-mails to author, Burleson Texas, Nov. 18 and 19, 2009; Timothy Brian Cole, Verification Transaction Detail, National Student Clearinghouse, Dec. 2, 2009.

9. Session, interview with author, Jan. 24, 2010; Timothy Brian Cole, "Information Releasable Under the Freedom of Information Act," National Military Personnel Records, St. Louis, Missouri, Jan. 18, 2010.; Blackburn, "Hope Deferred," part 1.

10. Cole's military records; Timothy Brian Cole's Police Report, Apr. 11,

1985, Police Department Records, Lubbock, Texas; Texas v. Cole, vol. VI, 737, 753–754; Blackburn, "Hope Deferred," part 1.

11. *Texas v. Cole*, vol. VI, 754 (quotation), 755.

12. Ibid., 755; Blackburn, "Hope Deferred," part 1 (quotation).

13. *Texas v. Cole*, vol. VI, 738, 768; Case Report Number 85-6814, prepared by Ronnie L. Goolsby, Lubbock Police Department, Apr. 11, 1985; Hendricks, e-mail to author, Nov. 18, 2009.

14. Patrick Aten, Assistant to the City Council, Lubbock, Texas (Paten@ mail.ci. lubbock.tx.us), e-mail to author, Burleson, Texas, July 22, 2009; "Population History of Selected Cities, 1850–2000," *Texas Almanac*, http:// www.texasalmanac.com/population [accessed July 22, 2009]; Sally Post, Director, Communications and Marketing, Texas Tech University, Lubbock, Texas (Sally.Post@ttu.edu), e-mail to author, Burleson, Texas, July 24, 2009; "Texas Tech University Fall Enrollment by Ethnicity since 1985," Texas Tech University, http://www. irim.ttu.edu/HistoryData.php [accessed July 24, 2009]; "Texas Tech University Spring Enrollment by Gender since 1926," Texas Tech University, http://www.irim.ttu.edu/HistoryData. php [accessed July 24, 2009]; "Texas Tech University Spring Enrollment since 1926," Texas Tech University, http://www.irim.ttu.edu/HistoryData.php [accessed July 24, 2009]; Tim Cole's Arrest Report dated Apr. 10, 1985, Police Department Records, Lubbock, Texas.

15. *Texas v. Cole*, vol. VI, 703 (first quotation); Blackburn, "Hope Deferred," part 1 (second quotation).

Chapter Two / Quagmire

1. Defendant's Documentary Evidence, Exhibit No. 3, *Texas v. Cole*, vol. IX, 81; *The University Daily*, Jan. 15, 1985; Elliott Blackburn, "Hope Deferred Series," part 1 of 3, *The Lubbock Avalanche-Journal*, June 28, 2008, http:// www.lubbockonline.com/stories/ 062808/ loc_296894153.shtml [accessed July 30, 2009]; Offense Report, Case Number MS 9C-1 and various supplements, Texas Tech University Police Department, Dec. 27, 1984–Jan. 21, 1985.

2. Offense Report, Case Number MS 9C-1, supplement, Dec. 27, 1984 (quotations).

3. Ibid. (quotation).

4. Ibid. (quotation).

5. Ibid.; Defendant's Exhibit No. 3, *Texas v. Cole*, vol. IX, 81.

6. Defendant's Exhibit No. 3; *Texas v. Cole*, vol. V, 497–498; Offense Report written by Jay Allen Parchman, Case Number 6-1, Texas Tech University Police Department, Jan. 21, 1985; Offense Report written by Jay Allen Parchman, Case Number 6-1, Supplement 6, Texas Tech University Police Department, Apr. 29, 1985.

7. Defendant's Exhibit No. 3; *The University Daily*, Jan. 15, 1985; Offense Report, Jan. 21, 1985; Offense Report, Apr. 29, 1985.

8. Defendant's Exhibit No. 3; *Texas v. Cole*, vol. V, 497; *The University Daily*, Jan. 15, 1985; Jan. 22, 1985; Jan. 30, 1985 (quotation); State's Exhibit No. S-9, Photograph of T. L. Clark, *Texas v. Cole*, vol. IX, 10; Offense Report, Jan. 21, 1985; Barbara Sucsy, Lubbock County District Clerk (BSucsy@co.lubbock. tx.us), e-mails to author, Burleson, Texas, Sept. 23 and Sept. 28, 2009; Case

Number 07-85-00274-CR (Terry Lee Clark), Texas Courts Online – Seventh of Court Appeals Case Management, http://www.7thcoa.courts.state.tx.us/ opinions/case.asp?FilingID=4483 [accessed August 20, 2009]; Grand Jury for the 140th Judicial District Court-Lubbock, Texas, indictment of Terry Lee Clark for the rape of Virgie Odom, Lubbock District Clerk's Office, Feb. 5, 1985; *The Lubbock Avalanche-Journal*, Sept. 11, 1986. According to the latter source, Terry Lee Clark "was found guilty in August 1985 of a January 1985 rape in Mackenzie State Park [Lubbock] and sentenced to 30 years in prison."

9. Offense Report, Apr. 29, 1985 (quotations); *Texas v. Cole*, vol. VI, 642; see vol. IX, 58 (State's Exhibit No. 51) for Tana Murphy's composite of her assailant.

10. Offense Report, Apr. 29, 1985 (quotation).

11. *The University Daily*, Jan. 22, 1985. The term, "Tech rapist," was widely used by the media to describe the assailant who abducted young women near the Texas Tech campus during the period extending from Dec. 27, 1984 through Mar. 25, 1985.

12. Tim Cole's Arrest Report, Number 85-1473, Lubbock Police Department File No. 15-8, Jan. 19, 1985; Tim Cole's Robbery Report, Number 85-1473, Lubbock Police Department File No. 3-20, Jan. 19, 1985; *Lubbock City Directory, 1985–1986* (Dallas: R. L. Polk & Company, 1986), section 3, 359; Blackburn, "Hope Deferred," part 1; *Texas v. Cole*, vol. V, 355–358. During Tim Cole's trial, Rosanna Bagby testified that the revolver held "one spent cartridge and it appeared to have been recently fired."

13. Tim Cole's Robbery Report, Jan. 19, 1985; *Lubbock City Directory, 1985–1986*, section 3, 324. To the author's knowledge, no one ever clarified to whom the revolver actually belonged, and the question, therefore, remains whether Tim Cole was confused when he provided his statement.

14. Tim Cole's Robbery Report, Jan. 19, 1985.

15. Tim Cole's Arrest Report, Jan. 19, 1985; Troy P. Burleson, "Punishment Range for a Class A Misdemeanor in Texas," Texas Criminal Attorney Blog, Oct. 23, 2008, http:// www.texascriminalattorneyblog.com/2008/10/punishment_range_for_a_class_a_misdemeanor_ in_texas.html [accessed August 8, 2009]; Photograph of Tim Cole, *Texas v. Cole*, vol. IX, 9. At this time, according to Captain Greg Stevens, Lubbock Police Department's Public Information Officer, all bookings by police personnel were done at the Lubbock County Sheriff's Office.

16. Tim Cole's Robbery Report, Jan. 19, 1985; *Texas v. Cole*, vol. V, 278; Motions and Orders to Dismiss Case Numbers 85-450602 and 85-450603, Minute Books 189/339 and 192/325, respectively, Lubbock County Clerk, Lubbock, Texas.

17. State's Exhibit No. 54, *Texas v. Cole*, vol. IX, 63–78; *The University Daily*, Feb. 4, 1985.

18. State's Exhibit No. 54, 62, 64 (second quotation), 67, 72 (first quotation); *The University Daily*, Feb. 4, 1985.

19. State's Exhibit No. 54, 65–66; Defendant's Exhibit No. 3, *Texas v. Cole*, vol. IX, 81; *The University Daily*, Feb. 4, 1985.

20. State's Exhibit No. 54, 65–66; Defendant's Exhibit No. 3; *The University Daily*, Feb. 4, 1985.

21. Defendant's Exhibit No. 3; Case Report Number 85-2627, Lubbock Police Department, Feb. 3, 1985 (quotation).

22. Defendant's Exhibit No. 3; Case Report Number 85-2627.

23. *Texas v. Cole*, vol. IX, 81 (first quotation); Defendant's Exhibit No. 3; Case Report Number 85-2627 (second quotation).

24. *Texas v. Cole*, vol. IX, 81; Defendant's Exhibit No. 3; Case Report Number 85-2627 (quotation).

25. *Texas v. Cole*, vol. IX, 81; Case Report Number 85-2627.

26. *The University Daily*, Feb. 14, 1985 (quotation).

27. Ibid., Feb. 15, 1985 (quotation).

28. Ibid., Feb. 14, 1985 (quotation).

29. Offense Report, Case Number R-60, Texas Tech Police Department, Mar. 6, 1985 (quotation); Blackburn, "Hope Deferred," part 1; *Texas v. Cole*, vol. VI, 750–752.

30. Offense Report, Case Number R-60 (quotation).

31. Offense Report, Case Number R-60 (quotation); Blackburn, "Hope Deferred," part 1; *Texas v. Cole*, vol. VI, 750–752.

32. Offense Report, Case Number R-60; *Texas v. Cole*, vol. VI, 752–753 (first quotation); "Schizophrenia," National Institute of Mental Health, http://www.nimh.nih.gov/health/topics/schizophrenia/index.shtml [accessed December 26, 2009] (second quotation). The mention of Tim Cole's diagnosis of schizophrenia is contained in a confidential memo that is not part of this narrative.

33. Offense Report, Case Number R-60 (quotation); Blackburn, "Hope Deferred," part 1.

34. *Texas v. Cole*, vol. VI, 735, 739–740, vol. IX, 82 (quotation). Mike Brown, Tim Cole's defense attorney, eventually introduced the referenced calendar into evidence as Defendant's Exhibit No. 4.

35. *Texas v. Cole*, vol. VI, 740–741 (quotation), 742.

36. Ibid.

37. Ibid., 668–675, 676 (quotation). The United States Football League played its games in the spring after the National Football League's regular season ended. During the television newscast pertaining to the MX Missile Program, Reggie Kennard stated that he and his brother had a brief family argument over whether the U.S. Air Force or the Army would control the project. Each had served, in some capacity, these respective services.

38. Ibid., 677, 742–746.

39. Ibid., 680, 746, 747 (quotations).

40. Ibid., 674, 681–683, 702, 747–748, 762.

41. Ibid., 763 (quotations).

Chapter Three / Into the Abyss

1. Michele Jean Murray, *Texas v. Cole*, vol. IV, 45 (quotation).

2. Margaret Ehlig (mdehlig@gccisd.net), e-mail to author, Burleson, Texas, Aug. 13, 2009; *Texas v. Cole*, vol. IX, 81; *Texas Birth Index*.

3. "Baytown, Texas," *Handbook of Texas Online*, http://www.tshaonline.org/handbook/online/articles/BB/hdb1.html [accessed August 10, 2009] (quotation); City of Abernathy, Texas Web Page, http://www.cityof

abernathy.org/[accessed August 10, 2009]; *Texas v. Cole*, vol. IV, 23–25, 29; Michele Murray's Intake Record, Lubbock Rape Crisis Center, Mar. 25, 1985. The latter source, of which a copy remains with the Innocence Project of Texas in Lubbock, reflects that two case workers, Jennifer Rosson and Kelley Johnson took the report at 1:27 a.m. There is also mention that Miss Murray resided at 349 Doak Hall, Texas Tech.

4. *Texas v. Cole*, vol. IV, 28 (quotation).

5. Ibid., 34 (first quotation), 35–36, 37 (second quotation); *The University Daily*, Mar. 26, 1985; Case Report Number 85-6814, prepared by Ronnie L. Goolsby, Lubbock Police Department, Apr. 11, 1985.

6. *Texas v. Cole*, vol. IV, 37 (quotation); Michele Jean Murray's Signed Affidavit, Lubbock Police Department Records, Apr. 9, 1985. The author has a copy in his possession.

7. *Texas v. Cole*, vol. IV, 37 (first quotation), 41 (second quotation); vol. VI, 542–547.

8. Elliott Blackburn, "Hope Deferred Series," part 1 of 3, *The Lubbock Avalanche-Journal*, June 28, 2008, http://www.lubbockonline.com/stories/062808/loc_296894153.shtml [accessed July 30, 2009] (quotation).

9. *Texas v. Cole*, vol. IV, 41.

10. Ibid., 42–43 (first quotation), 43 (second quotation), 44, 63–64, 80; *The University Daily*, Mar. 26, 1985.

11. *Texas v. Cole*, vol. IV, 47–48; vol. IX, State's Exhibit No. 25, Michele Murray's Intake Record (quotation); *The University Daily*, Mar. 26, 1985.

12. Justin Weaver, Meteorologist-in-Charge, National Weather Service, Lubbock, Texas, telephone interview with author, July 20, 2009; *Texas v. Cole*, vol. IV, 48; "Sun and Moon Data for One Day: Sunday, 24 March 1985," U.S. Naval Observatory, http://aa.usno.navy.mil/cgi-bin/aa_pap.pl [accessed July 22, 2009].

13. *Texas v. Cole*, vol. IV, 53 (quotations).

14. Ibid., 53 (quotation), 54–56.

15. Ibid., 57 (quotation).

16. Ibid., 57 (first and second quotations), 58 (third quotation).

17. Ibid., 59 (first and second quotations), 60–61 (third quotation), 62.

18. Ibid., 62 (quotations).

19. Ibid., 64 (first and second quotations), 65, 68–69 (third and fourth quotations); *The University Daily*, Mar. 26, 1985; Case Report Number 85-6814, prepared by Jamie Herrera, Lubbock Police Department, Mar. 25, 1985. When Michele Jean Murray mentioned the loop, she referred to Loop 289 in Lubbock.

20. *Texas v. Cole*, vol. IV, 71 (first quotation), 72, 73 (second quotation).

21. Ibid., 75, 80, 190–193, 194 (quotations).

22. Ibid., 165–166, 167 (first and second quotations), 168 (third quotation).

23. Ibid., 75, 79 (quotation), 80–81, 87, 195–198, 226; vol. IX, State's Exhibit No. 25. During her trial testimony, Michele Murray stated that the vaginal blood was definitely not produced due to her menstrual cycle. Also during the same testimony found on page 80, she explained that at no time during the entire three-hour ordeal did she stand beside her rapist, because instead of exiting the car and getting into the back of the car, she said, "We crawled over the seat."

24. *Texas v. Cole*, vol. IV, 198–201; Michele Murray's Intake Record; Case Report Number 85-6814, prepared by Jimmie Riemer, Lubbock Police Department, Mar. 25, 1985. Identification Technician Riemer later explained in court testimony (*Texas v. Cole*, vol. V, 521), "If we can find four or more points, we will save the card. If we can't find enough points that we can identify it, then we don't save it." In an interview with Ruby Session conducted by the author on Jan. 24, 2010, she stated that she had no idea how the empty Winston cigarette package got into Tim's car. "It could not have been Reggie's, either," she said, "because he smoked Kools."

25. *The University Daily*, Mar. 27, 1985 (quotation); Grand Jury for the 140th Judicial District, Lubbock, Terry Lee Clark Indictments, Feb. 5, 1985.

26. Case Report Number 85-6814, prepared by José Nevarez, Lubbock Police Department, Mar. 28, 1985; *Texas v. Cole*, vol. IV, 89–91, 222–225, 231; *The University Daily*, Apr. 2, 1985.

27. *Texas v. Cole*, vol. IV, 226, 227 (quotation).

Chapter Four / The Moth Effect

1. *Texas v. Cole*, vol. V, 350 (quotation).

2. "Moth," *World Book Online*, http://www.worldbook.com/wb/world book/cybercamp/html/walkmoth.html [accessed August 12, 2009].

3. *Texas v. Cole*, vol. V, 368–371, Case Report Number 85-6814, prepared by Ronnie L. Goolsby, Lubbock Police Department, Apr. 11, 1985 (quotation). The end of the last sentence of the quote (2-11 and 2-30) refers to the Lubbock Police Department case numbers that were assigned to Barclay and Murray, respectively.

4. Goolsby's Case Report Number 85-6814; *Texas v. Cole*, vol. IV, 257; vol. V, 280 (quotation).

5. *Texas v. Cole*, vol. V, 280–284, 327–328, 329 (quotation); Goolsby's Case Report Number 85-6814. Within the latter source, Detective Ronnie Goolsby pointed out that "Officer Bagby had been utilized in the area as a decoy for intelligence-gathering purposes so as to hopefully obtain actions from the person who had been committing the rapes as mentioned earlier in this report. Officer Bagby was dressed in plain clothes and had the general appearance of being a Tech student. She had made several trips back and forth across University to Week's Hall on Tech Campus to where her unmarked unit had been parked on the Church parking lot in the 1500 block of University."

6. Case Report Number 85-6814, prepared by Teddy Daniels, Lubbock Police Department, Apr. 3, 1985.

7. Goolsby's Case Report Number 85-6814.

8. Case Report Number 85-7944, Brenda Jones, Lubbock Police Department Records, Apr. 7–22, 1985 (quotation); *The Lubbock Avalanche-Journal*, Apr. 13, 1985.

9. Case Report Number 85-7944; *The Lubbock Avalanche-Journal*, Apr. 13, 1985.

10. Ibid.

11. Goolsby's Case Report Number 85-6814 (quotation).

12. Ibid. (quotation); *Texas v. Cole*, vol. IV, 236, vol. VI, 760–761.

13. *Texas v. Cole*, vol. V, 332, 333 (quotation).

14. Ibid., 333–337, 356; vol. VI, 760, 761 (quotation); Case Report Number 85-6814, prepared by Rosanna Bagby, Lubbock Police Department, Apr. 8, 1985.

15. *Texas v. Cole*, vol. V, 337 (quotation).

16. Ibid. (quotation); Bagby's Case Report Number 85-6814.

17. *Texas v. Cole*, vol. V, 338–339, 340 (first quotation), 341 (second, third, and fourth quotations); Bagby's Case Report Number 85-6814.

18. "She`s the Sheriff: Bastrop County`s Top Gun," *Bastropia.com*, Nov. 4, 2007, http://www.bastropia.com/news/shes-the-sheriff-bastrop-countys-top-gun.4.html [accessed September 1, 2009]; Heidi Templeton, Director of Public Relations, Truman State University, Kirksville, Missouri (heidi@truman.edu), e-mail to author, Burleson, Texas, Sept. 1, 2009.

19. *Texas v. Cole*, vol. V, 341, 342 (quotation); 353–355; Case Report Number 85-6814, prepared by George White, Lubbock Police Department, Apr. 08, 1985; Goolsby's Case Report Number 85-6814; Bagby's Case Report Number 85-6814.

20. *Texas v. Cole*, vol. V, 342–343 (quotations).

21. Goolsby's Case Report Number 85-6814; White's Case Report Number 85-6814; *Texas v. Cole*, vol. V, 389.

22. Goolsby's Case Report Number 85-6814 (first quotation); *Texas v. Cole*, vol. V, 273, 274 (second quotation); Case Report Number 85-7944.

23. Case Report Number 85-6814, prepared by George White, Lubbock Police Department, Apr. 9, 1985; *Texas v. Cole*, vol. V, 292–296; Captain Greg Stevens, interview with author, Aug. 18, 2009, Lubbock, Texas. During a visit to Lubbock in August 2009, the author scanned a copy of State's Exhibit No. 21 in which all of the photos are shown to be in color; all remain in his personal collection.

24. *Texas v. Cole*, vol. IV, 93 (first quotation), 94, 95 (second quotation); vol. V, 391–392; White's Case Report Number 85-6814, Apr. 9, 1985; Case Report Number 85-6814, prepared by José Nevarez, Lubbock Police Department, Apr. 9, 1985.

25. *Texas v. Cole*, vol. IV, 95 (quotation).

26. Ibid. (first quotation); Richard Willing, "Police Line-ups Encourage Wrong Picks, Experts Say," USA TODAY, Nov. 26, 2002, http://www.usatoday.com/news/acovtue.htm [accessed September 2, 2009] (second quotation); Michele Jean Murray's Signed Affidavit, Lubbock Police Department Records, Apr. 9, 1985. Reference the latter source, the author has a copy in his possession.

27. *Texas v. Cole*, vol. IV, 95 (first and second quotations), 96 (third quotation), 97; vol. IV, 490–491; *The Lubbock Avalanche-Journal*, Apr. 11, 1985; State's Exhibit No. 21, *Texas v. Cole*, vol. IX, 22; Nevarez' Case Report Number 85-6814.

28. *The Lubbock Avalanche-Journal*, Apr. 11, 1985; Goolsby's Case Report Number 85-6814.

29. Goolsby's Case Report Number 85-6814.

30. Ibid. (first three quotations contain inventory lists); *Texas v. Cole*, vol. IV, 395–396, 397 (fourth quotation), 398.

31. Goolsby's Case Report Number 85-6814; *Texas v. Cole*, vol. VI, 698–701.

32. Goolsby's Case Report Number 85-6814 (quotation); Case Number 85-450, 603 (Timothy Brian Cole's Case Information), Lubbock County Electronic Public Access to Court Records, https://apps.co.lubbock.tx.us/attorney/caseinfo.aspx [accessed September 7, 2009]; State's Exhibit No. 54, *Texas v. Cole*, vol. IX, 78.

33. Goolsby's Case Report Number 85-6814; *Texas v. Cole*, vol. V, 401.

34. Goolsby's Case Report Number 85-6814; Elliott Blackburn, "Hope Deferred Series," part 3 of 3, *The Lubbock Avalanche-Journal*, June 30, 2008, http://www.lubbockonline.com/ stories/063008/loc_297531088.shtml [accessed July 30, 2009] (quotation). The actual date of the on-camera interview is not shown, and even though the interviewer's name is not given either, Elliott Blackburn probably conducted it himself. Reggie Kennard said that through the years, he has never forgiven himself for telling his brother to sign the line-up waiver, and in fact, felt that he was to blame for Tim's ultimate verdict.

35. *Texas v. Cole*, vol. V, 404–405.

36. Goolsby's Case Report Number 85-6814 (quotation).

37. Ibid. (first quotation); Case Report Number 85-6814, Witness Affidavit, witnessed by Ronnie L. Goolsby, Lubbock Police Department, Apr. 10, 1985 (second quotation); *Texas v. Cole*, vol. IV, 98–101, 155 (third quotation).

38. Goolsby's Case Report Number 85-6814 (quotation); Ruby Lee Session, interview with author, Jan. 24, 2010, Fort Worth, Texas.

39. Blackburn, "Hope Deferred," part 3 (quotation).

40. Arrest Report, Number 67453 (LPD No. 81507), Jerry Wayne Johnson, Lubbock County Sheriff's Office, Apr. 10, 1985.

41. Affidavit for Arrest Warrant and Witness Statement by Brenda Jones, Case Report Number 85-7944, Lubbock Police Department Records, Apr. 11, 1985.

42. Case Report Number 85-7944, Brenda Jones, Lubbock Police Department Records, April 7–22, 1985; *The Lubbock Avalanche-Journal*, Apr. 13, 1985. A Lubbock County Grand Jury indicted Tim on the aggravated kidnapping charge, and, according to an article that appeared in the Sept. 19, 1986 Friday morning edition of *The Lubbock Avalanche-Journal*, it remained outstanding even after his conviction on the charge of aggravated sexual assault against Michele Murray. Eventually, the Jones case was dismissed.

43. *Texas v. Cole*, vol. V, 413–414, 415 (quotation), 416, 445–446.

44. Timothy Cole's Bail Bond, Apr. 17, 1985; *Texas v. Cole*, vol. VI, 756–757, 766–767; Session, interview with author, Jan. 24, 2010. A copy of Cole's bond is in the author's possession. During a follow-up telephone conversation on Jan. 25, 2010, the author reviewed with Tim's mother the common information found on the official bail bond record and an Inmate Report of Incarceration and Behavior report dated Nov. 5, 1986. Mrs. Session remembers the occasion a little differently. She claims that Reggie called her on Friday, which would have been Apr. 12, 1985, and informed her that Tim had been arrested. The next morning, Saturday, Apr. 13, she bought a ticket and flew to Lubbock, where she arranged for bail.

45. Session, interview with author, Jan. 24, 2010. At this point, however, the author has not located a police report to substantiate the account of the alleged rape that occurred during the Session family's flight back to Fort Worth.

Chapter Five / The Interim

1. *Texas v. Cole*, vol. V, 498 (quotation).
2. "Lubbock, Texas," *Handbook of Texas Online*, http://www.tshaonline. org/handbook/online/articles/LL/flu2.html [accessed October 25, 2009] (first, second, fourth, and fifth quotations); Michael T. Kingston, Ruth Harris, and Erma Bailey, eds., *The Texas Almanac, 1984–1985* (Dallas: *The Dallas Morning News*, 1985), 322 (third quotation).
3. *Texas v. Cole*, vol. V, 474; vol. VII, 41 (quotation).

Chapter Six / Adversaries and the Balance Wheel

1. Sir William Blackstone, *Commentaries on the Laws of England (1765–1769)*, vol. IV: chap. 27, http://www.lonang.com/exlibris/blackstone/ [accessed September 10, 2009] (quotation). In Blackstone's quote, the word "presumptive" is described by Merriam-Webster as "giving grounds for reasonable opinion or belief."
2. Case Number 85-403, 151 (Timothy Brian Cole's Case Information), Lubbock County Electronic Public Access to Court Records, https://apps. co.lubbock.tx.us/attorney/caseinfo.aspx [accessed September 7, 2009]; Dennis R. Reeves, Capital Public Defenders Office, Lubbock, Texas, telephone interview with author, Sept. 8, 2009; Ruby Lee Session, interview with author, Jan. 24, 2010, Fort Worth, Texas.
3. Richard E. Drain, *The Diamondbacks: The History of the 99th Bomb Group (H)* (Paducah: Turner Publishing, 1998), 79; *Texas Birth Index*; Jeff Blackburn, chief counsel, the Innocence Project of Texas, interview with author, Aug. 19, 2009, Lubbock, Texas; "Outstanding Young Lawyer Award Recipients," Lubbock County Bar Association, http://www. lcba.org/Docs/Award_Winners.pdf [accessed September 8, 2009]; Session, interview with author, Jan. 24, 2010.
4. "John T. Montford," Lubbock Centennial, 1909–2009, http://www. Lubbock centennial.com/citysmost/011109.shtml [accessed September 8, 2009] (first quotation); Elliott Blackburn, "Hope Deferred Series," part 1 of 3, *The Lubbock Avalanche-Journal*, June 28, 2008, http://www.lubbock online.com/stories/062908/loc_297196667.shtml [accessed July 30, 2009] (second quotation); *The Lubbock Avalanche-Journal*, Sept. 11, 1986.
5. "Honorable Jim Bob Darnell," 140th District Court, Lubbock County, http://www.co. lubbock.tx.us/DCrt140/Darnell_biography.htm [accessed July 24, 2009]; *Texas Birth Index*; "Outstanding Young Lawyer Award Recipients," 1981; "Hope Deferred Series," part 1 (quotations); Marilyn Lutter, Administrative Assistant, Lubbock County Criminal District Attorney's Office, telephone interview with author, July 27, 2009.
6. Resolution of the Lubbock County Bar Association in Memory of the Honorable Thomas L. Clinton, Lubbock County Bar Association, Lubbock, Texas, Dec. 15, 1993 (quotation); *Texas Birth Index*. During the war, Judge Clinton held the distinction of serving as an artillery officer under General George Patton's command.
7. *Texas v. Cole*, vol. III, 17; Indictment for the Offenses of Aggravated Sexual Assault, Aggravated Kidnapping, and Aggravated Robbery, June 5, 1985; Waiver of Arraignment, June 6, 1985; Criminal Docket, Case Number 85-

403, 151, entries for Nov. 1, 1985 and Apr. 21, 1986; Defendant's First Motion for Continuance and Waiver of Speedy Trial, June 11, 1986 (quotation). All of the aforementioned documents are included in the master file titled *Texas v. Cole*, located at the Lubbock District Clerk's Office.

8. Motion for Exculpatory Evidence, Aug. 29, 1986; Defendant's Motion for Notice of Evidence of Other Crimes, Sept. 5, 1986; Criminal Docket; *Texas v. Cole*, vol. II, 3. Both of the motions and the Criminal Docket are included in the master file titled *Texas v. Cole*, located at the Lubbock District Clerk's Office.

9. "Hope Deferred Series," part 1 (quotations); Elliott Blackburn, "Hope Deferred Series," part 3 of 3, *The Lubbock Avalanche-Journal*, June 30, 2008, http://www.lubbockonline. com/stories/063008/loc_297531088.shtml [accessed July 30, 2009].

Chapter Seven / The Trial–Day One
 1. *Texas v. Cole*, vol. III, 19 (quotation).
 2. Ibid., vol. II, 3–4, 5 (quotation), 6–16.
 3. Ibid., 16–17 (quotation).
 4. Ibid., 19 (first quotation), 19–20 (second quotation).
 5. Ibid., 20–22.
 6. Ibid., 25, 26 (quotation).
 7. Ibid., 26 (quotation).
 8. Ibid., vol. III, 10; Jury List, Cause Number 85-403, 151, 99th District Court, Lubbock County, Texas, Wednesday, Sept. 10, 1986; Defendant's Election to Have Jury Assess Punishment, Sept. 10, 1986 (first quotation); Application for Probation, Sept. 10, 1986 (second quotation). Both the Jury List and the Application for Probation are included in the master file titled *Texas v. Cole*, located at the Lubbock District Clerk's Office.
 9. *Texas v. Cole*, vol. III, 11–93.
 10. Ibid., 94–116, 117 (quotation).
 11. Ibid., 118–198.
 12. *The University Daily*, Sept. 10, 1985; *The Lubbock Avalanche-Journal*, Sept. 11, 1986; Jury List; Jury Chosen List, Cause Number 85-403, 151.
 13. *Texas v. Cole*, vol. IV, 3–6, 7 (quotation).
 14. Ibid., 7 (quotation).
 15. Ibid., 8–17.
 16. Justin Weaver, Meteorologist-in-Charge, National Weather Service, Lubbock, Texas (Justin.Weaver@noaa.gov), e-mail to author, Burleson, Texas, Sept. 18, 2009; *The Lubbock Avalanche-Journal*, Sept. 11, 1986.

Chapter Eight / The Trial–Day Two
 1. *Texas v. Cole*, vol. IV, 104 (quotation).
 2. *The Lubbock Avalanche-Journal*, Sept. 19, 1986.
 3. Ibid.; *Texas v. Cole*, vol. IV, 18–19, 20 (quotation).
 4. *Texas v. Cole*, vol. IV, 22–23, 24 (quotation).
 5. Ibid., 25, 26 (quotation).
 6. Ibid., 27–49, 50 (quotation).
 7. Ibid., 51 (first quotation), 53–54 (second quotation).

8. Ibid., 81 (first quotation), 82 (second quotation).

9. Ibid., 83 (quotation).

10. Ibid. (quotation).

11. Ibid., 84, 85 (first quotation); *The Lubbock Avalanche-Journal*, Sept. 12, 1986 (second quotation).

12. *Texas v. Cole*, vol. IV, 55–100, 101–102 (quotation).

13. Ibid., 101 (quotation).

14. Ibid., 65–68, 103–105.

15. Ibid., 105, 106 (quotation).

16. Ibid., 106 (quotation).

17. *The Lubbock Avalanche-Journal*, Sept. 11, 1986; Sept. 12, 1986; Sept. 15, 1986; *Texas v. Cole*, vol. IV, 107–122, 123 (first quotation), 124 (second quotation), 125–132.

18. *Texas v. Cole*, vol. IV, 133 (quotation), 134–138.

19. Ibid., 139 (quotation).

20. Ibid., 139 (quotation).

21. Ibid., 140–147, 148 (first quotation), 149 (second quotation).

22. *The University Daily*, Sept. 12, 1986; *The Lubbock Avalanche-Journal*, Sept. 12, 1986; *Texas v. Cole*, vol. IV, 150 (first quotation), 151 (second quotation), 152, 153 (third quotation).

23. *Texas v. Cole*, vol. IV, 153 (quotation).

24. Ibid., 154 (quotation); *The Lubbock Avalanche-Journal*, Sept. 12, 1986.

25. *Texas v. Cole*, vol. IV, 154 (quotation).

26. Ibid., 154 (first quotation), 155 (second quotation).

27. Ibid., 155 (quotation).

28. Ibid., 155 (quotation), 156–157.

29. Ibid., 157 (quotation).

30. Ibid., 158 (quotation).

31. Ibid., 159 (quotation).

32. Ibid., 159 (quotation).

33. Ibid., 160–161, 162–163 (quotation).

34. Ibid., 163 (quotation), 164.

35. Ibid., vol. VII, 32 (quotation).

36. *The Lubbock Avalanche-Journal*, Sept. 15, 1986; *Texas v. Cole*, vol. IV, 165–178, 179 (quotation).

37. *Texas v. Cole*, vol. IV, 179 (quotation).

38. Ibid., 180, 181 (quotation).

39. Ibid., 182, 183 (quotations).

40. Ibid., 183 (quotations).

41. Ibid., 184–185, 186 (first quotation), 187, 188 (second quotation).

42. Ibid., 190–214, 215 (quotation), 216–220.

43. Ibid., 222–244.

44. Ibid., 245, 246 (quotation).

45. Ibid., 246 (quotation).

46. Ibid., 247, 248 (quotations).

47. *The University Daily*, Sept. 12, 1986; *The Lubbock Avalanche-Journal*, Sept. 12, 1986; *Texas v. Cole*, vol. IV, 249–259, 260 (first quotation), 261, 262 (second quotation), 263–264.

Chapter Nine / The Trial–Day Three
1. *Texas v. Cole*, vol. V, 306 (quotation).
2. Justin Weaver, Meteorologist-in-Charge, National Weather Service, Lubbock, Texas (Justin.Weaver@noaa.gov), e-mail to author, Burleson, Texas, Sept. 18, 2009.
3. *Texas v. Cole*, vol. V, 271–272, 273 (first quotation), 275–276 (second quotation).
4. *The University Daily*, Sept. 16, 1986; *Texas v. Cole*, vol. V, 277–303.
5. *Texas v. Cole*, vol. V, 309–315, 316 (quotation), 317–326.
6. *The Lubbock Avalanche-Journal*, Sept. 15, 1986; *The University Daily*, Sept. 16, 1986; *Texas v. Cole*, vol. V, 327–350.
7. *Texas v. Cole*, vol. V, 351 (quotations).
8. Ibid., 291, 352 (first seven quotations); 353 (eighth quotation).
9. Ibid., 354, 355 (quotation), 356–358.
10. Ibid., 359, 360 (quotation).
11. Ibid., 360 (quotation), 361-366.
12. Ibid., 368–398, 399 (quotation).
13. *The University Daily*, Sept. 16, 1986; *The Lubbock Avalanche-Journal*, Sept. 16, 1986; *Texas v. Cole*, vol. V, 400–464.
14. *The University Daily*, Sept. 16, 1986; *The Lubbock Avalanche-Journal*, Sept. 16, 1986; *Texas v. Cole*, vol. V, 465–471, 472 (first and third quotations), 473–475, 476–477 (fourth quotation), 478 (fifth quotation); "Timothy Cole Exonerated 24 Years Later," KCBD.com, http://www.kcbd.com/Global/story.asp?S=9804937 [accessed November 12, 2009] (second quotation).
15. *The University Daily*, Sept. 16, 1986; *The Lubbock Avalanche-Journal*, Sept. 16, 1986; *Texas v. Cole*, vol. V, 479–482; Thomas J. Nichols, former Lubbock Chief of Police, telephone interview with author, Aug. 24, 2009.
16. *Texas v. Cole*, vol. V, 465–472, 483–494; Case Report Number 85-2627, Lubbock Police Department Records, Feb. 3, 1985 (quotation).
17. Case Report Number 85-2627, Lubbock Police Department Records, Feb. 3, 1985 (quotation).
18. *Texas v. Cole*, vol. V, 495–504, 505 (quotations).
19. Ibid., 505 (quotation).
20. Ibid., 506–507.
21. Ibid., 509–520, 521 (quotation), 522–535.

Chapter Ten / The Trial–Day Four
1. *Texas v. Cole*, vol. VII, 7 (quotation).
2. Ibid., vol. VI, 541-563, 564 (first quotation), 565–566 (second quotation).
3. Ibid., 564 (first quotation), 565–566 (second quotation).
4. Ibid., 567–579.
5. *The Lubbock Avalanche-Journal*, Sept. 17, 1986; *Texas v. Cole*, vol. VI, 580–582, 583 (quotation), 584–607; Jeff Blackburn, chief counsel, the Innocence Project of Texas, interview with author, Aug. 19, 2009, Lubbock, Texas.
6. *Texas v. Cole*, vol. VI, 608 (quotation), 609–619; *The Lubbock Avalanche-Journal*, Sept. 17, 1986.
7. *Texas v. Cole*, vol. VI, 620–622, 623 (first quotation), 624 (second quotation).
8. Ibid., 625–635, 636 (quotation), 637.

9. Ibid., 639–651.

10. Ibid., 652–658; *The Lubbock Avalanche-Journal*, Sept. 17, 1986.

11. *Texas v. Cole*, vol. VI, 659 (quotation), 660–666.

12. Ibid., 667–696; *The Lubbock Avalanche-Journal*, Sept. 17, 1986; *The University Daily*, Sept. 17, 1986.

13. *The University Daily*, Sept. 17, 1986; *Texas v. Cole*, vol. VI, 697–705; *The Lubbock Avalanche-Evening Journal*, Sept. 17, 1986.

14. *Texas v. Cole*, vol. VI, 706–730, 731 (quotation); *The Lubbock Avalanche-Journal*, Sept. 17, 1986; *The University Daily*, Sept. 17, 1986.

15. *Texas v. Cole*, vol. VI, 732, 733 (quotation), 734–735.

16. Elliott Blackburn, "Hope Deferred Series," part 2 of 3, *The Lubbock Avalanche-Journal*, June 29, 2008, http://www.lubbockonline.com/stories/062908/loc_297196667.shtml [accessed July 30, 2009]; Ruby Lee Session, interview with author, Jan. 24, 2010, Fort Worth, Texas; Ruby Session and family members, interview with Fil Alvarado, Fox 4 News (Dallas), Sept. 1, 2009, Fort Worth, Texas, also attended by the author. During the latter interview, Mrs. Session reiterated that her son had turned down a plea bargain, but in a letter to the author dated Aug. 14, 2009, Donna L. Clarke, Assistant Criminal District Attorney for Lubbock, Texas, said that nothing in the records substantiated that claim. Clarke, however, indicated earlier to the author that plea bargain offers would rarely be documented, especially those made verbally. During an interview conducted by the author on Jan. 24, 2010, Mrs. Session said that during the guilt or innocence phase of the trial, both she and Reggie, as witnesses for the defense, were sequestered, and therefore she did not hear any of the other witnesses testify.

17. *The Lubbock Avalanche-Journal*, Sept. 17, 1986; *The University Daily*, Sept. 17, 1986; *Texas v. Cole*, vol. VI, 736–748.

18. *Texas v. Cole*, vol. VI, 749–756, 757 (quotation); *The University Daily*, Sept. 17, 1986.

19. *Texas v. Cole*, vol. VI, 758–760, 761 (first quotation), 762 (second quotation).

20. Ibid., 763, 764 (quotation).

21. Ibid., 764 (quotation).

22. *The Lubbock Avalanche-Evening Journal*, Sept. 17, 1986; Ruby Lee Session, interview with author, Jan. 24, 2010, Fort Worth Texas. During this interview, Mrs. Session indicated that she never knew exactly why Mike Brown did not question Tim about the fact that Tim did not smoke.

23. *Texas v. Cole*, vol. VI, 765, 766 (first quotation), 767, 768 (second quotation).

24. *The University Daily*, Sept. 17, 1986; *The Lubbock Avalanche-Journal*, Sept. 17, 1986; *Texas v. Cole*, vol. VI, 768 (quotation).

25. *Texas v. Cole*, vol. VI, 770 (quotation).

Chapter Eleven / The Trial–Day Five

1. *The Lubbock Avalanche-Journal*, Sept. 17, 1986 (quotation).

2. *Texas v. Cole*, vol. VII, 3–4, 5 (third and fourth quotations), 6 (first quotation); Charge of the Court, Case Number 85-403, 151, item 9, master file titled *Texas v. Cole*, Lubbock District Clerk's Office, Sept. 16, 1986 (second quotation).

3. *Texas v. Cole*, vol. VII, 7 (quotation), 8–10; vol. IX, 31.

4. Ibid., vol. VII, 11–18; *The Lubbock Avalanche-Journal*, Sept. 17, 1986.

5. *Texas v. Cole*, vol. VII, 18 (quotations). To the author's knowledge, no one ever documented an explanation for how the empty Winston cigarette package came to be in Tim Cole's automobile.

6. Ibid., 19–22, 23 (first quotation), 24, 25 (second quotation), 26 (third quotation).

7. *The Lubbock Avalanche-Evening Journal*, Sept. 17, 1986; *Texas v. Cole*, vol. VII, 27 (first quotation), 28–34, 35 (second quotation), 36.

8. *Texas v. Cole*, vol. VII, 37 (quotation).

9. Ibid., 38 (quotation), 39–42; *The Lubbock Avalanche-Evening Journal*, Sept. 17, 1986.

Chapter Twelve / The Verdicts

1. *The Lubbock Avalanche-Journal*, Sept. 19, 1986 (quotation).

2. *Texas v. Cole*, vol. VII, 43–45; *The Lubbock Avalanche-Journal*, Sept. 18, 1986 (quotation).

3. *Texas v. Cole*, vol. VII, 46; *The Lubbock Avalanche-Journal*, Sept. 18, 1986; *The Lubbock Avalanche-Evening Journal*, Sept. 17, 1986. According to the latter source, "the two alternate jurors were released from duty as the panel retired shortly before 10:00 a.m."

4. *Texas v. Cole*, vol. VII, 46 (quotation); Guilty Verdict (Guilt or Innocence), Case Number 85-403, 151, master file titled *Texas v. Cole*, Lubbock District Clerk's Office, Sept. 17, 1986.

5. *The Lubbock Avalanche-Journal*, Sept. 18, 1986 (quotation).

6. *Texas v. Cole*, vol. VII, 47.

7. *The Lubbock Avalanche-Journal*, Sept. 18, 1986; *Texas v. Cole*, vol. VII, 47, 48 (quotation).

8. "Timothy Cole Exonerated 24 Years Later," KCBD.com, http://www.kcbd.com/Global/story.asp?S=9804937 [accessed November 12, 2009] (quotation). Jim Hansen is the current Justice of the Peace for Precinct Number 1 of Lubbock County, Texas.

9. *The University Daily*, Sept. 18, 1986 (first quotation); *The Lubbock Avalanche-Evening Journal*, Sept. 18, 1986 (second quotation); *The Lubbock Avalanche-Journal*, Sept. 18, 1986.

10. *The University Daily*, Sept. 18, 1986.

11. Elliott Blackburn, "Hope Deferred Series," part 1 of 3, *The Lubbock Avalanche-Journal*, June 28, 2008, http://www.lubbockonline.com/stories/062808/loc_296894153.shtml [accessed July 30, 2009] (quotation).

12. Ibid. (quotation).

13. *The University Daily*, Sept. 19, 1986 (quotation).

14. Ibid. (quotation).

15. Ibid. (quotation).

16. Jeff Blackburn, chief counsel, the Innocence Project of Texas, interview with author, Aug. 19, 2009, Lubbock, Texas; Natalie Roetzel, executive director, the Innocence Project of Texas, interview with author, Aug. 19, 2009, Lubbock, Texas; Ruby Lee Session, interview with author, Jan. 24, 2010, Fort Worth, Texas (quotation).

17. *Texas v. Cole*, vol. VIII, 3, 4–5 (quotations); Objections to Court's Charge

(Punishment), Case Number 85-403, 151, master file titled *Texas v. Cole*, Lubbock District Clerk's Office, Sept. 18, 1986.

18. *The Lubbock Avalanche-Evening Journal*, Sept. 18, 1986; *Texas v. Cole*, vol. VIII, 6–8.

19. *Texas v. Cole*, vol. VIII, 9 (quotation). Jim Bob Darnell did not ask Huckabee to elaborate on his statement regarding Tim Cole's reputation; therefore, the reason for the officer's judgment is unclear by reading the records. But obviously, in addition to the run-in with Texas Tech Police at the Biology Building on March 6, 1985, Huckabee must have recalled two prior campus-related episodes. According to Offense Report, Case Number 9-18, Texas Tech Police Department, Tim and a friend named Eric Menyard Wiley were written up for an Oct. 21, 1979, incident that occurred at 2:30 that morning. As Huckabee stopped them in a parking lot and asked for identification, the situation obviously escalated. According to the official police report, "Both subjects are to be referred to the Dean for failure to present identification for verification of their stated identity, for their uncooperative and abusive behavior, for giving false information to this officer, and for attempting to turn a routine parking lot interview into a racail [sic] confrontation." And according to Offense Report, Case Number 9-118 (Aggravated Assault), issued by the Texas Tech Police Department, William DeNike accused Tim of stabbing him in the right hip on Apr. 9, 1980. When officer Devitt interviewed Tim, "he stated that the incident started at Bromley Hall where the guys started picking on him because they saw him kissing on his white girl friend . . . ." When the author requested a copy of the final report reflecting a resolution of the latter, Ronald Seacrist, Texas Tech Police Chief, responded on Sept. 3, 2009. His department had no record of this offense, because "our criminal records go back to 1988." Either the matter was settled out of court or the charge was dropped, because prior to the Michele Murray case, Tim Cole had never been convicted of a felony.

20. *Texas v. Cole*, vol. VIII, 10–11, 12 (quotation); *The Lubbock Avalanche-Evening Journal*, Sept. 18, 1986.

21. *Texas v. Cole*, vol. VIII, 13.

22. Ibid., 14 (first quotation), 15, 16–17 (second quotation), 18–19,

23. Ibid., 20–21 (quotations), 22–24; *The Lubbock Avalanche-Evening Journal*, Sept. 18, 1986; *The University Daily*, Sept. 19, 1986.

24. *Texas v. Cole*, vol. VIII, 25 (first quotation), 26–30, 31 (second quotation), 32, 33 (third quotation), 34–36, 37 (fourth quotation); The Lubbock Avalanche-Evening Journal, Sept. 18, 1986; *The University Daily*, Sept. 19, 1986.

25. *Texas v. Cole*, vol. VIII, 37, 38 (first quotation), 39 (second quotation), 40 (third quotation); *The Lubbock Avalanche-Evening Journal*, Sept. 18, 1986; *The University Daily*, Sept. 19, 1986.

26. *Texas v. Cole*, vol. VIII, 41–42.

27. Ibid., 42, 43 (quotation); *The Lubbock Avalanche-Evening Journal*, Sept. 18, 1986; Guilty Verdict (Punishment), Case Number 85-403, 151, master file titled *Texas v. Cole*, Lubbock District Clerk's Office, Sept. 18, 1986.

28. *Texas v. Cole*, vol. VIII, 44–45, 46 (quotation).

29. Ibid., 46 (quotation).

30. Ibid., 47 (quotation); *The University Daily*, Sept. 19, 1986.

31. *The Lubbock Avalanche-Journal*, Sept. 19, 1986 (quotation).
32. Ibid. (quotations).
33. Ibid.

Chapter Thirteen / A Meaningless Victory

1. Mike Brown's letter to the Honorable Thomas Clinton, Lubbock, Texas, Oct. 13, 1986; Timothy Brian Cole Defendant's Motion for a New Trial, Case Number 85-403, 151, master file titled *Texas v. Cole*, Lubbock District Clerk's Office, Oct. 9, 1986 (quotations).

2. Charge of the Court on Punishment, item 1, Case Number 85-403, 151, master file titled *Texas v. Cole*, Lubbock District Clerk's Office, September 17, 1986; Notice of Appeal, Case Number 85-403, 151, master file titled *Texas v. Cole*, Lubbock District Clerk's Office, Oct. 15, 1986; Defendant's Motion for a Transcript of the Record and for Permission to Proceed on Appeal *In Forma Pauperis* with Appointed Counsel, Case Number 85-403, 151, master file titled *Texas v. Cole*, Lubbock District Clerk's Office, Oct. 15, 1986; "Compensation of Counsel Appointed to Defend," Tex. Cr. Code Ann. § 26.05: Texas Statutes — Article 26.05, http://codes.lp.findlaw.com/txstatutes/CR/1/26/26.05 [accessed December 14, 2009]; Commitment Pending Mandate, Case Number 85-403, 151, master file titled *Texas v. Cole*, Lubbock District Clerk's Office, Oct. 29, 1986; Order Appointing Counsel and Ordering Record on Appeal, Case Number 85-403, 151, master file titled *Texas v. Cole*, Lubbock District Clerk's Office, Dec. 3, 1986 (quotation); Timothy Brian Cole, letter to the Honorable Thomas L. Clinton, Jan. 15, 1987; Ferguson (FE), Texas Department of Criminal Justice, http://www.tdcj.state.tx.us/stat/unitdirectory/fe.htm [accessed October 30, 2009].

3. "Ferguson Prison Unit in Midway, Texas," http://www.prisontalk.com/forums/archive/index.php/t-110688.html [accessed October 30, 2009]; Elliott Blackburn, "Hope Deferred Series," part 2 of 3, *The Lubbock Avalanche-Journal*, June 29, 2008, http://www.lubbockonline.com/stories/062908/loc_297196667.shtml [accessed July 30, 2009] (quotation).

4. Blackburn, "Hope Deferred," part 2 (quotation).
5. Ibid. (quotation).
6. Cole letter to Clinton (quotation).
7. *Cole v. State*, 735 S.W.2d 686 (Tex.App.-Amarillo 1987) (quotations).
8. Ibid.
9. Ibid.
10. Ibid.
11. Ibid. (quotation).
12. Ibid.
13. Ibid.
14. *Cole v. State*, 839 S.W.2d 798 (Tex.Crim.App. 1990); Blackburn, "Hope Deferred," part 2; Diane Burch Beckham, "Long Wait Ends for Ruling on Lab Reports," *Texas Lawyer*, Oct. 26, 1992: 3. Consult the latter source for a full discussion on how the Court of Criminal Appeal's ruling affected future court cases.

Chapter Fourteen / The Repeat Offender

1. Elliott Blackburn, "Coming Clean," *The Lubbock Avalanche-Journal*, June

24, 2008, http://www.lubbockonline.com/stories/061007/reg_061007125. shtml [accessed July 30, 2009] (quotation).

2. Johnson, Jerry Wayne, Offender Information Detail, Texas Department of Criminal Justice, http://168.51.178.33/webapp/TDCJ/InmateDetails.jsp? sidnumber=02711498 [accessed July 26, 2009]. According to this source, Johnson was sentenced for the July 4, 1985, offense (Case Number 85-403, 280) on July 29, 1987, and for the Sept. 27, 1985 offense (Case Number 85-403, 696), he was sentenced on Apr. 9, 1987. Furthermore, the grand jury indictments for the July 1985 term in the 137th District Court in Lubbock show the rape victim in the first offense to be Rebecca Parker; and a second grand jury indictment for the July 1985 term in the 99th District Court, also in Lubbock, reflects the victim to be Tina Martin, a fifteen-year-old Estacado High School student. Miss Martin identified Johnson as her assailant by picking his picture out of a 1977 EHS yearbook, taken while Johnson was a student there.

3. *Texas Birth Index*; Elliott Blackburn, "Hope Deferred Series," part 2 of 3, *The Lubbock Avalanche-Journal*, June 29, 2008, http://www.lubbockonline. com/stories/062908/loc_297196667. shtml [accessed July 30, 2009] (quotation); Elliott Blackburn, "Hope Deferred Series," part 3 of 3, *The Lubbock Avalanche-Journal*, June 30, 2008, http://www.lubbockonline.com/stories/ 063008/ loc_297531088.shtml [accessed July 30, 2009]; Case Report Number 84-27308, Della Warner's file re: Jerry Wayne Johnson, Lubbock Police Department Records, Nov. 24, 1984; Case Report Number 85-15475, Rebecca Parker's and Johnny Ramos's file re: Jerry Wayne Johnson, Lubbock Police Department Records, July 5, 1985. In the latter source, Parker's signed affidavit indicated, "That's when he told us that the same thing had happened to him and his sister, a ways over in the same field where we were." Within the "Hope Deferred Series," part 3 of 3 article listed above, at the time that Johnson raped Michele Jean Murray, "he was working for a rental car company and on sick leave . . . . He lived and worked nowhere near campus."

4. Case Report Number 84-27308 (quotations).

5. Ibid.

6. Ibid. (quotation).

7. Case Report Number 85-15475, Johnny Ramos's statement.

8. Ibid. (quotation).

9. Ibid. (quotation); Officer Carter's statement.

10. Johnny Ramos's statement; Officer Carter's statement (quotation).

11. Johnny Ramos's statement; Officer Carter's statement; Grand Jury for the 137th Judicial District Court-Lubbock, Texas, Jerry Wayne Johnson indictments, Lubbock District Clerk's Office, Aug. 7, 1985; Johnson, Jerry Wayne, Offender Information; *Texas v. Cole*, vol. V, 476, 479–481. In spite of Ramos's uncertainty in identifying Johnson as his assailant, the district attorney's office referred the matter to the Grand Jury of the 137th District Court, and on Aug. 7, 1985, indictments were returned for the aggravated sexual assault on Parker and the aggravated kidnapping of Ramos. On July 29, 1987, the trial jury added an additional ninety-nine years for raping Parker, on top of the life sentence received already for the aggravated sexual assault on Martin.

12. Incident Report Number 85-6349, Missing Person Report contained in

Mary Louise Smith's Case File Number 85-21528 re: Jerry Wayne Johnson, Lubbock Police Department Records, Sept. 10, 1985.

13. Case File Number 85-21528 (quotations).

14. Ibid.

15. Ibid.

16. Ibid; Calvin Watkins, "Top Five Dallas Cowboys-Redskins Games at Texas Stadium," http://www.dallasnews.com/sharedcontent/dws/spt/football/cowboys/stories/092808dnspocowsider.140d701.html [accessed Apr. 5, 2010]. Watkins's article indicated that the Dallas Cowboys beat the Washington Redskins on the Sept. 9, 1985, Monday night football game at Texas Stadium in Irving by a score of 44 to 14. Detective Hudgens's report dated Sept. 14, 1985 indicated that Johnson and his wife, Jeanette Marie, did not live together, but she claimed to have visited her husband twice on Monday, Sept. 9, "the first time was about 4:00 p.m. and the second time about 9:00 p.m. and each time she was there for about an hour." She also vouched for the fact that Earl Harris "had gone by to see Jerry Wayne," because Harris verified that piece of information in a telephone conversation with her.

17. Blackburn, "Hope Deferred Series," part 2; Case Report Number 85-22931, Jerry Wayne Johnson, Lubbock Police Department Records, Sept. 27, 1985 (quotations).

18. Case Report Number 85-22931; Case Report Number 85-22994, Tina Martin's file re: Jerry Wayne Johnson, Lubbock Police Department Records, Sept. 27, 1985. The quotation is taken from Rosia Lee Taylor's notarized witness affidavit, Oct. 8, 1985.

19. Case Report Number 85-22994, Taylor's witness affidavit (quotations).

20. Ibid. (quotation).

21. Case Report Number 85-22994, Robert E. Moore, notarized witness affidavit, Oct. 17, 1985; William Glass and Officer Roberto Garcia, witness report, Sept. 27, 1985; Roberto Garcia, police report, Sept. 27, 1985 (quotation).

22. Glass and Garcia (quotation).

23. Case Report Number 85-22994, supplement report, Oct. 4, 1985 (quotation).

24. Ibid., Tina Martin, notarized witness affidavit, page 1, Oct. 8, 1985 (quotation).

25. Glass and Garcia (quotations).

26. Ibid., Juvenile Officer Rendleman's report, Oct. 4, 1985; Tina Martin, notarized witness affidavit, page 2, Oct. 8, 1985 (quotation); Carrol Thomas, notarized witness affidavit, Oct. 8, 1985. Dr. Thomas currently serves as superintendent of the Beaumont (Texas) Independent School District.

27. Case Report Number 85-22994, Joe Nevarez, Supplemental Report, Oct. 8, 1985; Jerry Wayne Johnson, Warrant of Arrest, Oct. 8, 1985; Johnson, Jerry Wayne, Offender Information; *Texas v. Cole*, vol. V, 474–482.

28. Case File Number 85-21528, Lucious Weatherspoon, notarized witness affidavit, Oct. 14, 1985; Sgt. Hoffman, supplemental report, Oct. 14, 1985; Sgt. Hargrave, supplemental report, Oct. 18, 1985; Case Number 85-403, 698 (Jerry Wayne Johnson's Case Information), Lubbock County Electronic Public Access to Court Records, https://apps.co.lubbock.tx.us/ attorney/caseinfo. aspx [accessed November 7, 2009]; *Texas v. Cole*, vol. V, 476.

29. Johnson, Jerry Wayne, Offender Information.

30. Tim Cole's letters to Wayne LeCroy, District Clerk, Lubbock, Texas, Jan. 4, 1988 and June 22, 1988; Daniel Unit (DL), Texas Department of Criminal Justice, http://www.tdcj.state.tx.us/stat/ unitdirectory/dl.htm [accessed November 11, 2009]; Blackburn, "Hope Deferred Series," part 2 (quotation); Coffield Unit (CO), Texas Department of Criminal Justice, http://www.tdcj. state.tx.us/stat/unitdirectory/co.htm [accessed November , 2009].

31. Ruby Lee Session, interview with author, Jan. 24, 2010, Fort Worth, Texas (quotation).

Chapter Fifteen / The Unlikely Ally

1. Jerry Wayne Johnson, letter to author, Burleson, Texas, Aug. 13, 2009 (quotation).

2. *Cole v. State*, No. 07-86-0258-CR, Court of Appeals for the Seventh District of Texas at Amarillo, Panel D, master file titled *Texas v. Cole*, Lubbock District Clerk's Office, Mar. 29, 1993: 13 (quotation).

3. Ibid.; Jerry Wayne Johnson, letter to Craig Watkins, Dallas County District Attorney, Dallas, Texas, June 30, 2008; Heather McDonald, memo to Natalie Roetzel, the Innocence Project of Texas, Lubbock, Texas, undated; Cause Number 95-550, 214, Jerry Wayne Johnson's Petition for Appointment of Counsel, Lubbock District Clerk's Office, Feb. 3, 1995; Cause Number 95-550, 214, Jerry Wayne Johnson's Petitioner's Affidavit of Inability to Pay Court Cost or to Retain Counsel, Lubbock District Clerk's Office, Feb. 3, 1995; Barbara Sucsy, Lubbock County District Clerk (BSucsy@co.lubbock.tx. us), e-mail to author, Burleson, Texas, Nov. 24, 2009.

4. Elliott Blackburn, "Coming Clean," *The Lubbock Avalanche-Journal*, June 24, 2008, http://www.lubbockonline.com/stories/061007/reg_061007125. shtml [accessed July 30, 2009] (quotation).

5. Cause Number 95-550, 214 (quotation); Johnson to Watkins.

6. Disciplinary Reports re: TDCJ-ID 435828, Timothy Brian Cole, Texas Department of Criminal Justice, Correctional Institutions Division, Huntsville, Texas, Nov. 5, 2009.

7. Jeff Blackburn, chief counsel, the Innocence Project of Texas, interview with author, Aug. 19, 2009, Lubbock, Texas; Jena A. Williams, "Cole Case," *Texas Monthly*, http://texasmonthly.com/2009-02-01/webextra17.php [accessed July 30, 2009] (quotation).

8. Elliott Blackburn, "Hope Deferred Series," part 2 of 3, *The Lubbock Avalanche-Journal*, June 29, 2008, http://www.lubbockonline.com/stories/ 062908/loc_297196667.shtml [accessed July 30, 2009] (quotations); Ruby Session and family members, interview with Fil Alvarado, Fox 4 News (Dallas), Sept. 1, 2009, Fort Worth, Texas, also attended by the author; No. D1-DC 08-100-051, Opinion and Order of the Court (Exoneration of Timothy Brian Cole), Judge Charles Baird, 299th District Court, Travis County, Texas, Apr. 7, 2009.

9. *Fort Worth Star-Telegram*, Dec. 7, 1999; Opinion and Order of the Court; Physician's Report on the Death of Tim Cole, Texas Department of Criminal Justice, Office of the General Counsel, Huntsville, Texas (quotation). The latter source revealed that "the triggering mechanism of the asthma attack in this

case remains obscure. Usually, an allergen to which a patient has been sensitized is the inciting antigen. However, in many cases, no allergen can be identified." The report went on to conclude that "the manner of death is natural."

10. Darrington Unit (DA), Texas Department of Criminal Justice, http://www.tdcj.state.tx.us/ stat/unitdirectory/da.htm [accessed November 10, 2009]; Physician's Report on the Death of Tim Cole [quotation].

11. Elliott Blackburn, "Hope Deferred Series," part 3 of 3, *The Lubbock Avalanche-Journal*, June 30, 2008, http://www.lubbockonline.com/stories/063008/loc_297531088.shtml [accessed July 30, 2009] (quotation). To some, the Grenada service statement reflected on Tim Cole's military marker might seem contradictory, given that this action did not begin until Oct. 25, 1983, sometime after Tim had left the military. In an interview conducted with Ruby Lee Session on Jan. 24, 2010, she explained the Army advised her that since her son served during the approximate time of this theater of operations, he was entitled to the "Grenada" designation.

12. Jerry Wayne Johnson, letter to Judge Cecil Puryear, 137th District Court, Lubbock, Texas, June 13, 2000 (quotations); Johnson to Watkins.

13. Cause Number 95-550, 214, Final Order by Judge J. Blair Cherry, Jr., 72nd District Court, Lubbock, Texas, Jan. 12, 2001 (quotation); Opinion and Order of the Court.

14. David Weeks, "Post-Conviction DNA Testings: More Questions Than Answers," State Bar of Texas, http://www.texasbar.com/Template.cfm?Section=Home&Template=/Content Management/ ContentDisplay.cfm&ContentID=5902 [accessed November 9, 2009] (quotation); Johnson to Watkins.

15. Blackburn, "Coming Clean" (first quotation); Johnson to Watkins (second quotation); "Texan Who Died in Prison Cleared of Rape Conviction," CNN.com, http://www.cnn.com/2009/CRIME/02/06/texas.exoneration/index.html#cnnSTCOther1 [accessed November 12, 2009] (third quotation); McDonald to Roetzel. The latter source indicates that "in 2007, Johnson's mother did an open records request for Cole's booking card," and that is how they found the Fort Worth address to which to send the letter.

16. Blackburn, "Hope Deferred Series," part 3 of 3 (quotation).

17. Ibid. (quotation).

18. Elliott Blackburn, "Inmate's Claims May Posthumously Clear Man of Lubbock Rape, *The Lubbock Avalanche Journal*, May 24, 2007, http://www.lubbockonline.com/stories/052407/ loc_052407028.shtml [accessed December 15, 2009] (quotation). Johnson's account of abducting Michele Murray from a "cold" church parking lot appears as contradictory, given that according to data supplied by the National Weather Bureau, the lowest temperature for that evening was no less than 56 degrees.

19. McDonald to Roetzel; Blackburn, "Coming Clean" (quotation).

20. McDonald to Roetzel; Blackburn, "Hope Deferred Series," part 3 of 3. According to the Innocence Project of Texas's web site, "Roetzel received her J.D. from the Texas Wesleyan University School of Law in 2007, where she co-founded the Wesleyan Innocence Project and was a member of the Wesleyan Law Review's editorial board."

21. Blackburn, "Coming Clean" (quotation).

22. *Fort Worth Star-Telegram*, Oct. 10, 2009 (quotation); Jeff Blackburn, Ruby Session, and Michele Murray Mallin, telephone interview with Tony Cox, National Public Radio, Sept. 23, 2008, http://www.npr.org/templates/story/story.php?storyId=94937062&ps=rs [accessed November 14, 2009].

23. Blackburn, "Hope Deferred Series," part 3 of 3 (quotation).

24. Johnson to Watkins (quotations); Jerry Wayne Johnson, letter to Heather McDonald or Jeff Blackburn, the Innocence Project of Texas, Lubbock, Texas, Jan. 9, 2008. In the latter source, Johnson took the opportunity to smear George White once more. During their meeting to discuss Cole's innocence, Johnson said, "White immediately began to read me my rights, couldn't remember it, couldn't locate the card he carries with it, and stated 'you understand what that is.'" This letter, however, never mentioned the alleged intimidation by the investigators that he so vividly pointed out in his June 30, 2008 communication with Craig Watkins, the Dallas County District Attorney.

25. Opinion and Order of the Court (quotation); Blackburn, Session, and Mallin, telephone interview with Cox; Johnson to Watkins.

Chapter Sixteen / Uncharted Ground
1. Jeff Blackburn, Ruby Session, and Michele Murray Mallin, telephone interview with Tony Cox, National Public Radio, Sept. 23, 2008, http://www.npr.org/templates/story/story.php?storyId= 94937062&ps=rs [accessed November 14, 2009] (quotation).

2. Elliott Blackburn, "Hope Deferred Series," part 3 of 3, *The Lubbock Avalanche-Journal*, June 30, 2008, http://www.lubbockonline.com/stories/063008/loc_297531088.shtml [accessed July 30, 2009] (quotation).

3. Ibid. (quotation). The web site of the Innocence Project of Texas indicates that Jeff Blackburn is "a successful criminal defense attorney who is responsible for securing the release of 35 people convicted as part of the drug sting in Tulia, Texas in 1999. The State Bar of Texas named him Criminal Defense Lawyer of the Year for 2002-2003, and he has been named a *Texas Monthly* "Super Lawyer" each year since 2003."

4. Posthumous Exoneration Sought Through Court of Inquiry," *Texas Lawyer*, July 7, 2008, http://www.law.com/jsp/tx/PubArticleTX.jsp?id= 1202422790640&slreturn=1 [accessed November 19, 2009] (quotation).

5. "Courts of Inquiry Conducted by District Judges," Tex. Cr. Code Ann. § 52.01: Texas Statutes—Article 52.01, http://codes.lp.findlaw.com/txstatutes/CR/1/52/52.01 [accessed November 15, 2009]; No. D1-DC 08-100-051, Opinion and Order of the Court (Exoneration of Timothy Brian Cole), Judge Charles Baird, 299th District Court, Travis County, Texas, Apr. 7, 2009 (first quotation); Crime Victims' Petition for a Court of Inquiry into the Conviction of Timothy Brian Cole and the Guilt of Jerry Johnson, 99th District Court, Lubbock County, Texas, June 26, 2008 (second quotation).

6. Robbins, "Posthumous Exoneration," July 7, 2008; Jerry Wayne Johnson's Motion in Opposition to Request for Court of Inquiry, 99th District Court, Lubbock County, Texas, July 10, 2008.

7. Blackburn, Session, and Mallin, telephone interview with Cox (first quotation); Blackburn, "Hope Deferred Series," part 3 of 3 (second quotation).

8. Opinion and Order of the Court.

9. Ibid. (first and second quotations); Dahlia Lithwick, "When Our Eyes Deceive Us," *Newsweek.com*, http://www.newsweek.com/id/189294 [accessed November 21, 2009] (third and fourth quotations). For a complete listing of Dr. Well's numerous works, the reader should consult his web site: http://www.psychology.iastate.edu/faculty/gwells/. One of the better articles on this particular subject is titled "Eyewitness Testimony," co-written by Dr. Wells and Elizabeth A. Olson. It can be accessed at http://www.innocenceproject.org/docs/Eyewitness_Testimony_Ann_Rev.pdf.

10. Jeff Blackburn, chief counsel, the Innocence Project of Texas, interview with author, Aug. 19, 2009, Lubbock, Texas; Opinion and Order of the Court; Carla Castaño, "Austin Judge Reverses Cole Conviction," KXAN.com, http://www.kxan.com/dpp/news/texas/Tim_Cole_exoneration_ hearing_continues [accessed November 25, 2009] (quotation).

11. Jordan Smith, "Cole's Posthumous Exoneration is First for Texas," *The Austin Chronicle*, http://www.austinchronicle.com/gyrobase/Issue/Story?oid=oid:740144 [accessed November 21, 2009] (quotation); Opinion and Order of the Court.

12. Opinion and Order of the Court (quotations).

13. Ibid.

14. Ibid.

15. Ibid.; "Judge's Ruling Clears Deceased Texas Prisoner and Emphasizes Need for Reform," the Innocence Project, http://www.innocenceproject.org/Content/1937.php [accessed October 30, 2009] (quotation).

16. "In Memory of the Life of Timothy Brian Cole," Senate Resolution 124, *Senate Journal*, Eighty-first Legislature—Regular Session, http://www.journals.senate.state.tx.us/sjrnl/81r/html/ 81RSJ02-04-F.HTM [accessed November 23, 2009]; Tim Cole Act, Senate Bill 2014, Texas Senate, http://www. legis.state.tx.us/billlookup/History.aspx?LegSess=81R&Bill=SB2014 [accessed November 23, 2009]; Tim Cole Act, House Bill 1736, Texas House of Representatives, http://www.legis.state.tx.us/ billlookup/History.aspx?LegSess=81R&Bill=HB1736 [accessed November 23, 2009]; Jordan Smith, "Tim Cole Act Becomes Law," *The Austin Chronicle*, http://www.austinchronicle.com/gyrobase/News/ Blogs?oid=oid:787201 [accessed November 23, 2009] (quotation); Dave Montgomery, "Tim Cole Act Sent to Governor by Senate," *Fort Worth Star-Telegram*, May 12, 2009; Jim Vertuno, "Tim Cole Act Signed into Law," *Fort Worth Star-Telegram*, May 28, 2009.

17. Vertuno, "Tim Cole Act Signed into Law," May 28, 2009 (quotations). According to the Innocence Project of Texas's web site, "The previous law, which was only available to living exonerees, was also amended by the Tim Cole Act to allow compensation to be paid to the estate of exonerees who pass away during their term of confinement."

18. "Judge's Ruling Clears Deceased Texas Prisoner and Emphasizes Need for Reform" (first quotation); "HB 498, Innocence Commission Passes Criminal Justice Committee," press release by Senator Rodney Ellis, Texas District 13, May 22, 2009, The Senate of Texas, http://www.senate.state.tx.us/75r/Senate/members/dist13/pr09/p052209a.htm [accessed November 24, 2009] (second quotation); "Statement of Sen. Rodney Ellis on the First Meeting of the Tim Cole Advisory Panel on Wrongful Convictions," press re-

lease by Senator Rodney Ellis, Texas District 13, Oct. 13, 2009, The Senate of Texas, http://www.ellis.senate.state.tx.us/pr09/p101309a.htm [accessed November 24, 2009].

19. Kelsey Heckel, "Tech Alumni Create Scholarship for Wrongly Convicted Lubbock Man," *The Daily Toreador* (Texas Tech), http://www.daily toreador.com/news/tech-alumni-create-scholarship-for-wrongly-convicted-lubbock-man-1.2110787 [accessed January 16, 2009] (quotation).

20. Ibid. (quotation).

21. Ibid. (quotation).

22. Elliott Blackburn, "Voters May Have Say in Helping Governor Clear Cole," *The Lubbock Avalanche-Journal*, Apr. 17, 2009, http://www.lubbockon-line.com/stories/041709/loc_430105473. shtml [assessed November 24, 2009]; *Fort Worth Star-Telegram*, May 12, 2009; Anna M. Tinsley, "Family Renews Its Push for a Pardon," *Fort Worth Star-Telegram*, July 2, 2009; Dave Montgomery, "Perry Can't Pardon Tim Cole, Office Says," *Fort Worth Star-Telegram*, June 5, 2009; "Perry Should Issue Posthumous Pardon," an editorial, DallasNews. com, http://www.dallasnews.com/sharedcontent/dws/dn/opinion/editorials/stories/DN-pardon_15edi.State.Edition1.2addc7d.html [accessed November 25, 2009] (quotation); Anna M. Tinsley, "Review: Perry Can Give Posthumous Pardons," *Fort Worth Star-Telegram*, July 9, 2009.

23. Opinion No. GA-0754, "Authority of the Governor to Grant a Post-humous Pardon," Greg Abbott, Attorney General of Texas, Jan. 7, 2010 (first quotation); Jeff Carlton, "AG: Governor Can Pardon Dead Man Exonerated by DNA," WCFCourier.com, http://www. wcfcourier.com/news/national/arti-cle_bef6f650-1ee5-5c87-861e-b8511e5d3ce5.html [accessed January 7, 2010] (second quotation).

24. "Gov. Perry Grants Posthumous Pardon for Innocence to Tim Cole," press release from the Office of the Governor Rick Perry, Mar. 01, 2010, http://governor. state.tx.us/news/ press-release/14312/ [accessed March 01, 2010]. Through discussions with family members, the author has personal knowledge as it relates to Ruby Session's surgical procedure.

25. "Gov. Perry Grants Posthumous Pardon for Innocence to Tim Cole," (quotation).

Epilogue

1. Gregory Stevens, Captain, Public Information Officer, Lubbock Police Department, Lubbock, Texas (GStevens@mail.ci.lubbock.tx.us), e-mail to au-thor, Burleson, Texas, Oct. 28, 2009.

2. *Texas v. Cole*, vol. V, 416–417 (quotation).

3. Elliott Blackburn, "Coming Clean," *The Lubbock Avalanche-Journal*, June 24, 2008, http://www.lubbockonline.com/stories/061007/reg_061007125. shtml [accessed July 30, 2009] (quotation).

4. Elliott Blackburn, "Cole Family Wants Explanation," *The Lubbock Avalanche-Journal*, Sept. 26, 2009, http://www.lubbockonline.com/sto-ries/092609/loc_497543690.shtml [accessed November 27, 2009] (quotations); Jeff Blackburn, chief counsel, the Innocence Project of Texas, telephone inter-view with author, Jan. 5, 2010.

5. Jeff Blackburn, Ruby Session, and Michele Murray Mallin, telephone interview with Tony Cox, National Public Radio, Sept. 23, 2008, http://www.npr.org/templates/story/story.php?storyId= 94937062&ps=rs [accessed November 14, 2009]; Wade Goodwyn, "Family of Man Cleared by DNA Still Seeks Justice," National Public Radio, Feb. 5, 2009, http://www.npr.org/templates/story/ story.php?storyId=100249923 [accessed November 25, 2009] (quotation); Ruby Session and family members, interview with Fil Alvarado, Fox 4 News (Dallas), Sept. 1, 2009, Fort Worth, Texas, also attended by the author.

6. Cory Session, interview with author, Sept. 1, 2009, Fort Worth, Texas; Don Teague, "Texas Wrestles with Wrongful Convictions," CBSNews.com, May 9, 2009, http://www.cbsnews.com/stories/ 2009/05/09/eveningnews/ main5003683.shtml [accessed November 25, 2009] (quotation); Elliott Blackburn, "Cole's Family Finds A Little Closure in Lubbock," *The Lubbock Avalanche-Journal*, Feb. 13, 2009, http://www.lubbockonline.com/stories/ 021309/loc_387479461.shtml [accessed November 25, 2009].

7. Ruby Lee Session, interview with author, Jan. 24, 2010, Fort Worth, Texas (quotations).

8. Session and family members, interview with Alvarado (quotation).

9. The author attended Governor Perry's news conference and has personal knowledge about the family trip to Mount Olivet Cemetery.

GLOSSARY

While the author does not intend the following words, terms, and phrases to be inclusive of all legal terminology, these are some of the most commonly used within this publication. The quoted definitions are provided by USLEGAL.COM; legal-dictionary.thefreedictionary.com, and World Law Direct. For further reference, I recommend their web sites:

> http://definitions.uslegal.com
> http://legal-dictionary.thefreedictionary.com
> http://www.worldlawdirect.com

Aggravated Kidnapping. Kidnapping that involves use of a deadly weapon.

Aggravated Sexual Assault. Typically defined as a sexual assault that maims, wounds, or disfigures the victim, or involves a victim who is physically or mentally incapacitated. It may also be defined to include a sexual assault that is aided or abetted by another person, occurs during commission of another crime, or involves use of a deadly weapon.

Aggravated Theft. Theft that involves use of a deadly weapon.

Bill of Exception. A legal pleading filed to complain on appeal about a matter that would not otherwise appear in the record. It is a statement of objections to the decision, or instructions of a judge in the trial of a dispute.

Burden of Proof. Refers to the duty on a party in a case to submit sufficient evidence on an issue in order to avoid dismissal of the claim.

Charge to the Jury. The process whereby a judge addresses the jury before the verdict. During the charge, the judge summarizes the case and gives instructions to the jury concerning such matters as the RULES OF LAW that are applicable to various issues in the case.

Continuance. Postponement of a date of a trial, hearing or other court appearance. An order for a continuance may be requested from the court by one of the parties, or the parties may agree to . . . a continuance. A continuance may be requested for various reasons, such as unavailability of an attorney or interested party, necessity of extra time to prepare for the matter, and others.

Docket. An official court record book which lists all the cases before the court and which may also note the status or action required for each case log containing brief entries of court proceedings. The docket is kept by the clerk of the court and should contain the names of the parties, and an entry of every proceeding in the case.

Exculpatory Evidence. Applied to evidence which may justify or excuse an accused defendant's actions, and which will tend to show the defendant is not guilty or has no criminal intent.

Extraneous Evidence. Inessential or unrelated to the topic or matter at hand; irrelevant.

Felony. An offense for which a sentence to a term of imprisonment in excess of one year is authorized. Felonies are serious crimes, such as murder, rape, or burglary, punishable by a harsher sentence than that given for a misdemeanor.

Grand Jury. A panel of citizens that is convened by a court to decide whether it is appropriate for the government to indict (proceed with a prosecution against) someone suspected of a crime.

Hearsay Rule. A rule of evidence which prohibits admitting testimony or documents into evidence when the statements contained therein are offered to prove their truth, and the maker of the statements is not able to testify about it in court. Hearsay is "second-hand" information.

Indictment. A formal accusation, issued by a grand jury based upon a proposed charge, witnesses' testimony and other evidence presented by the public prosecutor (District Attorney). It is the grand jury's determination that there is enough evidence that the defendant committed the crime to justify having a trial. In order to issue an indictment, the grand jury does not make determination of guilt, but only the probability that a crime was committed, that the accused person did it, and that he/she should be tried.

In Forma Pauperis. A Latin term meaning "in the form of a pauper," referring to a party to a lawsuit who gets filing fees waived by filing a statement, often in the form of an affidavit, declaring . . . inability to pay. Indigency, or lack of ability to pay, is a legal reason for having certain required fees waived, being declared eligible for free services, or appointment of legal counsel.

In Liminie. Latin for "at the threshold," referring to a motion before a trial begins.

Legalese. The specialized vocabulary of the legal profession, especially when considered to be complex or abstruse.

Modus Operandi. A characteristic pattern of methods of a repeated criminal act, used to identify the culprit. It is often referred to as "M.O."

No Bill. A term that the foreman of the Grand Jury writes across the face of a bill of indictment (a document drawn up by a prosecutor that states formal criminal charges against a designated individual) to indicate that the criminal charges alleged therein against a suspect have not been sufficiently supported by the evidence presented before it to warrant his or her criminal prosecution.

Presumptive. Providing a reasonable basis for belief or acceptance.

Probative Value. Probative, in evidence law, means tending to prove something. Therefore, evidence or testimony with no probative value may be objected to as immaterial and not admissible or will be stricken from the record if objected to by opposing counsel. The probative value of proposed evidence must be weighed by the trial judge against prejudicing in the minds of jurors toward the opposing party or criminal defendant.

Reasonable Doubt. The standard of proof that must be met in order to convict a criminal defendant of a crime.

Redirects. A redirect examination is the second direct examination of a witness after the cross-examination. Redirect examinations are usually limited to the matters that were covered during cross-examination.

Remand. To send back. An appeals court may remand a case to the trial court for further action if it reverses the judgment of the lower court.

Res Gestae. A legal term meaning "things done." In evidence law, it is used to refer to words spoken that are so closely connected to an event that they are considered part of the event, and their introduction does not violate the hearsay rule.

Rule of Lenity. Under the common law rule of lenity, courts must strictly construe penal statutes in order to avoid a violation of the due process rights of the accused. Thus in criminal cases where two reasonable interpretations of a penal statute exist, one inculpating and the other exculpating a defendant, a court must employ the less harsh reading.

Speedy Trial. In criminal prosecutions, a defendant has a right to demand a trial within a short time under the Sixth Amendment of the U.S. Constitution. The Sixth Amendment states, "In all criminal prosecutions, the accused shall enjoy the right to a speedy and public trial, by an impartial jury of the State and district wherein the crime shall have been committed, which district shall have been previously ascertained by law, and to be informed of the nature and cause of the accusation; to be confronted with the witnesses against him; to have compulsory process for obtaining witnesses in his favor, and to have the assistance of counsel for his defense."

True Bill. The agreement of a grand jury that probable cause exists to order a defendant to stand trial on the charges in the indictment. When this occurs, the grand jury is said to have "indicted" the defendant; the defendant can then be brought to trial.

Voir Dire. A Latin term meaning "to see or speak." It is a legal procedure conducted before trial in which the attorneys and the judge question prospective jurors to determine if any juror is biased and/or cannot deal with the issues fairly, or if there is cause not to allow a juror to serve.

Waiver of Arraignment. To call an accused person before a court to answer the charge made against him or her by indictment, information, or complaint. An arraignment may also be waived in a less formal manner, such as by the voluntary entry of a plea, by failing to call the court's attention to a defect in the proceedings at the proper time, by announcing readiness for trial, by going to trial without objection, or by filing motions and obtaining rulings on issues of law in the case.

BIBLIOGRAPHY

All report numbers identified as 85-6814 are associated directly with the Timothy Brian Cole case, and others, unless further indicated, are assumed to be as well.

Collected Documents and Books

Affidavit for Arrest Warrant and Witness Statement by Brenda Jones. Case Report Number 85-7944. Lubbock Police Department Records, April 11, 1985.

Application for Probation. Master file titled *Texas v. Cole*. Lubbock District Clerk's Office, September 10, 1986.

Arrest Report, Number 67453 (LPD No. 81507). Jerry Wayne Johnson. Lubbock County Sheriff's Office, April 10, 1985.

Arrest Report, Number 85-1474. Lubbock Police Department File No. 15-8, January 19, 1985.

Bail Bond, dated April 17, 1985. A copy is in the author's possession.

Case Report Number 84-27308. Della Warner's file re: Jerry Wayne Johnson. Lubbock Police Department Records, November 24, 1984.

Case Report Number 85-2627. Margaret Russo's report. Lubbock Police Department Records, February 3, 1985.

Case Report Number 85-6814. Michele Murray's report, prepared by Jamie Herrera. Lubbock Police Department Records, March 25, 1985.

_____. Michele Murray's report, prepared by Jimmie Riemer. Lubbock Police Department Records, March 25, 1985.

_____. Michele Murray's report, prepared by José Nevarez. Lubbock Police Department Records, March 28, 1985.

_____. Michele Murray's report, prepared by Teddy Daniels. Lubbock Police Department Records, April 3, 1985.

_____. Michele Murray's report, prepared by George White. Lubbock Police Department Records, April 8, 1985.

225

_____. Michele Murray's report, prepared by Rosanna Bagby. Lubbock Police Department Records, April 8, 1985.

_____. Michele Murray's report, prepared by George White. Lubbock Police Department Records, April 9, 1985.

_____. Michele Murray's report, prepared by José Nevarez. Lubbock Police Department Records, April 9, 1985.

_____. Michele Murray's report, prepared by Ronnie L. Goolsby. Lubbock Police Department Records, April 11, 1985.

Case Report Number 85-15475. Rebecca Parker's and Johnny Ramos's file re: Jerry Wayne Johnson. Lubbock Police Department Records, July 5, 1985.

Case Report Number 85-21528. Mary Louise Smith's file re: Jerry Wayne Johnson. Lubbock Police Department Records, September 10, 1985.

Case Report Number 85-22931. Jerry Wayne Johnson. Lubbock Police Department Records, September 27, 1985.

Case Report Number 85-22994. Tina Martin's file re: Jerry Wayne Johnson. Lubbock Police Department Records, September 27, 1985.

Case Report Number 85-7944. Brenda Jones. Lubbock Police Department Records, April 7–22, 1985.

Cause Number 95-550, 214. Jerry Wayne Johnson's Petition for Appointment of Counsel. Lubbock District Clerk's Office, February 3, 1995.

_____. Jerry Wayne Johnson's Petitioner's Affidavit of Inability to Pay Court Cost or to Retain Counsel. Lubbock District Clerk's Office, February 3, 1995.

_____. Final Order by Judge J. Blair Cherry, Jr., 72nd District Court, Lubbock, Texas, January 12, 2001.

Charge of the Court on Guilt or Innocence. Case Number 85-403, 151. Master file titled *Texas v. Cole*. Lubbock District Clerk's Office, September 16, 1986.

Charge of the Court on Punishment. Case Number 85-403, 151. Master file titled *Texas v. Cole*. Lubbock District Clerk's Office, September 17, 1986.

Cole, Timothy Brian. "Information Releasable Under the Freedom of Information Act." National Military Personnel Records, St. Louis, Missouri, January 18, 2010.

_____. Verification Transaction Detail. National Student Clearinghouse, December 2, 2009.

Cole v. State, 735 S.W.2d 686 (Tex.App.-Amarillo 1987).

_____, 839 S.W.2d 798 (Tex.Crim.App. 1990).

_____. No. 07-86-0258-CR. Court of Appeals for the Seventh District of Texas at Amarillo, Panel D. Master file titled *Texas v. Cole*. Lubbock District Clerk's Office, March 29, 1993.

Commitment Pending Mandate. Case Number 85-403, 151. Master file titled *Texas v. Cole*. Lubbock District Clerk's Office, October 29, 1986.

Cox Broadcasting Corp. v. Cohn, 420 U.S. 469 (1975).

Crime Victims' Petition for a Court of Inquiry into the Conviction of Timothy Brian Cole and the Guilt of Jerry Johnson. 99th District Court, Lubbock County, Texas, June 26, 2008.

Criminal Docket, Case Number 85-403, 151. Master file titled *Texas v. Cole*. Lubbock District Clerk's Office, November 1, 1985 and April 21, 1986.

Defendant's Election to Have Jury Assess Punishment. Master file titled *Texas v. Cole*. Lubbock District Clerk's Office, September 10, 1986.

Defendant's First Motion for Continuance and Waiver of Speedy Trial. Master file titled *Texas v. Cole*. Lubbock District Clerk's Office, June 11, 1986.

Defendant's Motion for a New Trial. Case Number 85-403, 151. Master file titled *Texas v. Cole*. Lubbock District Clerk's Office, October 9, 1986.

Defendant's Motion for a Transcript of the Record and for Permission to Proceed on Appeal *In Forma Pauperis* with Appointed Counsel. Case Number 85-403, 151. Master file titled *Texas v. Cole*. Lubbock District Clerk's Office, October 15, 1986.

Defendant's Motion for Notice of Evidence of Other Crimes. Master file titled *Texas v. Cole*. Lubbock District Clerk's Office, September 5, 1986.

Disciplinary Reports re: TDCJ-ID 435828, Timothy Brian Cole. Texas Department of Criminal Justice, Correctional Institutions Division, Huntsville, Texas, November 5, 2009.

Drain, Richard E. *The Diamondbacks: The History of the 99th Bomb Group (H)*. Paducah: Turner Publishing, 1998.

Frazier v. U.S., 419 F.2d 1161, 1176 (D.C. 1969).

Grand Jury for the 99th Judicial District Court-Lubbock, Texas. Jerry Wayne Johnson indictment. Lubbock District Clerk's Office, November 7, 1985.

Grand Jury for the 137th Judicial District Court-Lubbock, Texas. Jerry Wayne Johnson indictments. Lubbock District Clerk's Office, August 7, 1985.

Grand Jury for the 140th Judicial District Court-Lubbock, Texas. Terry Lee Clark indictments. Lubbock District Clerk's Office, February 5, 1985.

Guilty Verdict (Guilt or Innocence). Case Number 85-403, 151. Master file titled *Texas v. Cole*. Lubbock District Clerk's Office, September 17, 1986.

Guilty Verdict (Punishment). Case Number 85-403, 151. Master file titled *Texas v. Cole*. Lubbock District Clerk's Office, September 18, 1986.

Indictment for the Offenses of Aggravated Sexual Assault, Aggravated Kidnapping, and Aggravated Robbery. Master file titled *Texas v. Cole*. Lubbock District Clerk's Office, June 5, 1985.

"Justice." *The Random House College Dictionary*, 1968.

Kingston, Michael T., Ruth Harris, and Erma Bailey, eds. *The Texas Almanac*, 1984–1985. Dallas: *The Dallas Morning News*, 1985.

Lubbock City Directory, 1985–1986. Dallas: R. L. Polk & Company, 1986.

Michele Jean Murray's "Intake Record." Lubbock Rape Crisis Center, March 25, 1985. A copy is retained by the Innocence Project of Texas in Lubbock within Tim Cole's master file.

_____. Signed affidavit. Lubbock Police Department Records, April 9, 1985.

Motion for Exculpatory Evidence. Master file titled *Texas v. Cole*. Lubbock District Clerk's Office, August 29, 1986.

Motion (Jerry Wayne Johnson's) in Opposition to Request for Court of Inquiry. 99th District Court, Lubbock County, Texas, July 10, 2008.

Motions & Orders to Dismiss Case Numbers 85-450602 and 85-450603. Minute Books 189/339 and 192/325, respectively. Lubbock County Clerk. Lubbock, Texas.

No. D1-DC 08-100-051, Opinion and Order of the Court (Exoneration of Timothy Brian Cole). Judge Charles Baird, 299th District Court, Travis County, Texas, April 7, 2009.

Notice of Appeal. Case Number 85-403, 151. Master file titled *Texas v. Cole*. Lubbock District Clerk's Office, October 15, 1986.

Objections to Court's Charge (Punishment). Case Number 85-403, 151. Master file titled *Texas v. Cole*. Lubbock District Clerk's Office, September 18, 1986.

Offense Report, Case Number 6-1, Supplement 6 (Tana Murphy). Texas Tech Police Department, January 21, 1985 and April 29, 1985.

Offense Report, Case Number 9-18. Texas Tech Police Department, October 21, 1979.

Offense Report, Case Number 9-118. Texas Tech Police Department, April 9, 1980.

Offense Report, Case Number MS 9C-1 and various supplements (Velma Chavez). Texas Tech Police Department, December 27, 1984–January 21, 1985.

Offense Report, Case Number R-60. Texas Tech Police Department, March 6, 1985.

Opinion No. GA-0754. "Authority of the Governor to Grant a Posthumous Pardon." Greg Abbott, Attorney General of Texas, January 7, 2010.

Order Appointing Counsel and Ordering Record on Appeal. Case Number 85-403, 151. Master file titled *Texas v. Cole*. Lubbock District Clerk's Office, December 3, 1986.

Physician's Report on the Death of Tim Cole. Texas Department of Criminal Justice. Office of the General Counsel, Huntsville, Texas.

Resolution of the Lubbock County Bar Association in Memory of the Honorable Thomas L. Clinton. Lubbock County Bar Association, Lubbock, Texas, December 15, 1993.

Robbery Report, Number 85-1473. Lubbock Police Department File No. 3-20, January 19, 1985.

The State of Texas v. Terry Lee Clark, 140th Judicial District Court case number 85402763, trial transcript. Lubbock: Lubbock County District Clerk, 1985.

The State of Texas v. Timothy Brian Cole, 99th Judicial District Court case number 85-403, 151, trial transcript. 9 vols. Lubbock: Lubbock County District Clerk, 1986.

Waiver of Arraignment. Master file titled *Texas v. Cole*. Lubbock District Clerk's Office, June 6, 1985.

Witness Affidavit, witnessed by Ronnie L. Goolsby. Lubbock Police Department Records, April 10, 1985.

Magazine and Newspaper Articles
Bechham, Diane Burch. "Long Wait Ends for Ruling on Lab Reports." *Texas Lawyer*, October 26, 1992: 3.

Montgomery, Dave. "Tim Cole Act Sent to Governor by Senate." *Fort Worth Star-Telegram*, May 12, 2009.

———. "Perry Can't Pardon Tim Cole, Office Says." *Fort Worth Star-Telegram*, June 5, 2009.

Tinsley, Anna M. "Family Renews Its Push for a Pardon." *Fort Worth Star-Telegram*, July 2, 2009.

———. "Review: Perry Can Give Posthumous Pardons." *Fort Worth Star-Telegram*, July 9, 2009.

Vertuno, Jim. "Tim Cole Act Signed into Law." *Fort Worth Star-Telegram*, May 28, 2009.

Newspapers/Television/Online News Sources
Austinchronicle.com (*The Austin Chronicle*).
CBSNews.com (CBS News).
CNN.com (CNN).
DallasNews.com (*The Dallas Morning News*).
Fort Worth Star-Telegram, December 07, 1999–October 10, 2009.
GoSanAngelo.com (*Standard Times*, San Angelo).
KCBD.com (Channel 11–Lubbock).
KXAN.com (Channel 36–Austin).
Lubbockcentennial.com (*The Lubbock Avalanche-Journal*).
Lubbockonline.com (*The Lubbock Avalanche-Journal*).
MyFoxDFW.com (Fox 4, Dallas/Fort Worth).
NPR.org (National Public Radio).
Newsweek.com (*Newsweek*).
Newyorktimesonline.com (*New York Times*).
Texasmonthy.com (*Texas Monthly*).
The Lubbock Avalanche-Journal, April 11, 1985–December 31, 2009.
The Lubbock Avalanche-Evening Journal, September 17–18, 1986.
The University Daily (Texas Tech-Lubbock), January 15, 1985–September 19, 1986.
USAtoday.com (*USA Today*).
Wcfcourier.com (*Waterloo-Cedar Falls Courier*, Waterloo, IA).

Letters, E-Mails, and Memoranda
Barbara Sucsy, Lubbock County District Clerk (BSucsy@co.lubbock.tx.us), e-mails to author, Burleson, Texas, September 23, September 28, 2009, and November 24, 2009.
Debbie Ray, Deputy Program Monitor, Office of Administrative Monitor for Use of Force, Texas Department of Criminal Justice, Huntsville, Texas, letter to author, Burleson, Texas, August 3, 2009.
Donna L. Clarke, Assistant Criminal District Attorney, Civil Division, Lubbock, Texas, letter to author, Burleson, Texas, August 14, 2009.
Gilbert "Gib" Weaver, Superintendent, TTUISD, Lubbock, Texas (gilbert.weaver@ttu.edu), e-mail to author, Burleson, Texas, November 4, 2009.
Gregory Stevens, Captain, Public Information Officer, Lubbock Police Department, Lubbock, Texas (GStevens@mail.ci.lubbock.tx.us), e-mails to author, Burleson, Texas, September 4, 2009 and October 28, 2009.
Heather McDonald, memo to Natalie Roetzel, the Innocence Project of Texas, Lubbock, Texas, undated. Author has a copy in his possession.
Heidi Templeton, Director of Public Relations, Truman State University, Kirksville, Missouri (heidi@truman.edu), e-mail to author, Burleson, Texas, September 1, 2009.
Jerry Wayne Johnson, letter to Judge Cecil Puryear, 137th District Court, Lubbock, Texas, June 13, 2000, attached to Cause Number 95-550, 214.
_____, letter to Heather McDonald or Jeff Blackburn, the Innocence Project of

Texas, Lubbock, Texas, January 9, 2008. Author has a copy in his possession.

_____, letter to Craig Watkins, Dallas County District Attorney, Dallas, Texas, June 30, 2008. Author has a copy in his possession.

_____, letter to author, Burleson, Texas, August 13, 2009.

Justin Weaver, Meteorologist-in-Charge, National Weather Service, Lubbock, Texas (Justin.Weaver@noaa.gov), e-mail to author, Burleson, Texas, September 18, 2009.

Margaret Ehlig, Librarian, Robert E. Lee High School, Baytown, Texas (mdehlig@gccisd.net), e-mail to author, Burleson, Texas, August 13, 2009.

Mike Brown, letter to the Honorable Thomas Clinton, Lubbock, Texas, October 13, 1986. Author has a copy in his possession.

Patrick Aten, Assistant to the City Council, City of Lubbock, Lubbock, Texas (PAten@mail.ci.lubbock.tx.us), e-mail to author, Burleson, Texas, July 22, 2009.

Ronald Seacrist, Chief, Texas Tech Police Department, Lubbock, Texas (ronald.seacrist@ttu.edu), e-mail to author, Burleson, Texas, September 3, 2009.

Sally Post, Director, Communications and Marketing, Texas Tech University, Lubbock, Texas (SALLY.POST@ttu.edu), e-mail to author, Burleson, Texas, July 24, 2009.

Sandra K. Murphy, Administrator, Offender Grievance Program, Texas Department of Criminal Justice, Huntsville, Texas, letter to author, Burleson, Texas, August 4, 2009.

Timothy Brian Cole, letter to the Honorable Thomas L. Clinton, January 15, 1987. Author has a copy in his possession.

_____, letters to Wayne LeCroy, District Clerk, Lubbock, Texas, January 4, 1988 and June 22, 1988. Author has copies in his possession.

Timothy L. Hendricks, Senior Business Assistant, Office of the Registrar, Texas Tech University, Lubbock, Texas (timothy.hendricks@ttu.edu), e-mails to author, Burleson Texas, November 18 and November 19, 2009.

Interviews

Blackburn, Jeff. Chief Counsel, the Innocence Project of Texas. Interview with author, August 19, 2009, Lubbock, Texas.

_____. Telephone interview with author, January 5, 2010.

_____, Ruby Session, and Michele Murray Mallin. Telephone interview with Tony Cox, National Public Radio, September 23, 2008. http://www.npr.org/templates/story/story.php?storyId=94937062&ps=rs [accessed November 14, 2009].

Lutter, Marilyn. Administrative Assistant, Lubbock County Criminal District Attorney's Office. Telephone interview with author, July 27, 2009.

Nichols, Thomas J. Former Chief of Police-Lubbock. Telephone interview with author, August 24, 2009.

Reeves, Dennis R. Capital Public Defenders Office, Lubbock, Texas. Telephone interview with author, September 8, 2009.

Roetzel, Natalie. Executive Director, the Innocence Project of Texas. Interview with author, August 19, 2009, Lubbock, Texas.

Session, Cory. Interview with author, September 1, 2009, Fort Worth, Texas.
Session, Ruby Lee. Interview with author, January 24, 2010, Fort Worth, Texas.
_____. Telephone interview with author, January 25, 2010.
_____ and family members. Interview with Fil Alvarado, Fox 4 News (Dallas), September 1, 2009, Fort Worth, Texas. The author also attended.
Stevens, Captain Greg. Public Information Officer, Lubbock Police Department. Interview with author, August 18, 2009, Lubbock, Texas.
Weaver, Justin. Meteorologist-in-Charge, National Weather Service, Lubbock, Texas. Telephone interview with author, July 20, 2009.

Unpublished Sources
Cole v. State, Cause No. 07-86-0258-CR on remand from the Texas Court of Criminal Appeals, unpublished opinion, issued March 29, 1993.

Web Sources
Ancestry.com. *Texas Birth Index, 1903-1997* [database on-line]. Provo, UT, USA: The Generations Network, Inc., 2005. Original data: Texas. *Texas Birth Index, 1903-1997*. Texas: Texas Department of State Health Services. Microfiche [accessed July 29, 2009].
"Baytown, Texas." *Handbook of Texas Online*. http://www.tshaonline.org/handbook/online/ articles/BB/hdb1.html [accessed August 10, 2009].
Blackburn, Elliott. "Cole Family Wants Explanation." *The Lubbock Avalanche-Journal*, September 26, 2009. http://www.lubbockonline.com/stories/092609/loc_497543690.shtml [accessed November 27, 2009].
_____. "Cole's Family Finds A Little Closure in Lubbock." *The Lubbock Avalanche-Journal*, February 13, 2009. http://www.lubbockonline.com/stories/021309/loc_387479461.shtml [accessed November 25, 2009].
_____. "Coming Clean." *The Lubbock Avalanche-Journal*, June 24, 2008. http://www.lubbock online.com/stories/061007/reg061007125.shtml [accessed July 30, 2009].
_____. "Hope Deferred Series," part 1 of 3. *The Lubbock Avalanche-Journal*, June 28, 2008. http://www.lubbockonline.com/stories/062808/loc_296894153.shtml [accessed July 30, 2009].
_____. "Hope Deferred Series," part 2 of 3. *The Lubbock Avalanche-Journal*, June 29, 2008. http://www.lubbockonline.com/stories/062908/loc_297196667.shtml [accessed July 30, 2009].
_____. "Hope Deferred Series," part 3 of 3. *The Lubbock Avalanche-Journal*, June 30, 2008. http://www.lubbockonline.com/stories/063008/loc_297531088.shtml [accessed July 30, 2009].
_____. "Inmate's Claims May Posthumously Clear Man of Lubbock Rape. *The Lubbock Avalanche-Journal*, May 24, 2007. http://www.lubbockonline.com/stories/052407/loc_ 052407028.shtml [accessed December 15, 2009].
_____. "Voters May Have Say in Helping Governor Clear Cole." *The Lubbock Avalanche-Journal*, April 17, 2009. http://www.lubbockonline.com/stories/041709/loc_430105473.shtml [assessed November 24, 2009].
Blackstone, Sir William. Commentaries on the Laws of England (1765-1769). 4 vols. http:// www.lonang.com/exlibris/blackstone/ [accessed September 10, 2009].

"Brenham, Texas." *Handbook of Texas Online.* http://www.tshaonline.org/ handbook/online/ articles/BB/heb11.html [accessed July 29, 2009].

Capitol Almanac, 4–10. *Standard Times* (San Angelo). http://www.gosan angelo.com/news/2009/apr/10/capitol-almanac-4-10/ [accessed November 24, 2009].

Carlton, Jeff. "AG: Governor Can Pardon Dead Man Exonerated by DNA." WCFCourier.com. http://www.wcfcourier.com/news/national/article_ bef6f650-1ee5-5c87-861e-b8511e5d3ce5.html [accessed January 7, 2010].

Case Number 07-85-00274-CR (Terry Lee Clark). Texas Courts Online – Seventh of Court Appeals Case Management. http://www.7thcoa.courts. state.tx.us/opinions/case.asp?FilingID=4483 [accessed August 20, 2009].

Case Number 85-403, 151. Timothy Brian Cole's Court Cases. Lubbock County Electronic Public Access to Court Records. https://apps.co.lubbock.tx.us/ attorney/caseinfo.aspx [accessed July 23, 2009].

_____. Timothy Brian Cole's Crime Events. Lubbock County Electronic Public Access to Court Records. https://apps.co.lubbock.tx.us/attorney/ crimeevents.aspx [accessed July 28, 2009].

Case Number 85-450, 603 (Timothy Brian Cole's Case Information). Lubbock County Electronic Public Access to Court Records. https://apps.co. lubbock.tx.us/ attorney/caseinfo.aspx [accessed September 7, 2009].

Castaño, Carla. "Austin Judge Reverses Cole Conviction." KXAN.com. http://www.kxan.com/dpp/news/texas/Tim_Cole_exoneration_hearing _continues [accessed November 25, 2009].

"City of Abernathy, Texas." Abernathy Web Site. http://www.cityof abernathy.org/ [accessed August 10, 2009].

Coffield Unit (CO). Texas Department of Criminal Justice. http://www. tdcj.state.tx.us/stat/ unitdirectory/co.htm [accessed November 8, 2009].

"Compensation of Counsel Appointed to Defend." Tex. Cr. Code Ann. § 26.05: Texas Statutes—Article 26.05. http://codes.lp.findlaw.com/txstatutes/ CR/1/26/26.05 [accessed December 14, 2009].

"Courts of Inquiry Conducted by District Judges." Tex. Cr. Code Ann. § 52.01: Texas Statutes—Article 52.01. http://codes.lp.findlaw.com/txstatutes/ CR/1/52/52.01 [accessed November 15, 2009].

Daniel Unit (DL). Texas Department of Criminal Justice. http://www.tdcj. state.tx.us/stat/ unitdirectory/dl.htm [accessed November 11, 2009].

Darrington Unit (DA). Texas Department of Criminal Justice. http://www. tdcj.state.tx.us/stat/ unitdirectory/da.htm [accessed November 10, 2009].

"Ferguson Prison Unit in Midway, Texas." http://www.prisontalk.com/ forums/archive/index.php/t-110688.html [accessed October 30, 2009].

Ferguson Unit (FE). Texas Department of Criminal Justice. http://www. tdcj.state.tx.us/stat/ unitdirectory/fe.htm [accessed October 30, 2009].

"Gerald Myers, Director of Athletics Biography." Texas Tech University. http://www.irim.ttu.edu/ SACSFocusReport/PDF/GeraldMyersBio.pdf [accessed August 5, 2009].

Goodwyn, Wade. "Family of Man Cleared by DNA Still Seeks Justice." National Public Radio, February 5, 2009. http://www.npr.org/templates/ story/story.php?storyId=100249923 [accessed November 25, 2009].

"Gov. Perry Grants Posthumous Pardon for Innocence to Tim Cole," press release from the Office of the Governor Rick Perry, March 01, 2010. http://governor.state.tx.us/news/ press-release/14312/ [accessed March 01, 2010].

"HB 498, Innocence Commission Passes Criminal Justice Committee." Press release by Senator Rodney Ellis. Texas District 13, May 22, 2009. The Senate of Texas. http://www.senate.state. tx.us/75r/Senate/members/dist13/pr09/p052209a.htm [accessed November 24, 2009].

Heckel, Kelsey. "Tech Alumni Create Scholarship for Wrongly Convicted Lubbock Man." *The Daily Toreador* (Texas Tech). http://www.daily toreador.com/news/tech-alumni-create-scholarship-for-wrongly-convicted-lubbock-man-1.2110787 [accessed January 16, 2009].

"Honorable Jim Bob Darnell." 140th District Court, Lubbock County. http://www.co.lubbock.tx. us/DCrt140/Darnellbiography.htm [accessed July 24, 2009].

Innocence Project of Texas. http://ipoftexas.org/about-us/ [accessed October 10, 2009].

"John T. Montford." Lubbock Centennial, 1909–2009. http://www.lubbock-centennial.com/ citysmost/011109.shtml [accessed September 8, 2009].

Johnson, Jerry Wayne. Offender Information Detail. Texas Department of Criminal Justice. http://168.51.178.33/webapp/TDCJ/InmateDetails.jsp?sidnumber= 02711498 [accessed July 26, 2009].

_____. Taped confession and comments about Tim Cole's innocence, undated. http://link. brightcove.com/services/player/bcpid1137960457?bctid= 1636542748 [accessed September 28, 2009].

"Judge's Ruling Clears Deceased Texas Prisoner and Emphasizes Need for Reform." The Innocence Project. http://www.innocenceproject.org/Content/1937.php [accessed October 30, 2009].

Lanehart, Chuck. "Bobby Rogers." Lubbock Criminal Defense Lawyers Association. http://lcdla. org/2007/08/07/bobby-rogers/ [accessed August 30, 2009].

Lithwick, Dahlia. "When Our Eyes Deceive Us." Newsweek.com. http://www.newsweek.com/id/ 189294 [accessed November 21, 2009].

"Lubbock, Texas." *Handbook of Texas Online.* http://www.tshaonline.org/handbook/online/ articles/LL/flu2.html [accessed October 25, 2009].

"Moth." World Book Online. http://www.worldbook.com/wb/worldbook/cybercamp/html/ walkmoth.html [accessed August 12, 2009].

"Outstanding Young Lawyer Award Recipients." Lubbock County Bar Association. http://www. lcba.org/Docs/Award_Winners.pdf [accessed September 8, 2009].

"Perry Should Issue Posthumous Pardon," an editorial. DallasNews.com. http://www.dallasnews. com/sharedcontent/dws/dn/opinion/editorials/stories/DN-pardon_15edi.State.Edition1. 2addc7d.html [accessed November 25, 2009].

"Population of Selected Cities, 1850–2000." Texas Almanac. http://texas-almanac.com/population [accessed July 22, 2009].

"Rape." *New York Times Online.* http://health.nytimes.com/health/guides/specialtopic/rape/overview.html?inline=nyt-classifier [accessed July 19, 2009].

Posthumous Exoneration Sought Through Court of Inquiry." Texas Lawyer,

July 7, 2008. http://www.law.com/jsp/tx/PubArticleTX.jsp?id=12024 22790640&slreturn=1 [accessed November 19, 2009].

"In Memory of the Life of Timothy Brian Cole." Senate Resolution 124. Senate Journal. Eighty-first Legislature—Regular Session. http://www.journals. senate.state.tx.us/sjrnl/81r/html/ 81RSJ02-04-F.HTM [accessed November 23, 2009].

"Schizophrenia." National Institute of Mental Health. http://www.nimh. nih.gov/health/topics/schizophrenia/index.shtml [accessed December 26, 2009].

"She`s the Sheriff: Bastrop County`s Top Gun." Bastropia.com, November 4, 2007. http://www.bastropia.com/news/shes-the-sheriff-bastrop-countys-top-gun.4.html [accessed September 1, 2009].

Smith, Jordan. "Cole's Posthumous Exoneration is First for Texas." *The Austin Chronicle*. http://www.austinchronicle.com/gyrobase/Issue/Story?oid= oid:740144 [accessed November 21, 2009].

———. "Tim Cole Act Becomes Law." *The Austin Chronicle*. http://www. austinchronicle.com/gyrobase/News/Blogs?oid=oid:787201 [accessed November 23, 2009].

"Statement of Sen. Rodney Ellis on the First Meeting of the Tim Cole Advisory Panel on Wrongful Convictions." Press release by Senator Rodney Ellis. Texas District 13, October 13, 2009. The Senate of Texas. http://www.ellis. senate.state.tx.us/pr09/p101309a.htm [accessed November 24, 2009].

"Sun and Moon Data for One Day: Sunday, 24 March 1985." U.S. Naval Observatory. http://aa. usno.navy.mil/cgi-bin/aa_pap.pl [accessed July 22, 2009].

Teague, Don. "Texas Wrestles with Wrongful Convictions." CBSNews.com, May 9, 2009. http://www.cbsnews.com/stories/2009/05/09/evening news/main5003683.shtml [accessed November 25, 2009].

"Texan Who Died in Prison Cleared of Rape Conviction." CNN.com. http://www.cnn.com/ 2009/CRIME/02/06/texas.exoneration/index. html#cnnSTCOther1 [accessed November 12, 2009].

Texas Crime Rates 1960–2008. http://www.disastercenter.com/crime/ txcrime.htm [accessed November 17, 2009].

"Texas Tech University Fall Enrollment by Ethnicity since 1985." Texas Tech University. http://www.irim.ttu.edu/HistoryData.php [accessed July 24, 2009].

"Texas Tech University Spring Enrollment by Gender since 1926." Texas Tech University. http://www.irim.ttu.edu/HistoryData.php [accessed July 24, 2009].

"Texas Tech University Spring Enrollment since 1926." Texas Tech University. http://www. irim.ttu.edu/HistoryData.php [accessed July 24, 2009].

Tim Cole Act. House Bill 1736. Texas House of Representatives. http:// www.legis.state.tx.us/ billlookup/History.aspx?LegSess=81R&Bill=HB 1736 [accessed November 23, 2009].

Tim Cole Act. Senate Bill 2014. Texas Senate. http://www.legis.state. tx.us/billlookup/History.aspx?LegSess=81R&Bill=SB2014 [accessed November 23, 2009].

"Timothy Cole Exonerated 24 Years Later." KCBD.com. http://www.kcbd.com/Global/story. asp?S=9804937 [accessed November 12, 2009].

Watkins, Calvin. "Top Five Dallas Cowboys-Redskins Games at Texas Stadium." http://www. dallasnews.com/sharedcontent/dws/spt/football/cowboys/stories/092808dnspocowsider.140d701.html [accessed April 5, 2010].

Weeks, David. "Post-Conviction DNA Testings: More Questions Than Answers." State Bar of Texas. http://www.texasbar.com/Template.cfm?Section=Home&Template=/Content Management/ContentDisplay.cfm&ContentID=5902 [accessed November 9, 2009].

Wells, Dr. Gary L., Distinguished Professor of Liberal Arts and Sciences, Department of Psychology, Iowa State University, Ames, IA. http://www.psychology.iastate.edu/faculty/gwells [accessed November 16, 2009].

_____ and Elizabeth A. Olson. "Eyewitness Testimony." http://www.innocence project.org/docs/ Eyewitness_Testimony_Ann_Rev.pdf [accessed November 21, 2009].

Williams, Jena A. "Cole Case." *Texas Monthly.* http://texasmonthly.com/2009-02-01/webextra17. php [accessed July 30, 2009].

Willing, Richard. "Police Line-ups Encourage Wrong Picks, Experts Say." *USA TODAY.* http://www.usatoday.com/news/acovtue.htm [accessed September 2, 2009].

INDEX